FAMILY ROMANCE

ALSO BY JOHN LANCHESTER

Fragrant Harbor
Mr Phillips
The Debt to Pleasure

FAMILY ROMANCE

A Love Story

❋

JOHN LANCHESTER

A MARIAN WOOD BOOK

Published by G. P. Putnam's Sons
a member of Penguin Group (USA) Inc.
New York

A Marian Wood Book
Published by G. P. Putnam's Sons
Publishers Since 1838
a member of the Penguin Group
Penguin Group (USA) Inc., 375 Hudson Street, New York, New York 10014, USA • Penguin
Group (Canada), 90 Eglinton Avenue East, Suite 700, Toronto, Ontario M4P 2Y3, Canada
(a division of Pearson Penguin Canada Inc.) • Penguin Books Ltd, 80 Strand, London
WC2R 0RL, England • Penguin Ireland, 25 St Stephen's Green, Dublin 2, Ireland (a division
of Penguin Books Ltd) • Penguin Group (Australia), 250 Camberwell Road, Camberwell,
Victoria 3124, Australia (a division of Pearson Australia Group Pty Ltd) • Penguin Books
India Pvt Ltd, 11 Community Centre, Panchsheel Park, New Delhi–110 017, India • Penguin
Group (NZ), Cnr Airborne and Rosedale Roads, Albany, Auckland 1310, New Zealand
(a division of Pearson New Zealand Ltd) • Penguin Books (South Africa) (Pty) Ltd,
24 Sturdee Avenue, Rosebank, Johannesburg 2196, South Africa

Penguin Books Ltd, Registered Offices:
80 Strand, London WC2R 0RL, England

Library of Congress Cataloging-in-Publication Data

Lanchester, John.
Family romance : a love story / John Lanchester.
p.   cm.
"A Marian Wood book."
ISBN-13: 978-0-399-15300-6
ISBN-10: 0-399-15300-4
1. Lanchester family.   2. Lanchester, John—Family.   3. British Empire—
Hong Kong—Biography.   4. Great Britain—Ireland—Biography.
5. Colonialism.   6. Great Britain—Biography.   I. Title.
CT787.L   2007   2006041666
941.08209'2—dc22

Printed in the United States of America
1   3   5   7   9   10   8   6   4   2

This book is printed on acid-free paper. ∞

BOOK DESIGN BY AMANDA DEWEY

While the author has made every effort to provide accurate telephone numbers and
Internet addresses at the time of publication, neither the publisher nor the author
assumes any responsibility for errors, or for changes that occur after publication.
Further, the publisher does not have any control over and does not assume any
responsibility for author or third-party websites or their content.

For Finn and Jesse

"If I am ever kidnapped or taken hostage," my mother told me, "and they allow me to communicate with you, but I can't say what's happened or where I am, what I'll do is, I'll deliberately make a grammatical mistake. For instance, I'll say 'between you and I' instead of 'between you and me.' So if you ever speak to me over the phone and I sound a bit strained and I say 'between you and I,' you'll know I'm being held hostage. Will you remember that?"

"Okay, Mum," I said.

PROLOGUE

· I ·

ONE OF THE MOST FAMOUS THINGS ever written about family life is the opening sentence of *Anna Karenina*. "All happy families resemble one another, each unhappy family is unhappy in its own way." It's a magnificent line, so sonorous and resonant that it makes it easy for us not to notice it isn't true. Part of its falsehood lies in the fact that happy families aren't especially alike, any more than unhappy ones are unalike. But at a deeper level, the falsehood lies in the idea that a family is either happy or unhappy. Life, family life, just isn't that simple. Most families are both happy and unhappy, often intensely so, and often at the same time. A sense of safety can be a feeling of trappedness; a delight in routine can be suffocating boredom; a parent's humor and unpredictability can be a maddeningly misplaced childlikeness—and in many cases, the feeling is simultaneous. I was both happy and unhappy as a child, just as my parents were both happy and unhappy, and just as almost everyone else is.

Another way in which our family resembled everyone else's was that we had secrets. All families have secrets. Sometimes they are of the variety that a family keeps from outsiders; sometimes they are the sort that a family keeps from itself; sometimes they are the sort to whose presence no one consciously admits. But they are almost always there. People have a deep need for secrets. The question is what to do with them and about them, and when to let them go.

MY PARENTS' ASHES are interred in the graveyard of All Saints' Church at Manfield in North Yorkshire. Neither of them had any connection with the place in life, and it is in that sense an arbitrary place for them to have ended up. My mother was born in Ireland, my father in Africa, and neither of them ever lived anywhere near Manfield. But they moved around a lot, and came to be people who didn't have too strong a link with anywhere, so I don't think the arbitrariness of the location is inappropriate. Besides, Manfield is where the Lanchesters' grave is: my father's father and great-grandparents, and then back again for two more generations, are all buried there. His grandfather is the only immediate ancestor to be elsewhere. Some of the graves have been shifted over the years, pushed up against the church wall to—among other things—make the graveyard easier to mow. But the Lanchesters' grave was spared that, and lies where it always has, under the south wall of the high-windowed, grim eighteenth-century church.

"It's a cold place," my mother said to me, the day that we buried my father's ashes in the summer of 1984, several months after his death. "I don't like the idea of him being cold."

"It's where he wanted to be," I said, which was true.

I didn't, and don't, have the same consolation about my mother's ashes ending up at All Saints'. I interred them there in the summer of 1998, and it was a mistake. She didn't want her ashes to go there, because she didn't want to be cremated. In the immediate aftermath of her death, though, I was so upset that I didn't read the will closely enough to notice its very first sentence: "I ask that my body be buried." It used to be an important piece of Catholic doctrine, that cremation was wrong because it prevented the body's rising from death at the Last Judgment. But I am not a Catholic, and in my distress simply missed the statement and its importance. So I interred her ashes in the summer of 1998, in the same grave where she and I had put my father's ashes fourteen years before.

That day, the day I interred my mother's ashes, I had a sense of being oppressed by things I wanted to talk about and could not. The mistake I had made in having her cremated was on my conscience, but since I did not know the priest— had met him right there and then for the first time—I felt it would be too much to explain in the fifteen or so minutes we had together. There was also the fact, not at all important but very hard to get out of my mind, that the priest was wearing army boots and combat trousers under his cassock. I noticed this as we stood beside the grave, reading a shortened form of the burial service. No doubt I wouldn't have spotted it if I hadn't already been looking down at the small hole in the grave, just big enough to cover the little wooden box that contained my mother's ashes. I began to wonder whether it would seem out of turn to ask why he was wearing combat clothes. Was it some new thing that priests did, making some point about being a soldier for Christ? I did hope not. And he seemed a nice, mild-mannered, gentle man, not the sort for wild evangelical gestures. Or perhaps it was me? Funeral rites often have an air of strangeness and unreality about them; sometimes you lose your hold on what is normal and what isn't. I had a sudden, vivid memory of the day after my father died, when the local Church of England vicar came to the door to offer comfort. Because my parents had only just moved into the house, he had no idea who we were. My mother was somewhere upstairs, so I made tea. In a very English way we made small talk. Then he picked up a photograph of my father from the bookcase.

"I hope you don't mind me asking," he said, "but are you Jewish?"

It was about twelve hours since my father had died. I had been up all night dealing with police, ambulance men, and the doctor. I was numb to my bones, so numb I didn't know quite what to say other than:

"I don't mind you asking, but no, I'm not Jewish."

"Oh," he said. Pause. "Because you look Jewish." Pause. "I hope you don't mind my asking again, but was your father Jewish?"

By now wondering where this was going, I said, "No . . ."

"Oh," he said. Pause. "Because he looks Jewish." Pause. "Because *I'm* Jewish."

At this point he was visibly expecting me to break down and admit that I, too, was Jewish but had been too shy to admit it.

Standing by the family grave, I had a flashback to that moment. The Church of England seemed to generate a strange force-field involving eccentricity and embarrassment and nobody's ever knowing quite what to say. It might be perfectly normal for a Church of England priest to be wearing combat clothes under his clerical outfit. But I found it hard to concentrate on the words of the service, there in the cold Yorkshire graveyard.

In the event, the nice priest cleared things up, just after putting the clod of earth over the small wooden box containing my mother's ashes.

"Thought I should say about the outfit," he said. "I serve in the Territorials. Mechanical engineering. I'm off now to repair some motorbikes."

"Thanks," I said.

"What would you like to have written on the grave?" he then asked. And that was the next thing I did not want to talk about. The gravestone lists the names and ages of all the Lanchesters buried there. But both my mother's name and her age were now in question. A month before, five days after she died, I had found out that both the name and the date of birth I had known my mother by were false. What I didn't know was when or why or how she had taken a false identity, and what it meant for the story of her life, and my father's life, and mine. I also knew that finding all that out was going to take some work. My immediate dilemma was whether to give the dates that corresponded to her legal identity—and which contradicted all the documents I had had to show in arranging the interment, and also contradicted all the stories she had told about her life—or to tell the truth. The story of our lives is not the same as the story we tell about our lives.

"Can I get back to you on that?" I asked the priest. He looked a little surprised, but he said, "Of course."

So I set out to find the story of my mother's life, which is also the story of my father's life, and to an extent far greater than I realized when I began this journey, the story of mine, too. This book is that story. It has involved three kinds of detective work for me. One is close to actual detective work: finding out what my parents did, and what was done to them. This is fairly straightforward for my father, and not at all so for my mother, who covered her traces well and never gave anything away. For my mother's earlier life, my main sources have been conversations with family members; a short account of my mother's life written by my aunt Peggie and followed by a formal interview with her; and a set of letters that Peggie gave me. For the later part of my mother's life, for my father's life, and for my parents' lives after marriage, a camphor-wood chest full of family papers has been my primary source. The second kind of detective work is emotional: trying to find out what they felt about what happened, and why they did the things they did. And then there's the third strand: trying to work out what I feel and think. That is something we all need to do about who we are and where we come from. I believe that everyone should do this, or something close to it. We should all know our families' stories, all the more so if nobody tells them to us directly and we have to find them out for ourselves.

But before I tell the story of our family, I need to explain a little about what my parents were actually like.

· 2 ·

I DON'T REMEMBER how I found out that my mother was, or rather had been, a nun.

When you're a child, the way you learn something attaches itself to the thing you've learned. Straightforward stuff, like the things you learn in school, doesn't need a label or a warning; you know you can let it out in a fashion as uncomplicated as the way you let it in. Your times tables, the capital of Nicaragua: this is knowledge that might be useful in the classroom but is not dangerous or psychically important.

The things you learn in the playground have a higher sense of risk and a lower sense of reliability, and you need them in a more urgent way. How to make friends, who your friends are, and who they aren't, and who are friends who turn out not to be friends, and what happens when you are picked on, and maybe what happens when you pick on someone else, and how to behave in any and all these combinations of circumstances: none of these things is officially taught, but they are among the most important you will learn. We learn them in the social world, and we learn at the same time that the social world can be a merciless place, and that is something none of us ever entirely forgets.

And then there are the things that are whispered about in the playground, or among friends, and that have a sense of danger and unreliability about them right from the start. They might not be true, but they are explosive; their potential to be explosive is not reduced even if they are not true. These things often have to do with sex, or money, and they always have to do with secrets. Children know that the adult world is full of secrets, and they know that secrets are thrilling and explosive and dangerous, even if they don't quite know what the secrets are finally about, or why it is that they are so dangerous.

As time goes by, our sense of home life shifts along this axis. At first everything about home and our parents seems straightforward: things are the way they are. Then we gradually realize that there are reasons why things are the way they are, and that other people's lives are not quite the same as ours, in ways that are both interesting and, potentially, disturbing: Why doesn't Ryan have a daddy, and why does Lisa's mummy cry all the time, and why does my daddy walk out of the room whenever someone on the telly talks about wanting to buy a new car? We gradually sense that our own family, our own lives, are not quite like other families, other lives. And then, often, if we are either lucky or unlucky—I'm still not quite sure which—we learn that there are things about our families, our lives, that are secret, not just private but secret, and they have a dangerous charge about them. They are things we are not supposed to talk about, or even to think about. So we learn not to.

That, I think, is how I came to sort of know that my mother had been a nun, without knowing where or when or for how long or what it meant. Nietzsche said that ignorance is as structured as knowledge. I've come to agree. The things you don't know are very often the things you have chosen not to know. At a broad historical level, they are the things for which any era is judged most harshly by those that follow: not for the things that people genuinely didn't know, but for the things right in front of them that they chose not to see. At a personal level, too, some of the most important truths in our lives are the ones right in front of us, that we won't think about and can't face. The thing we most can't face is always the thing directly facing us.

So, about my mother's having been a nun. I'm sure I wasn't directly told. My parents didn't much go in for directly telling me things. More likely, I was allowed to overhear certain things, and had certain other hints dangled in front of me, and I was encouraged to figure things out for myself. The truth was allowed to emerge, over time, through hints and allusions and half-stories and implication. Some dots were scattered around, and I was given an opportunity, if I felt so inclined, to connect them. This method, of telling me without telling me, had the effect of making things seem to be a big deal, because if something wasn't a big deal, I could be told about it more simply. So I knew that it was a big deal that my mother had been a nun. It was something that had been crucially important to her, and that explained a lot about her. But I still don't know how I knew.

I suppose that's partly because children have different degrees of knowing. I didn't know it as a simple, taken-for-granted fact, like the facts that we lived in Hong Kong, and that I was an only child, and that my mother was Irish. It also wasn't known in the way that you half know something isn't true, like the tooth fairy or Santa Claus or heaven, which is where both my grandfathers were—had been since before I was born. It was somewhere in the middle, in the category of things I knew but wasn't supposed to ask about, like why my father spoke Japanese and could do judo but my grandmother wouldn't have anything Japanese in the house, so we used to have to hide my record player and television when she came to stay; or why the people who lived in the next house along Middle Gap Road and had a Saint Bernard called Portnoy had given him "a very silly name" (though when I asked why it was silly, my mother wouldn't tell me); or why my mother's name was Julie even though her initials were B.T.J.; or where babies came from.

I must have known by the time I was ten, because that's when I was sent to boarding school eight thousand miles away in England, and I knew by then. I also knew that I wasn't supposed to tell anyone. It wasn't a secret, exactly, but it was private. My mother was proud of the fact and also close to ashamed of it. I was aware of these prescriptions and restrictions without their having been discussed; as a child, I was super-alert to the distinctions about what you could and couldn't say. My mother never spoke of it to anyone apart from my father and me, and even to us she did not speak openly.

I remember a conversation between my parents, when a letter arrived from my grandmother in County Mayo. This would date from the period when I was still piecing together the fact that Mum had been a nun, I think, or perhaps it comes from just after the time I worked it out.

"Anything in it?" asked Dad. He had come home from work, drunk a dry martini, and changed out of his suit.

"No, and for once there's nothing about Jane," said Mum. My mother was the oldest child in a family of eight, seven of them girls, and Jane was her youngest sister. Jane was a nun who worked with the poor in Peru. My grandmother was known for writing what amounted to poison-pen letters. The sting would come in the end, in a throwaway remark or post-script: "I was so sorry to hear about your husband's drinking, everyone in the family is praying for you" was an example, from a letter to a woman who had no idea that her spouse had gone back on the bottle. My grand-mother would always mention Jane in her infrequent letters to my mother, by way of—my mother felt—taunting her about her own fail-ure or apostasy. The emotional violence compressed into a short remark or observation was part of my mother's formative training in family life. I had never met my grandmother, and didn't until I was nineteen and went to Ireland on my own for the first time, but I knew to fear and dis-trust her.* And in fact, even knowing all the things I know now, and all the things that weren't quite as my mother told them, I know that my mother, who feared nobody, feared her own mother. She must have had her reasons.

---

*That was my mother's version. Others in the family agree that Molly Gunnigan, my grandmother, could write a mean letter—"stinker" was the family term. But they say that the mechanism worked a bit differ-ently. My cousin Siobhán put it like this: "The thing is, Mam would get cross about something, and she would sit down and pen a letter, and it would say all these terrible things, and then she would go down to the letter box and put it in and that would be the end of it as far as she was concerned. It would be a kind of explosion, it was her way of letting off steam. And then it was over. Of course, the trouble was, two days later someone would go downstairs and find this terrible thing waiting for them on the doormat and whereas Mam would regard it by now as something that was in the past, done and dusted, the person get-ting the letter would be inclined to feel differently."

"No mention of Jane? Perhaps she's run off with a priest," joked my father. As it turned out some time later, she had—which is no doubt one reason I remember this conversation. After a catastrophic Peruvian earthquake in 1974, which involved Jane in intensely demanding relief work, she fell in love with a man named Pat Brady, a strong, intelligent, and alarmingly good-looking missionary priest. My mother always had a special degree of feeling about her youngest sibling, who was also her goddaughter and whom she had taught, when she was a young nun and Jane was a pupil at her convent school—hence, perhaps, her mother's needling on the subject. But all this was something I learned only later; at the time I remember noticing that the mention of Jane's vocation was used somehow as a dig at my mother, and thinking, Can that possibly mean she was once a nun, too?

But I'm sure I was never directly told. That wasn't the way we did things. For instance, I was never told in as many words that my father had had a heart attack in 1974 while I was away at boarding school. It was something I was allowed to work out, to gather, to infer. It was a bad heart attack, and it permanently affected his health—he took early retirement five years later, and died of another heart attack four years after that, at the age of fifty-seven—but the mere fact that something was very, very important was no guarantee that my parents would approach it directly. If anything, the reverse was true. Looking back at my childhood, I have the feeling that much of the most important information I was given, I wasn't given. I was shown the dots and had to construct the picture for myself.

It's not that my parents were evasive. They weren't shifty. They did not duck and weave. But there were topics that did not come up, or that came up only with great difficulty and in a way that made it clear it would be better for all parties if they did not come up again. Important subjects by definition carried a powerful charge of feeling, and that made them difficult and dangerous; and if a thing is dangerous, then it is sensible not to do it unless you have to. Better to put it off, or approach it indirectly, or allow people (i.e., me) to work things out for themselves; better still to avoid the subject, if at all possible. My father used to tell the story of a tutor at his university, a Viennese professor of something or other. Once there was a general conversation about what people would have, if they could have anything in the world. There were some surprising answers— a youngish woman don said she wanted an enormous wine cellar. When it came to the old Viennese professor, he sucked on his pipe for a moment, then said, "Well, if I could really have anything I wanted, anything at all, I think I would choose . . . *permanent* delusions of grandeur."

Dad loved that story. He liked it because it was funny, but I think he liked also the idea of a permanent state of feeling that excluded difficulty or pain. For instance, he could never bring himself to discuss money. He could talk about it in the abstract, in relation to businesses in the news, or tax policy, or things like that. But he couldn't bear to talk about money in any personal context, anything to do with his income or—and this was a particular issue—my pocket money. I wasn't allowed to ask for money or to mention it. The subject caused Dad too much pain. It touched on things from his own childhood, to do with the fact that his father had used money as a means of control and interference.

What was odd about this was that my father worked for a bank. Dealing with money was what he did all day, every day, for his entire working life. And yet he couldn't bear to speak of it at home. As a teenager, when I was home from school, I would resort to simply stealing money from his wallet rather than putting him and me through the impossible ordeal of my asking for it. I would steal it resentfully, too, from the wallet he left openly on the hall table. I didn't want to steal, but I felt that I had no choice, and that the whole episode was showing both our characters in their least good light. I now see that the banking and the not being able to discuss money were tightly linked: he had gone to work in a bank because his father had bullied him into doing a job that would keep him grounded in the real world—which, in his father's view, meant a job that was all about money. The memory of that, and all it implied, was so painful for Dad that if I ever mentioned money to him, he was overpowered by flashbacks from his youth and sent into a profound gloom. Working with money all day and not being able to talk about it were at some psychic level part of the same deal.

My father, whom I loved deeply and whose memory I revere, was not a direct man. He was open and friendly in manner, unstuffy and funny, and he was also that rarest of all things, a good listener. But when there was any sense of difficulty about a conversation, he found it impossible to address himself to it head-on. It's not so much that he disliked confrontation with other people as that he disliked confronting himself, the parts of himself—anger or sadness or simple embarrassment—that he did not want to encounter. The one time I remember him trying directly to tackle a subject he would have preferred to avoid was during a summer holiday in England when he and I had a talk about sex. At least, that's what I realized, years later, it had been. Part of the trouble was that before he began, he took the precaution of getting comprehensively sloshed. My father never slurred or rambled or fell over or lost himself in drink; indeed, he never seemed that different, only a little more cheerful. It certainly didn't make him any more direct; but perhaps it helped him to think he had been more direct. On this occasion, my mother had gone to bed, saying over her shoulder to him, "If he was a girl I would have done it." He sat down with me in the kitchen, offered me a beer, and while fiddling with his own glass of dark rum, his inexplicable preferred nightcap, told a long, rambling, difficult-to-follow story about some rowers he had known at university in Melbourne who had, the night before big races, used to do this thing, which was a silly thing, but anyway, they had tied strips of towel to their backs, so that if they lay on their backs during the night they would be uncomfortable and would turn over, because it was while you lay on your back at night that you might have certain sorts of dreams, they sometimes, you know, and they thought that, you know, would sap their strength, ha-ha, wasn't that silly, the idea that it might sap their strength, even though they had a point, and anyway . . . We chatted on for a bit more and then went to bed.

I didn't have a clue what Dad was talking about. This was 1978, and I was sixteen. It was years later—this isn't a figure of speech: it was five years later, when I was at university in 1983—when somebody asked me whether I had ever had any formal sex education. No, I said, not a word, and as for my parents—and then I had a sudden flash of memory, and it hit me that my father's mumblings on the subject of towels and rowers at the University of Melbourne had been an attempt to fill me in on the details of human sexual reproduction, with special reference to the subject of puberty. I realized that my father had been talking about, or trying to talk about, wet dreams. When the rowers lay on their backs they had wet dreams. Hence the toweling strips, to stop them from lying on their backs. This was Dad's attempt at my sexual education. The sudden memory of his sweetness, gentleness, and chronic inability to tackle difficult subjects made me laugh aloud. To fill your son in on the details of how sex works in such a way that he realizes what you are talking about only five years later—now, that's good going.

My mother's gift for avoiding subjects was very different from my father's. She would never have left things like that. If she brought up a subject, you knew it had been brought up. You could sense the formidable head teacher she had been. But she was very, very, very good—a genius—at not bringing things up. She had the ability to make certain subjects unbroachable. My mother didn't quite have, as Steve Jobs of Apple Computer is said to have, a Reality Distortion Field, an aura that causes people near him to agree with his version of reality, in preference to the generally agreed-upon version outside his head. But she did have a kind of Inquiry Suppression Field, in which there were things you couldn't ask, psychic places you couldn't go, and wishes you were not allowed to acknowledge or voice.

"I want to ask your mother things about her childhood," a friend once told me, "but I can't. I don't know how she does that."

"Me neither," I said.

She had an ability to ensure not so much that certain topics were off-limits as that they just did not exist. It wasn't so much that she would dodge a subject, or evade it, as that she would behave as if it were not there, and do so with an absolute conviction that was impossible to challenge. Or at least that I found impossible to challenge. Even having a desire implied that there was something you wanted that she hadn't anticipated, which meant that it was in some sense a criticism of her. And you couldn't criticize her, implicitly or explicitly, ever. She had a talent for making tiny actions or exchanges carry a tremendous weight of emotional violence. At the same time, if you tried to explain why something was so violent, you wouldn't be able to. There was never anything you could call her on, since everything was unspoken and implicit. She managed to preserve total deniability.

There is no word for "no" in Irish. If someone asks you a direct question, "Are you going out tonight?" you can't just say, "No," you have to incorporate the question in your answer: "I am not going out." Even if you want flatly to contradict somebody, you have, at least partly, to incorporate or acknowledge that person's wishes by speaking them out loud. I'd be reluctant to make too large a general point about this, but it does often seem to me that this provides a clue to the Irish way of relating, which is keener to divert and deflect, to digress and elaborate and distract, than to confront. An Irish talker, if he doesn't like where you are headed, is not likely to stand directly in the way of your intention, but he is quite likely to come along beside you and give you a nudge, so you end up somewhere you weren't expecting or intending to be. Certainly that's what my mother was like. You knew where you were, and you knew where the "Keep Out" signs were, too, even if you didn't know the reason for them.

The zone of undiscussability blended into her preferred mode of getting what she wanted, which was to treat you with fait accompli. She was a master of the fait accompli—it was her favorite tactic for getting you to do something she suspected you didn't want to do. It's a highly effective tactic, too, if you don't mind the furious resentment it will cause. The key point is never to ask for something, because that implies the possibility that somebody might say no. Don't ask if someone will be home for dinner, just tell the person what you're cooking. Don't ask for help going to the supermarket, just announce that it's time to leave. Don't ever admit that there are things to discuss. Don't ever say good-bye.

What this leads to is a relationship that proceeds by negatives. It was almost impossible to have an explicit argument with Julie, but you could certainly have bitter, explosive, violent rows—only they tended to be carried out not in the medium of language. The preferred method for her to express anger involved sulking, silence, distance, and omission, and this became the only effective way of communicating these feelings back at her. She couldn't be outfought—she couldn't be fought at all—and she was devastatingly good at being unhappy at people. But you could simply not be there; you could not be there physically, insofar as it was possible, and when you had to be there physically you could learn not to be there emotionally. So I did that. I rose to Olympic standards at that. Our arguments tended to fall into patterns of explosive but silent withdrawal, with her sulking and me absent. And none of this, obviously, was ever discussed.

Well, that's families, I suppose. A book that gave a true and full account of any family's inner life would have to be able to explain how a remark that is short, plain, and apparently neutral—"There's that draft again"—can have in it a thousand-page history of rage and hate and emotional violence. It would have to capture that family atmosphere, of all the time spent together blending into a miasma of exhausting, exhaustive intimacy, combined with all the ways in which family members, who feel that they know one another so well they could die of boredom, also hardly know one another at all. But nobody would want to read that book; it would be too familiar.

I'll have to just ask you to take my word for my mother's force of personality. It was something you could sense in her speech. In rendering it I find it hard not to resort to italics. She often spoke with great emphasis; she never qualified or dithered, and she had no use for *rather*s or *somewhat*s or *very*s. "If I'm ever caught up in a disaster, a fire or earthquake or something," she once told me, "and they ask me what it was like—heaven help them if they ask me, 'How did you feel?'—but if they ask me what it was like, I'll just say, '*It was bad.* Just that. *It was bad.*'"

"Okay, Mum," I said.

In the days when she was drinking most—this would be the seventies and early eighties, when she would go through half a bottle of sherry a day, hardly ever more and not often less—I would sometimes tentatively raise the question of whether she really, truly wanted me to go to the fridge and pour her another glass. When I did that, she always said one of two things. If she was cooking, she would turn away from the stove or chopping board toward me and say, with maximum emphasis, *"The laborer is worthy of her hire."* (She was citing the Gospel according to Luke.) My favorite, though, was the other one, when she wasn't cooking. If I "cast nasturtiums," as she called it, she would waggle her empty glass and less crossly but more defiantly say, *"And is there balm in Gilead?"* This was intended to be, and somehow managed to be, a complete answer.*

It would be giving a misleading impression of her if I failed to convey just how entertaining, how funny, how alive she was. She was tricky, moody, difficult, powerful, superstitious, neurotic, and she projected an emotional force-field that was like something out of *Star Trek*; but she was also brilliant, funny, and invariably quick to see a point and get a joke. She was one of the best talkers I've ever known; she was famous for it. She loved a drink and loved a good meal. Most of all, though, I remember the talk. Or rather, I don't remember it, exactly, since good talk is the most evanescent thing in the world, so bound up as it is with timing and mood—but I do remember Julie's catchphrases, things she could be relied on, with absolute fidelity, to say in specific circumstances. Whenever she saw something unexpectedly expensive—when she peered over my shoulder to look at a car magazine, say, and found a picture of a Ferrari with a £150,000 price tag—she would firmly announce: "I'll have half a dozen." Whenever someone had a name that was definitely, irrevocably Irish—for instance the current Cardinal Archbishop of Westminster, the wonderfully named Cormac Murphy-O'Connor—she would say, "Good Turkish name." Whenever something came up that she should have

---

*Thanks to searchable online Bibles, I now know that this was my mother's riff on Jeremiah 8:22. The longer passage reads:

"When I would comfort myself against sorrow, my heart is faint in me. Behold the voice of the cry of the daughter of my people because of them that dwell in a far country: Is not the Lord in Zion? Is not her king in her? Why have they provoked me to anger with their graven images, and with strange vanities? The harvest is passed, the summer is ended, and we are not saved. For the hurt of the daughter of my people I am hurt; I am black; astonishment hath taken hold on me. Is there no balm in Gilead? Is there no physician there? Why then is not the health of the daughter of my people recovered?"

I admire my mother for deploying the prophet Jeremiah to eulogize Tío Pepe sherry.

known but didn't, she would say—it was the punch line of an old, old joke—"God bless us and save us, said poor Mrs. Davis, I never knew herrings [pronounced "herons"] was fish." Whenever I was hungry and cleared my plate, she would say, "Poor boy, he lost his appetite and found a horse's." Whenever I praised her cooking, or she thought something hadn't turned out as well as I thought it did, she would say, "Hunger is good sauce." When she offered you something and you said you didn't want it, she would say, with comedy disappointment that also managed to be real disappointment, "Be like that." Whenever anyone gave any indication of snobbery or class prejudice, she would say, "God bless the squire and his relations, and keep us in our proper stations." Whenever anyone dropped or broke anything, she would say—alluding to an old cartoon— "The happy home." Whenever anyone said anything critical of *The Guardian,* she would say, "*The Guardian* has been a good friend to Ireland." Once every six months, she would say, "Don't forget, if you're ever in trouble, you can always turn to the J's"—meaning the Jesuits, of whom she had a high opinion, based on the Jesuit priests she had known. "They can be relied on." To which I would say, "If they're so great, why does everybody hate them?" To which my mother, calmly: "That is their cross."

Ireland was a big subject. I was brought up with a profound ambivalence about Ireland and Irishness. On the one hand, my mother was deeply proud of being Irish; she talked about Ireland all the time, sought out the company of Irish friends wherever she went—"the Murphia," my father called them—and had the habit common to people from small countries of thinking that everyone else comes from them, too. "That man has spent time in Ireland as a child," she would say to me about someone overheard asking directions in the street; or, "He's from Cork," of a man behind us in the queue for the Star Ferry in Hong Kong; or, "That's a Kerry name," of somebody mentioned in the *South China Morning Post.* This drove me nuts as a child, but what drove me even more nuts was the extent to which she was right—when I got older and bolder, I would go up to people and say, "Excuse me, my mother is from Mayo, and she says you're from Wexford, is that right?" I gave up after three or four goes because it turned out that she had been right every time. Now

I'm the one who's prone to saying things like, "Sullivan? That's a Cork name," while my family around me grimace and flinch. She loved Irish talk and was proud of Irish writing and Irish attitudes—or some of them, anyway. A certain kind of Irish male omniscience used to irritate her, but it was more than balanced by the pride she exhibited in such things as the fact that the Irish word for "generous" is the same as that for "princely." Her Irish itself was pretty good; when we went to the Gaeltacht, the Irish-speaking part, of County Galway, I was deeply impressed by how well she got by in Irish. Once, in a bar in Buncrana, in Donegal, a man, clearly not quite believing her to be Irish (though we'd gone there with friends who were well known in the area), spoke to her in the language, and she unhesitatingly, and at some length, spoke back in Irish. She was proud of all that.

But there was a shadow side to her attitude to Ireland and, in particular, to her family. I was brought up to believe that I should not trust them. This wasn't a question of specifics, apart from the warning that one of her sisters was a "troublemaker": the one, it turned out, to whom she had been closest, the one without whom she would have found it virtually impossible to leave the convent—a deeply unfair assessment, it seems to me now. Occasionally she would tell me something more directly: when my wife and son and I moved to a larger house in 1998, she, with her inimitable maximum firmness, gave me her policy about the family: *"Never let them know you have a spare room."* But that was her comedy mode. There was something darker and not quite explicit about her sense of her family, something I got from her without its being spelled out: there was a source of danger, of unreliability, of potential treachery and ill will. That was it more than anything else: the feeling was that they did not always wish her well.

I must have known, in some way and at some level, that the version she gave of her life didn't quite add up. I'm not saying that it made no sense at all, or that she seemed shifty—just that, thinking about it now, I could and perhaps should have sensed that she wasn't an entirely reliable narrator. Not a wholly unreliable one, but not a wholly reliable one. Somewhere in the middle. There were few outright giveaways, but one of them should have been the confusion about her birthday. This was always celebrated on December 5, even though her passport said it was February 16. That was, she said, because of a cock-up with the registration of her birth. She was born in December 1929. But her father took months to get around to the chore of registering her. He was supposed to christen her Julia, but when he eventually went to the registrar, months after the birth, both of them were drunk, and the registrar wrote the date of registration on the birth certificate, instead of the date of birth. So my mother always celebrated her birthday on December 5, not February 16, when her birth had been erroneously registered. Her father got the name wrong, too, since it had been agreed that she would be known as Julia, but he forgot to write that on the form, so the birth certificate gave only her secondary names, Bridget and Teresa; the Julia was added as her confirmation name when she was eleven. That didn't seem as odd as it might have seemed to me, since my father's given name was George William, but he was only and always known as Bill. There were other oddities, too, related to the time she had spent in India as a missionary, and a vagueness about the relevant dates. When clues or hints were dropped—my wife, Miranda, in the aftermath of a conversation with one of my cousins at a family wedding, speculated that my mother must be older than she said, because her younger brother was about to have his seventieth birthday—I reacted with irritation. Her informant must have been drunk. I'd seen my mother's passport, I had a copy of her birth certificate. I *knew* how old she was.

I suppose what all this boils down to is, my mother didn't want to tell me, and I didn't want to know. I could tell there were "Keep Out" signs around areas of her life, and I was happy to keep out. When you're a child, your parents seem such fixed and immutable beings that it never occurs to you that they are living their lives, too. Some of this perhaps is protective: you protect them from your curiosity, and you protect yourself also. There seems to be a built-in limit to what you want to know about your parents. Then, later in life, as you become a grown-up yourself, you are increasingly curious about those other grown-ups, whom you know better than anyone else but also, in many ways, don't really know at all. We react to our parents so much as parents that it's easy to forget that they are also human beings. When I was younger, I had absolutely no idea whatsoever about my parents' lives; it would barely have occurred to me that either of them actually had a life. That was the degree of ignorance, half chosen, half imposed, with which I looked at them.

ONE OF THE THINGS I have noticed about my novels, in the course of writing this book, is that they all concern people who can't quite bring themselves to tell the truth about their own lives. The narrative they give about themselves is broken or damaged. It's not so much that they are "unreliable narrators"—a term I've always thought, at this point in history, wildly naive, since it implies the existence of an opposite thing, the reliable narrator, in whom no one any longer believes. My narrators aren't unreliable in that sense, but they all tell stories about themselves that have pieces missing, because they can't bear to tell the whole story. They are not liars, yet they can't tell the whole truth. I've come to realize that this interest in damaged, untellable life stories comes from my parents, and especially from my mother. I grew up with a sense that there was another, fuller, darker narrative looming behind the various shorter stories she told so well and so funnily.

LOOK WHAT
YOU MADE ME DO

❧

· I ·

JULIA IMMACULATA GUNNIGAN was born on December 5, 1920, at Lurgan, Kilkelly, in County Mayo, in the West of Ireland. That might sound like fairly straightforward information, but for reasons that will become clear, it isn't, at least not to me. Julia's true name and birthday were things I found out only after she died. If there was a special typeface for things my mother didn't tell me, the next hundred-odd pages of this book would be almost entirely in that face.

Julia was the first child of Patrick Gunnigan, a farmer, and his wife, Molly, whose maiden name was Waldron. Julia was baptized on December 8 at the parish church in Aghamore, three and a half miles from home. The day of her baptism was the feast of the Immaculate Conception—thus her middle name, Immaculata.

The Gunnigans and the Waldrons have an unsummarizably complicated family tree. What makes the chart of relationships so difficult to follow is intermarriage. For instance, Pat Gunnigan, my mother's father, was the son of John Gunnigan, who had two sisters, both of whom married men named John Waldron. The resulting family tree resembles those of European royal families or particle physics, and only one man, my uncle John Gunnigan, is known to understand it. Suffice it to say that at the time of my mother's birth, the Gunnigans of this branch were, and had been for some years, farmers, with a holding of about a hundred acres, at Lurgan. The farm is now run by my cousin Pat, who like me is the great-great-grandson of the first Gunnigan known to have lived there. That man, Tim (known as Thaig Mór, "Big Tim"), in 1873 built the house that is still the Gunnigan family home. At the time of Julia's birth, it had no running water and no electricity.

Mayo is a character in this story. Mayo, Maigh Eo in Irish, means "plain of the yew trees," a name that is romantic and evocative and that bears no relation to present-day reality. Basically, Mayo is a bog. In case you're wondering why County Mayo is so boggy: I asked a plant expert, who happens to be a paleobotany expert and an archaeologist and also my cousin Siobhán. Apparently it's because Mayo used to be completely covered in forest—hence, "plain of the yew trees." (Though they weren't all yew trees; yew would have been chosen for the name because it had strong magical and ritual associations. Actually most of the lost forest was oak.) During the Bronze Age the trees were cut down to make fires to smelt tin and copper. So no more trees. Since forest catches seventy percent of the rain that falls on it, deforestation leads pretty directly to the creation of bogs, which are composed of dead plants that don't rot, as they are soaking wet and are trapped under other dead plants. So Mayo is a bog because people made it one. The poor quality of the soil is a dominant fact of life here. Bogs are not good for growing much of anything except peat for the fire.

There are patches of beautiful scenery along the Mayo coast, and one spectacularly desolate area in the northwest of the county, out past Belmullet, where you drive for what feels like hours of bog to get to a Neolithic settlement called Céide (pronounced Cagey) Fields, one of the bleakest and most remote-feeling places I have been. The Stone Age settlers who lived there five thousand years ago depended on the cattle they raised—something that the Céide Fields Visitor Centre points out in a note stating that "cattle raised on standing grass are still the most important element in the Irish economy." There can't be too many places on the planet with that degree of economic continuity. But this continuity also has its postmodern aspects. Near the Gunnigan home is a place called Ballyhaunis, as sleepy and homogeneous a Mayo town as could be imagined—albeit with a pub where they serve the best pint of Guinness I've ever had. But Ballyhaunis also has a mosque, built because Knock airport opened a market for the export of halal meat to the Middle East, and it was far more economical to do the halal slaughtering in situ. So the demand for halal meat created a supply of halal slaughter men, which led to the opening of a mosque to accommodate their religious needs. Being imam of the Ballyhaunis mosque must be one of the Muslim world's odder jobs.

I've come to love the landscape of Mayo, and the other kinds of middling Irish landscape I associate with it. This isn't the Ireland that photographs so beautifully and about which people endlessly bang on: the Burren or the Giant's Causeway, the Ring of Kerry or the coves of Cork, the Twelve Bens of Connemara or the Cliffs of Moher in Clare. It is a landscape that doesn't look or feel like anything much—it feels like nowhere in particular. And because of the slow-moving traffic and poor single-lane roads, it takes forever to cross; as an Irish friend of mine says, you look at the map and things seem close together, but then when you're driving across the midlands you realize that Ireland is actually the biggest country in the world.

There is another way, though, in which Ireland is the biggest country in the world. Irish place names are immensely specific and connect directly to a past in which every feature of the landscape, every hillock or field, had a sense of story and memory attached. Brian Friel captures this in his great play *Translations,* in which the characters describe the incarnate specificity of the Irish landscape. Imagine if every place near you was called the Hill, or Tim's Field, or Big Oak, or Narrow Ford—it gives everywhere in Ireland an extraordinary sense of inhabited density. (Before the Famine, Ireland was one of the most densely populated countries in Europe, with a population at its height of almost 10 million; today it's only forty percent of that.) Ireland is dense, crowded, full, *written*. Everywhere in it is somewhere. And yet so much of it feels and looks like nowhere; and that somewhere/nowhere feeling is, for me, at its strongest in the anonymous bogs and near-bogs of inland Mayo.

At the time of my mother's birth and for some generations before, the standard smallholding in this area was twenty-one acres. The land would usually have been rented by a peasant from a landlord, who in this part of Mayo would have been from the Beatty family. In some places twenty-one acres is a good small-size holding on which to raise a family and grow a variety of crops. Here in boggy Mayo, it means marginal subsistence farming. Life here is hard, and for generations it has been. The Gunnigans, with a holding of a hundred acres, regarded themselves as relatively well-off.

The great issue was, and always had been, the land. Memories here were long, and many of them concerned grievances involving the land and the aftermath of the Famine, which had begun in 1845—not all that long ago, in Irish terms. I have a photograph of one of my mother's younger sisters standing with a neighbor who was born during the Famine. The years that followed were bitterly hard, and the accumulated grievances found a particular focus on the matter of evictions. These reached a peak in 1850, during which 20,000 families (more than 104,000 people) were evicted from their farms for nonpayment of rent. Emigration raged during these and subsequent decades. Mayo was a birthplace of the Land League, the body formed to fight for what came to be called "tenant right"—mordantly, and not inaccurately, summarized by the dark-hearted Lord Palmerston as "landlord wrong." The League lobbied for the Three F's, "free sale, fair rent, fixity of tenure," and it did so through a mixture of legal, semi-legal, and illegal tactics, one of which has passed into the language as boycott, after the estate supervisor whose job was to collect rents around Lough Erne, about thirty miles from Lurgan. This was in the period known as the Land War. Julia grew up hearing about the importance of the struggle for land reform, and about the heroic involvement of various family members. One of them, her grandmother Nora Drudy, as a girl had spent a month in jail for scattering sheep that the sheriff and police were trying to seize from a neighbor's land during a rent strike in 1887. Nora hid a sheepdog under her skirts and then let it go to disperse the livestock. On her return from prison in Dublin, she was greeted with bonfires; she is a family heroine to this day. The political was in this sense local and specific: it was about the right to own the land you farmed, and had farmed for generations; the objection to colonial rule flowed from, and grew out of, specific local injustices.

Julia was born in 1920, during the Anglo-Irish War. In that year the Black and Tans, irregular paramilitaries attached to the British army, were deployed, and their indiscriminate sectarian violence was starting to turn the tide of the conflict in favor of the rebels. The reality was that the British could not lose a military conflict, but they could lose a political one. They could lose both the consent of the governed and the will to govern. This, broadly speaking, is what happened. On November 21, two weeks before Julia was born, Michael Collins's team of gunmen assassinated a dozen undercover British agents in Dublin, and the Black and Tans the same day fired into a crowd gathered for a football match in Croke Park there. The resulting introduction of martial law was the beginning of the end for British rule. By 1921 the war of independence was over, to be succeeded by the civil war between the followers of Éamon de Valera, who rejected the terms of the treaty with the British (especially the oath of loyalty to the crown), and those of Michael Collins, who accepted the treaty on the basis that it was the best—not to mention the only—available deal. The consequences were played out over the subsequent decades of Irish history, but in the meantime, for Irish small farmers, there was a much more important and more local consequence of these great events: the Land Commission, founded in 1923, began the process of giving 450,000 acres of land to the people who lived on it and worked it.

In 1919, Patrick Gunnigan met a young woman named Molly Waldron. She was the oldest daughter of a relatively well-off local family, brought up in a house called Mount View in the village of Aghamore, about four miles from Lurgan. Her father was headmaster of the local primary school, and as such a figure of both means and respect; even when money was tight, the Waldrons had two servants. Molly's father was the illegitimately descended grandson of the local landlords' misbehaving scion, Dominic Beatty, who did not survive the experience of being sent to the Crimean War "to cool off" (as my uncle puts it). By the standards of the time and place, the Beattys behaved well by Dominic's illegitimately born daughter, letting her use the family surname and giving her money; there may also have been continuing financial support. It should be said that Molly vigorously denied this. But even if there was, it would have alleviated the hardness of life rather than annul it. Molly's father was one of twelve surviving children, born to a woman (the illegitimate Beatty daughter) who was married at sixteen and dead, exhausted by childbirth, at forty-six.

However the family was able to afford it, Molly went to Dublin to train and then work as a teacher. Unfortunately she failed an exam—her eyes were bad and she couldn't read the questions, according to family lore—and she was able to get only a so-so job in Dublin. When she came home for a holiday, she was introduced to Patrick Gunnigan, her near neighbor and distant relative; they married on November 5, 1919.

It would be a little too stark to say that Molly's marriage to Pat constituted coming down in the world. A farmer of his scale was a figure of substance in rural Mayo. Besides, there was a streak of poetry in the Gunnigans, and a streak of high-mindedness as well. On his mother's side, Pat was a Greally, and no fewer than five of his maternal uncles were priests. One of them, Canon John Greally, was the parish priest at Knock, site of the important Catholic shrine not far from Lurgan.* Tim, Pat's brother, had followed in the family tradition and become a priest, too. He was the curate at Westport, on the Mayo coast. Father Tim was an intelligent man,

---

*Canon John had helped buy the land where the Knock Basilica and Pilgrimage Centre now stand, and the money with which he had done so had been made thanks to a brilliant investment in Courtaulds—hence, in nylon stockings. This was a family secret / family joke.

Knock is worth a visit for two groups in particular: (1) devout Catholics; (2) connoisseurs of religious kitsch and the all-round bizarre. Last time I was there, I had just driven past a flashing neon sign for the Padre Pio Rest Home (which in my memory had illuminating on/off stigmata, though I'm told I imagined that detail), when I was nearly killed by a carful of nuns, smiling beatifically as they went the wrong way around a roundabout. My cousins tell me that nuns are notoriously dangerous drivers.

fastidious and scholarly, with a clerically dry sense of humor. He was to rise to become a papal monsignor, a figure of some local importance, and one who never lost a tart edge. He may have shared the family's political sympathies, and after the Easter Rising in 1916, at which point he was a junior priest at Dunshaughlin, he cycled twenty miles to Dublin to provide spiritual comfort for the men facing execution.* That was something he would not talk about.

Pat was not an intellectual like his brother Tim, but he was a hardworking farmer of good local repute. This, as the American anthropologist

---

*I know that the historiography around this subject is enormous, but I pass on this as a near-contemporary memory. According to my mother, the thing that changed Ireland most was not the Easter Rising but the executions after it. People had mixed feelings about the Rising, coming as it did during World War I, and involving as it appeared an element of fanaticism and wishful thinking. But then the rebels were shot, over several days, in what seemed a cruel, disproportionate, and excruciatingly protracted punishment, and Ireland changed.

Conrad Arensberg made clear in his 1936 study on the West of Ireland, *The Irish Countryman,* was crucial. A man's position was decided by the interplay of three closely related things: "land," "blood," and "local standing." Pat stood to inherit some land, his family was known and respected, and his own reputation was sound. Molly would be the first of the six Waldron daughters to be married. She was twenty-four, young by the standards of Ireland, which at this time had the highest average age for marriage in the world, 29.1 years old for women and 34.9 for men. All in all, Pat was a good catch. The new Mr. and Mrs. Gunnigan settled down at Lurgan and set about having a family. Their first child, my mother Julia, was born on December 5, 1920.

It is only in a certain sort of fiction that marriage automatically constitutes a happy ending. Life for the Gunnigans did not suddenly become easy. Pat was a subsistence farmer, what would in other parts of the world be known as a peasant. The family cows were the key livestock. In the words of Conrad Arensberg: "The small farmer cultivates a 'garden' of oats, rye, potatoes, cabbage and turnips, and devotes his pasture and the hay of his fields to milch cattle. He sells his cows' increase each year. He keeps large numbers of hens and a few pigs. But the milch cow is the center round which this economy revolves. Nearly all he raises he consumes at home; his family and his farm animals take the greater part of his produce. It is only his surplus and his annual crop of calves which break out of the circle of subsistence and in so doing bring him the only monetary income he receives." The great event, as my mother remembered it, was the slaughter of a pig. The butcher would come to the farm, once or twice a year, kill a pig, and make every bit of it into food. Right to the end of her life, my mother could recite what would happen to the various parts of the animal: the hocks would be salted for gammon, the back would be cured for bacon, the head would be boiled for head cheese, the crubeens—that's the beautiful Irish word for pig's feet—would be breaded and fried, the blood would be mixed with oatmeal for black pudding, other bits would be made into sausages. "Then we'd make up a little parcel, wrapped in a handkerchief, with a little piece of all the different cuts, and take it to the neighbors, and when they killed a pig they'd do the same thing." The only things the family regularly bought, rather than grew or made, were tea, sugar, and soap. Everything else came from the farm. Some variety in the diet was supplied by fish, caught legally or poached, and from the birds and rabbits Pat shot for the pot. He was a legendarily good shot: if he could see something, he could hit it.

A man's life on the farm was determined by the routine of the seasons. He would do different types of work at different times of the year. By contrast, a woman's routine was determined by the hours of the day: its structure was given by the regular demands of the twenty-four hours, and especially by the children. The pattern in Ireland was not only for late marriage—this was partly because of the need to pass on the family farm in dowry settlements, so parents waited before entering into the semi-arranged marriages common in the countryside—but also for large families. Molly Waldron had bucked the first trend by marrying relatively early, but she did not buck the second. She was pregnant more or less once a year from 1920 on. Julia's birth was followed by the births of Noreen, Mary, Bernie, Peggie, Dilly, John—finally a boy to inherit the farm—and last, in 1934, Jane. In addition, Molly had five miscarriages and stillbirths, for a total of thirteen pregnancies. The fact that this was not unusual for the time and place did not make it any easier.

This is not a book about the Gunnigans. I have not tried to give a rounded, overall account of their lives—though that would be an amazing story, one that described the astonishing changes in Ireland in the past three-quarters of a century or so. The difference between the Ireland into which my mother and her siblings were born and the Ireland in which my cousins live is extraordinary and exhilarating. In some people's versions, the old Ireland would seem lighter, and the new Ireland darker, than they do to me; but I am my mother's son. Other family members see things differently, and remember things differently. This means not simply that specific events and actions struck them in different ways, but that the main incidents, the turning points and plot points, were different. Family life is not a neutral reality that we can achieve by research and consensus, but a story, in which the characters and the crucial actions are different depending on who is telling the story. This is my mother's story, and not a consensus version.

In my mother's account, there was a division of qualities between the parents. The Gunnigans were the good—the humanly good—side of the family. Her father was a kind man, or as kind as he was allowed to be by the need to work all the time and keep up a stern front. He was fond of my mother. One day when she had a rash, he took her aside, so that the other children in the family wouldn't hear and laugh at her, and told her that the best thing was to dab a little of her own urine on it. When my mother told that story, the affection in her voice was for the fact that he had shielded her from ridicule.

That was Gunnigan through and through. So were the family jokes. When my mother was three, she tripped and fell down the short, steep staircase of the house—a feature to this day. She landed on her head. As people rushed toward little Julia, her grandfather announced, "Oh, don't bother, she's bound to be dead."

On the other side were the Waldrons. Family memories diverge over the question of Molly, my mother's mother. It would not be too much of an exaggeration to say that my mother hated her. Julia certainly feared and distrusted her; she saw her mother as a spreader of gossip, a great one for rummaging through people's secrets, a reader of other people's letters and diaries, malicious, a troublemaker who took great pleasure in the trouble she made. This fed into the sense of what Ireland and Irishness meant for Julia. In my mother's stories, Ireland was a sad and glorious place, and being Irish was something to be proud of: she was, and she hoped I was, too. But it was also a place to be careful of and to keep your distance from. People wishing one another ill featured a lot in my mother's stories—envy and malice were vivid realities to her. And that was somehow connected to Ireland and to her experiences with her mother. Families could be trouble: there was a connection between Ireland and that fact as well. Things like wills had endless potential to make difficulty.

Julia felt that her mother resented her and did everything she could to hold her down. It may well be that Molly took out on her oldest

daughter her own resentment at being trapped and hemmed in. The dis-like my mother felt for her mother sometimes expressed itself in a dislike for all the Waldrons. In my mother's account they were hard people: they could be mean, mean-minded, practical, ungenerous. In later life, when she was angry with me, she would tell me that I was behaving like a "typical"—or sometimes she would use the word "real"—Waldron. This was not intended as a compliment. But I never heard my mother voice any actual complaints against any of her other Waldron relatives, many of whom had been very kind to her. So this was really just a way of talk-ing about her mother. Almost the only favorable thing she said about Molly was that she was a very good cook. The division was simple: Gun-nigan father nice, Waldron mother nasty.

That's not how others remember it. My aunt Peggie has a great deal of sympathy for her mother. "I know Mum could be infuriating—I can understand Julia in many ways—but Mum had a very tough life. She'd been brought up in Mount View, in a comfortable home by West of Ireland farmhouse standards. Then, when she married, she came to this absolutely bleak, comfortless home." Comfortless: that seems a fair summary of the incessant round of work, pregnancy, child-rearing, in a tiny and very spartan home, not much changed since its construction in 1873, lacking running water and power. By rural custom and precept, "one woman in the house must always be working." That, for a woman brought up to expect to be a schoolteacher, who had given up a job in Dublin for marriage, meant a hard life. Making the food grown on the farm stretch to feed the whole family, adjusting clothes for hand-me-downs for the younger children, mending everything that broke—these were now her crucial skills.

Life was hard. That is the key point. I don't want to belabor this, since it has been a recurrent feature of writing about Ireland since the revival of Gaelic literature in the 1900s. As soon as people began composing prose memoirs in Irish, a tidal wave of books vied with one another in their description of just how extravagantly difficult the protagonist's upbringing had been—walking ten miles to school, dining off the smell of cabbages, et cetera. This trend was parodied, devastatingly, by Flann O'Brien in *An Béal Bocht* (*The Poor Mouth*), whose title comes from the great Irish expression for complaining about how hard a time you're having—"giving it the poor mouth." In the novel, instead of walking miles to school, O'Brien's characters have to swim in from the island of Aran—that sort of thing. One might have hoped that *The Poor Mouth* would have put a permanent end to people's giving it the poor mouth, but not so, as the success of Frank McCourt's memoirs show. It's a pity O'Brien didn't live to parody that.

I don't want to overstress a thoroughly stressed fact. Still, life *was* hard, and this made a hardness enter into people. There was a mixture of objective poverty and a cultural narrowness, directed particularly toward women and intensified through the various pieties—Catholic, nationalist, Gaelicist, traditionalist—of the newborn Irish Free State. It is the world depicted in Patrick Kavanagh's masterpiece *The Great Hunger,* in which the hunger is both literal and imaginative, a longing for something more, something bigger. And this hardness contributed to a hardness in Julia's character. This is an Irish trait about which the Irish don't write or talk, but it's something I've often noticed: a bleak, adamantine toughness; a refusal to yield anything to circumstances (which is usually good) or weakness (which is usually good) or anybody else (which is sometimes good) or one's own better nature (not so good) or love (not good at all). Julia's dominant memory of her childhood was that it was hard, cold, comfortless, and unloving. When I once asked her whether she had been happy as a child, she said that she had not. I asked her why.

"Because I was ignored. And it isn't very nice being ignored."

My mother never felt she had had her mother's love; she never felt she had had a moment's undivided attention from anyone in her childhood, ever. You might say that the oldest daughter in a family of eight children living on the edge of subsistence will be bound to feel that, and you might be right. But the hardness of which I write was strongly present in her upbringing. Her father, Pat, she loved, and felt loved by, but she also felt him as an absence, and the reality for a farmer of his time was that life was an unremitting struggle to survive and provide. She felt it especially of her mother, who came across to her as hard, dark, bitter, unyielding, merciless, remorseless, and ruthless. And my mother could be some of these things, too, and knew it, and it was not her preferred truth about herself.

The route out was education. Nobody needed to tell Julia that, she figured it out for herself. She thrived on her first experience of the outside. There is a beautiful observation in Arensberg's *The Irish Countryman*: "At four in the 'evening,' as the countryman divides the day, the children arrive from school, to be fed and questioned. For they are important purveyors of news." Julia loved this sense of contact with the world. She did exceptionally well in school, and soon came home with praise and prizes. She had a phenomenal memory and was a champion retainer of facts and a star reciter of poetry. To the end of her life she could recite yardfuls of the verse she had learned as a child, and she had a big line in Edwardian and Victorian narrative poetry; "The Green Eye of the Little Yellow God" was a particular favorite. (The author of that poem, J. Milton Hayes, also wrote "The Whitest Man I Know." I don't think you need to have read it to feel that you've read it.) My wife's name is Miranda; my mother would often have to be prevented from reciting the whole of Hilaire Belloc's poem "Tarantella" ("Do you remember an inn, Miranda? / Do you remember an inn?") to her. "Horatius" and "The Charge of the Light Brigade" were also set pieces. These would be performed at family concerts, and to "entertain" visitors.

"Julia was a very bright child," my aunt Peggie remembers. "Everybody said that." Until the age of eleven, she was educated at the National School in Dugara. This was a walk of about a mile each way. She was immediately and lastingly at the top of her class. The open nature of academic competition suited her, and the attention and praise she earned through her success in the school suited her as well. This is another point over which memories diverge. My mother, as I've said, saw her childhood as one long immersion in being neglected and ignored. That's not exactly how other members of the family remember it. "Julia was the bright one, the clever one, the one that was always trotted out for visitors," one of her sisters recalls. She would be brought to the parlor and encouraged to go through her paces. Sixty years later, there was still an edge of sibling competition to these memories. Pat and Molly, in this version of events, doted on Julia's deeds: "Everything she did was then repeated."

In 1932, at the age of eleven, Julia won a place as a day pupil at the Convent of Mercy in Ballyhaunis. This small market town, now with its mosque, is about fifteen miles from the family home in Lurgan. It was a good school, run by the Sisters of Mercy. Julia went to stay with her mother's brother Tony Waldron, then a young G.P. just setting out in practice. (Tony died while I was writing this book, in 2005, at the age of 101. The Waldrons are very long-lived: at the time of this writing, my mother's aunt Nora is still alive at ninety-eight.) Another of her mother's siblings, her sister Biddy, was staying with him as his housekeeper. Julia moved in with them for the duration of the school term and continued to do well, better than well, in school. There was a national essay competition, on some patriotic subject or other, and Julia won it. This was a famous event in the family. It was "absolutely wonderful, that Julia was so very clever and so very bright," Peggie recalls.

At thirteen, Julia changed schools again, when she won a place at the Presentation convent in Tuam. This time she would be a boarder. She would spend twenty-four hours a day in the atmosphere of a missionary nuns' school.

The Sisters of the Presentation of the Blessed Virgin Mary are a religious order with Irish origins. The founder was a Cork woman, Nano Nagle, born in 1718, who received her religious education in France and then went home and dedicated her life to education and to the poor. At the time it was illegal to educate Catholic children; the penalty for doing so was exile and confiscation of property. Nano Nagle went ahead and did it anyway, which is why she recently came first in a poll to identify the greatest Irish person in history. (I find this a less depressing choice than the permanent British option, Winston Churchill.) She founded what was initially a branch of the Ursuline Sisters, and in 1775, when the Ursulines were forbidden to break their contemplative way of life to work with the poor, she established the Sisters of Charitable Instruction of the Sacred Heart of Jesus, which became the Order of the Presentation of the Blessed Virgin Mary. From its inception it has been an order with a strong bias toward education. It is not as well known or as prominent as its male equivalent, the Christian Brothers, but nonetheless has had a considerable presence in Ireland and as a missionary order abroad. The first overseas branch was founded in Newfoundland in 1833, followed by India (1842), San Francisco (1854), Tasmania (1856), and so on. The glory and wonder and drama of these missions were constant subjects in the school. Nuns returning from the missions would regularly give talks to the pupils. "It's very difficult to imagine, it's very difficult to explain to anyone without the background," says Peggie. "If you were at boarding school in Ireland, several times in the year nuns from the missions would come looking for postulants." A postulant is a trainee nun, one who has gone into the convent but has not yet "taken the habit" and sworn the vows that commit her to the order and to a life of poverty, chastity, and obedience. "You'd get a long talk about how wonderful the life was, the marvelous possibilities, they'd show you photographs of things they did, and tell you stories. So if you were in a convent boarding school, you were fired with this idea of how wonderful it would be to go on the missions. I imagine a lot of very unsuitable people went into convents, not having a clue of what they were letting themselves in for at a very early age. They'd grown up totally sheltered."

Sheltered in one way; exposed, or indoctrinated, in another. It might not be true to call Ireland in the mid-1930s the most Catholic country in the world. But in other countries with a strong Catholic presence there was also forceful opposition to Catholicism; there were strands of secular, left-wing, anticlerical thought, ranging from mild atheistic dissent to outright militant communism. That was not the case in Ireland. The ascent to power of Éamon de Valera's government in 1932, the anti-treaty body having reincarnated itself as Fianna Fáil, saw Catholicism and nationalism locked in an inseparably tight clinch. The Church had been courageous as the embodiment of national identity all through the dark years of the penal laws and the deliberate, violent suppression of Irish identity through religion, language, education, and economics. Now the Church was garnering its reward at the center of a state that was, if not exactly theocratic, then not far from it; the least you could say is that it was distinctly, defiantly unsecular. The air was heavy with piety: a peculiar and deeply Irish national Catholic piety. The new state religion was religion and the state. The intensity of feeling and the monolithic character of this new state, and its attitudes to women, at times conspire to seem, to a contemporary observer, close to some versions of Islam. Julia, like everyone else, but especially everyone else in a convent boarding school in the West of Ireland, drew in this mixture with every breath. A bright girl and a devout one, she was constantly being prompted to ask herself whether she might have that most exciting, most noble thing of all: a religious vocation.

When trying to understand the pressures on Julia, one must add to this the fact that by 1936 she was the oldest of a family of eight children, of whom seven were girls. It would not be fair to call this a disaster, but it did not make life simple for the Gunnigans. The house was small, and already so full that one of the younger children was sent to be brought up by her Waldron grandparents. The farm could not support more adults. The girls had to be married off; this was not a choice, it was a basic fact of economics. But the supply of available men was strictly finite, and so were opportunities to meet them; and in these circumstances Irish men were marrying later and later. (It's still true today in rural Ireland. The tongue-tied, solitary farmer, depressed and wordless and unable to meet women, is a rural Irish cliché with a sound basis in truth.)

The obligation to leave home was a particular imperative in the mid-1930s. One of the first things de Valera did after winning the election in 1932 was to stop the annuity the Free State had been paying to the British treasury. (This was part of the complex deal whereby the Free State bought out the freeholds that had belonged to absentee landlords.) The result was economic sanctions of such severity that they amounted to economic war—and since Britain was not just Ireland's main trading partner but essentially its only one, taking ninety-six percent of its exports, the effects were devastating. A punitive duty on cattle was catastrophic, and the value of Irish agricultural exports fell by two-thirds. For people like the Gunnigans, the impact was felt directly. These years are to this day known as the "Hungry Thirties."

So more than ever, the children of the family "must travel." But what did that, in practice, mean? For male children of a rural Irish family, the most prestigious and respected career choice was the priesthood; for female children, it was to become a nun. For the Gunnigans, a role model was close at hand in the form of Father, later Monsignor, Tim Gunnigan, my mother's uncle. "He was obviously marked out to be a priest from the time he was about twelve and sent to a diocesan college and then on to Maynooth and so on," one of Tim's nieces told me, before adding: "Even he, poor lad, had probably very little choice." Tim was the most admired member of the family, and would have made the convent seem both an admirable and a conceivable choice—provided always, of course, that the young woman in question was able to detect in herself the sincere glimmerings of a religious vocation.

Julia spent hours trying to distinguish between what was a real impulse to a vocation and what was her rational mind telling her that a vocation would be an immensely useful thing for her to have; what was real religious feeling and what was convenience. And mixed in with the desire to do what was right in the eyes of God, and her conscience, and beneficial to her family, was a voice, so quiet and unfamiliar at this time in her life that she would have had trouble hearing it, asking, But what about me? It was a sentiment she was trained not to have, and not to consider important if she did have it; but there it was, and like many such questions it did not become easier to ignore just because it was so quiet. In fact, the quietness of its insistence was part of what gave it force: But what about me?

At sixteen, Julia had no experience of the wider world. (Her only long-distance expedition had been a trip to Dublin to attend the Eucharistic Congress in 1932.) But she knew that a wider world did exist. In one sense, joining a religious order was a way of experiencing that world, especially if she joined an order with missions abroad. The price paid for this, however, was to spend her life in what amounted to a form of confinement, psychological as much as institutional. People joining religious orders didn't see it that way consciously; but they knew that they would never be free again. This was about three decades before Vatican II, and the vow of obedience meant what it said. Julia contemplated it with elation but also with real fear.

She struggled with these questions. It was difficult to unpick what was hers—her hopes, her beliefs, her needs—and what belonged to the culture; and what needs and hopes belonged to her family rather than to her. What belonged to whom? It's hard enough to untangle now, almost seventy years later. It must have been even harder at the time. But Julia made her decision. She told her family and the sisters at her convent school that she believed she had a vocation and that she wanted to be a nun. Her plan was to join the Sisters of the Good Shepherd as a postulant at their convent in New Ross, County Wexford. Her intention was to leave school before the end of her course of studies and join the convent immediately. This was the early summer of 1937, and Julia was sixteen years old.

THIS IS ANOTHER POINT of family history at which memories diverge. Julia was adamant that she was forced into the convent by family pressure. It was her family's needs and expectations that drove Julia into the convent at sixteen. But that is not how others remember it.

"Father Tim and my parents were against it," says Peggie. "My mother tried to persuade her to wait for a couple of years, at least to do her Leaving Cert." The Leaving Certificate was the set of exams at the end of Irish secondary education, at which Julia had been expected to excel. Without it she would have no formal qualifications. "But Julia didn't want to. At this stage my mother and father were very proud of her and very pleased that she was doing this wonderful thing that was great kudos for the family." Although there was no visible explicit pressure, there were expectations that Julia could gratify by taking the habit. So both accounts are probably right: my mother told the truth when she said there was pressure, and Peggie is accurate in her memory that her parents said they did not want Julia to go.

This is my mother's story, and I do not wish, in telling it, to trespass on anyone's privacy any more than I must. But I feel I have to mention here that four of the Gunnigan sisters became nuns. This must surely reflect a considerable degree of family pressure, as well as the example of the girls' great-uncles the Greally brothers—even if none of it was conscious or explicit. In any case, as soon as she made her decision, Julia became the family heroine. She was made godmother to her newborn youngest sister, Jane. Her choice was a source of enormous pride, and relief and sadness, too. This particularly affected Pat. His grief on the day Julia left to join the Good Shepherds was something the children had not seen before. "I would have been going on for ten," Peggie says. "I remember it distinctly. They went in a hired car—I remember the hired car coming to the gate. And it was the only time in my life I'd seen my father crying. It horrified me, and I couldn't believe that my father was crying. And my mother went with her."

The Sisters of the Good Shepherd earn a rave review in the *Catholic Encyclopedia* of the early twentieth century:

> The aim of this institute is to provide a shelter for girls and women of dissolute habits, who wish to do penance for their iniquities and to lead a truly Christian life. Not only voluntary penitents but also those consigned by civil or parental authority are admitted. Many of these penitents desire to remain for life; they are admitted to take vows, and form the class of "magdalens," under the direction of the Sisters of the Good Shepherd. They are an austere contemplative community, and follow the Rule of the Third Order of Mount Carmel. Prayer, penance and manual labour are their principal occupations. Many of these "magdalens" frequently rise to an eminent degree of sanctity. Besides girls and women of this class, the order also admits children who have been secured from danger, before they have fallen or been stained by serious crime. . . . Besides the three ordinary vows of poverty, chastity and obedience, the Sisters of the Good Shepherd take a fourth vow, namely, to work for the conversion and instruction of "penitents"—a vow which makes this order one of the most beautiful creations of Christian charity.

I can state with absolute confidence that the Good Shepherds are no longer seen as "one of the most beautiful creations of Christian charity." The order's main work was in running institutions that have now, thanks to Peter Mullan's incendiary film *The Magdalene Sisters,* become deservedly notorious. The Magdalene asylums were essentially prisons for girls and women who had done things that people who had power over them did not approve of. In some instances young women were sent to the asylum for such crimes as going to the cinema without permission. (That earned one woman, Mary Morris, a future campaigner against the Magdalene asylums, two years' incarceration.) The imprisonment was all the more terrible for being enforced not by any legal authority but through the psychological terror inflicted by Church authorities. It was coercion pure and simple, without even a legal gloss. The asylums were instruments of punishment and control and misogyny, disguised as charitable institutions. The incident that brought them more recently to notice took place in 1993, when a convent sold land to a property developer, who, in the course of excavations, discovered dozens of unmarked graves. These belonged to "penitents" who had died in the asylum and whose deaths had passed without notice, remark, or redress.

Thanks to *The Magdalene Sisters,* the cruelty of the asylums to their inmates is now known. The story that has not been told, however, is of the cruelty and violence that took place among the nuns who ran them. The source of this was not so much malice as the inbuilt authoritarian animus of an institution dedicated to controlling every moment of the lives of its functionaries, body and soul. It was this for which Julia was entirely unprepared. She had no idea what was entailed by the order's vows: the finality and irreversibility and completeness of the submission involved. This would have been the case in any monastic order, but in one following the Rule of Saint Francis de Sales it was especially marked.

To laypeople it may seem as if monks and nuns in general follow the same sorts of rules and lead similar lives. This is not the case. The crucial determining factor for any monastic order is which Rule it follows, this being a set of instructions that not only shapes the broad direction of the community, in terms of mission work or prayer or teaching or the like, but also gives detailed and explicit prescriptions for how every day is to be spent, what the members of the order wear, at what hour they get up in the morning and go to bed at night, when and how they pray, what they eat, when they speak, when or whether they are allowed leisure or exercise or conversation. The seventeenth-century Rule of Saint Francis de Sales exchanged some of the external strictures and "mortifications" of the Order of Saint Augustine, such as rising to pray in the middle of the night, in favor of an increased emphasis on internal mortification. In other words, it was meant to be physically easier but psychologically more rigorous. The sisters took vows that were renewed every year for five years and then confirmed in perpetuity. They wore a complicated habit, a garment of outstanding symbolic importance; as I've said, for a nun the equivalent process to being ordained was "taking the habit." Nuns were not allowed to own property of any sort; rooms, beds, rosaries, crosses, and pictures were regularly changed to prevent the development of any sense of individual ownership. Obedience was stressed even more than elsewhere in monastic orders, and as each convent was both cloistered from the outside world and subject only to its own authority—there was no superior general for the order, and convents were self-governing—the authority of the mother superior was absolute. There was no possibility of appeal or complaint for any reason, ever. The day began at five a.m. and ended at ten p.m. and was divided into fifteen-minute installments, every one of them filled with an allotted physical or spiritual task. The sisters were allowed two "recreations" a day of an hour each, the only time they were allowed to choose their own topics of thought or, up to a point, conversation: they were permitted to speak "with cordiality and simplicity only of agreeable and piously cheerful topics." As the *Catholic Encyclopedia* proudly says, these rules "overlook nothing which could mortify the spirit."

I don't know anything about any of this from my mother. She never spoke about her time as a Good Shepherd. I did not even know she had been in the Good Shepherd convent in New Ross until after her death. As for the impact all this had on Julia, there is almost no direct evidence for it, apart from her actions and two documents, the only contemporary evidence of what was on her mind that year. The first is a letter written not long after she had entered the convent. The occasion was her sister Bernie's twelfth birthday. Julia herself was not yet seventeen.

Good Shepherd Convent
New Ross
24th October 1937

My dearest Bernie,

Another year has passed and again I wish you many happy returns of the day and every blessing and happiness during the year you are beginning. I hope that you will enjoy your birthday very much and that you will get very nice things for it.

Thanks very much for your nice letter—I was delighted to hear from you—you are a splendid hand at giving news God bless you! I always enjoy your letters. I had a letter from Mary [their sister] on Tuesday and she told me that she got you a lovely new red coat and that you are well able to swank it—well I bet Daddie will have fun when you go home so. [Bernie was at boarding school.] I got a box of sweets from Mary too—wasn't she great? God bless her.

How are you getting on at school yourself? Now get good marks again this year like you did last year and keep on at the hard work and get your Inter.-Cert and then who knows but you might come to St Anne's when you are old enough if it be God's Will. [In other words, Julia was hoping that Bernie would enter the convent, too.]

Yes, I am very happy here and very thankful to God for bringing me here. Bernie dear if you did come you would never be sorry, but anyhow we will have to wait until you are old enough first.

Do you know what I have just noticed—that next Monday is November's Day [All Saints']—well now aren't you lucky, that means that you will be going home on Friday for the week-end and you will be home for nearly three days. If you aren't having the time of your lives of it 'tis no day. And you will be able to show off your new coat too. My dear but won't you feel posh. Aren't they having the Mission at home this fortnight and you will be home for the finishing of it too. Tell Mammie that I asked her to let you go on Sunday night as a birthday present and I bet you will be let go.

When you go home too, will you tell Peggie & Dillie that I am expecting to hear from them or I won't remember any more birthdays and tell Peggie that she is to write the letter herself and not get Mammie to do it for her. Tell Daddie that I said 'Up Kerry' & that I did not mean a bit of it and better luck Mayo next year. Tell them thanks for their letter and all the news and I will write soon. Write soon again and make your letter longer next time and if you please don't mind telling me that you suppose I am fat—you know well I am and I know it myself too.

I will again wish you a very happy birthday and many happy returns. God bless you all.

Ever lovingly yours

Julia

One has to realize a few things about this letter before one tries to take it at face value. A postulant was allowed to write only one letter home a week, at an allocated time (usually Sunday). The letter was read by the postulant mistress. A postulant was not allowed to mention anything that happened in the convent; she was explicitly forbidden to discuss her own feelings. So this letter was never going to be a howl of pain. Nonetheless, it is not the work of a young woman who has any idea what she is doing. Julia has vowed the rest of her life away and seems not to recognize it. The charm and sweetness of the letter, and the implied hint of trouble to come, lie in the fact that it is entirely devoted to things from which its author is now cut off. The Good Shepherds were an enclosed order, and the only contact Julia would have with her family from now on would be through letter and the occasional, extraordinarily infrequent visit. Letters in both directions were opened and read—there was an explicit ban on privacy in the order's emphasis on "common life"—so if Julia was unhappy she could not show it here. But it does look as if she was still in the honeymoon period of her time with the Good Shepherds. She would hardly have dangled the idea of Bernie's entering the convent herself one day if she had been miserable. And the fact that she is able to solicit a favor on Bernie's behalf ("Tell Mammie that I asked her to let you go on Sunday night as a birthday present and I bet you will be let go") is a sign that her domestic stock is high.

It is in the nature of life in an enclosed order that nothing can be known about what happens there, except what the participants themselves choose to tell. The only other document touching on this period in Julia's life is a short story of more than twenty years later, when she was living in London and beginning to write autobiographical fiction. The story was written and broadcast on the BBC under the pseudonym Shivaun Cunningham. It is one of only two written accounts she gave of her life as a nun. Again, I saw it only after her death.

Minding Mother Margaret
by Shivaun Cunningham

Mother Margaret looked me up and down. 'Put your hands under your cape, Sister,' she ordered. 'It's a cold day, and they'll be warmer that way; besides, postulants aren't supposed to walk swinging their arms.' I tucked my hands under the waist-length cape, only to whip them out again in a flash as Mother Margaret threw her veil back, hitched up her habit, and said, 'Me crutches dear, get me m' crutches, I'm goin' for a walk.' It was my first day in the convent, and instead of sending me to the school to teach, as I had expected, I had been told that I was to 'mind' Mother Margaret. Mother Superior had just taken me along to present me to Mother Margaret, and I was sorrier than ever that I hadn't been sent out to take a class. She was small, broad rather than fat, forthright in manner, and quite ugly-looking. She seemed to read my thoughts as I stood there. 'All right,' she said. 'We'll make the best of each other, and don't forget I like my tea hot and strong and not slopped in the saucer.'

Mother was old, eighty-two, I believe, 'a member of an old county family, my deah,' as she soon and often told me. She had slipped on one of the polished corridors of the convent some months before my entrance and broken her hip. This accident kept her in bed for several weeks, but now she was mobile again—with crutches—and something of a hazard to ordinary convent routine. So Mother Superior decided that the newest postulant should look after her. Luckily for me, Mother Margaret approved of the decision. 'I know the Cunninghams,' she declared, when the Reverend Mother brought me along to meet her, 'an old family, decent stock—is your face painted, child?' I assured her that it wasn't, and hoped that Mother Superior believed me, and then we got down to the business of going for a walk.

The walk was taken on the long upstairs corridor which ran the entire length of the convent. Mother Margaret's crutches made it impossible for her to go downstairs. I gave her the crutches and steered her out the door and along the corridor. 'Did you attend a ball before you entered?' she asked as we progressed. 'Well,' I stammered, quite unprepared, 'there was a party or two last week.' 'When I was a girl,' she went on, 'I went to all the balls. My poor father, God rest his soul, was one of the Ffrenches of Frenchpark—old county family—you know, my mother was just a peasant girl—pah—he believed in the social graces, he made me practise the piano and do watercolours for four hours every day, and then he allowed me to go to the county balls. Just before I entered,' Mother Margaret went on, 'I attended a ball at Mooncoin House—very fetching I looked, in a simple white dress with a rose over me ear—I had hair like yours then, m'dear—tuck it in, like a good child, the cap is supposed to hide it. I was, if I may say so, the belle of the ball, a gentleman there . . .'

Here Mother Margaret interrupted herself as another old nun passed by—unattended and crutchless. 'Do you see her?' she whispered hoarsely. She didn't wait for an answer. 'There she goes—the deaconess from Waterford, and her great-grandfather was a stableboy at Curraun House.' I discovered afterwards that there had developed in recent years a feud between these old souls, both very conscious of their superior birth, both in their eighties and bosom friends in their youth. I found out, too, that this feud was a very personal one in which no other member of the community dared even seem to take sides. Any criticisms made were made by themselves of each other, and each was quick to defend the other from the slightest censure by anyone else. 'Ah, the old stock,' sighed Mother Margaret as the deaconess passed by. 'Now my family could . . .' 'But the ball, Mother,' I ventured, 'did you enjoy it?' 'I always enjoyed meself, child: me poor father, God rest his soul, used to say it was a sign of good breedin' to enjoy yourself. Very fetchin' I looked, with a simple white dress and a rose over me ear—turn your toes out, child. I remember when I entered I was quite knock-kneed—after all the ridin', you know—the Duhallow hounds—me father was master—old county family.' 'But the ball, Mother,' I tried again: 'You looked lovely.' Would I never hear the end of the story? 'Ah yes, the ball. A gentleman there paid very marked attention to me, Sister; it was just before I entered. He took me in to supper, booked all the waltzes in my programme—do you waltz, child? A most graceful dance. Very fetchin' I looked, just a simple white dress.' 'And a rose over your ear,' I finished, hoping to get to the next part of the story. 'Yes, a rose over my ear, very fetchin' too. Me poor father always admired me hair—called it me crownin' glory, you know. Push your shoulders back, child. You should always watch your deport-ment, dear—sign of good breedin'. I never slouched.'

'But the ball, Mother,' I urged. 'Ah yes,' she went on. 'A gentleman there paid me very marked attention—very eligible, a very good catch. He took me to supper and after that he said, "Please, may I have the plea-sure of the last dance, and then I shall escort you to your home, and to-morrow I shall call at Frenchpark and speak to your father!" Very correct he was—get me my hankie, dear, and turn your toes out.' Mother blew her nose vigorously. I waited, tongue almost hanging out for the story to go on. 'He was going to offer for me, Sister,' she continued. 'And I said to him, "You needn't bother. I'm joining the convent in a few days." "Why didn't you tell me that at half past seven this evening and not have me wasting my night?" said he.' Mother Margaret sighed. 'Crazy about me he was, dear. I remember after I entered I was given charge of the play-ground at dinner. Very fetching I was, in me postulant's cap. This gentle-man, from a very good family too, child, came to Castleport (this was the town where our convent was situated) for the races. He dined with His Grace the Archbishop and afterwards, do you know what he did, Sister?

He came to the back gate and peeped into the playground just to get a glimpse of me in my postulant's dress. Crazy about me, he was, dear—put your shoulders back, now.'

This was the first time I heard Mother Margaret tell her story, but I listened to it every day for the next six months that I looked after her, and it never changed by so much as a syllable. Not that Mother's behaviour was usually as predictable as the next line of her story.

There was the day the Papal Nuncio called. A visit from a church dignitary, especially one such as the Nuncio, was usually a highlight of convent life, and it was customary to summon the sisters by ringing, not the ordinary single bell, but the two main bells. Double bells was a signal for everyone to drop what she was doing and come quick. Well, on this particular day, the Nuncio's visit was a private one. He was not meeting the entire community—just the Mother Superior and her assistants—or so he thought. He reckoned without Mother Margaret. Mother's cell, as a nun's tiny room is called, was situated to the front of the convent and gave her a clear view of the main door.

I was occupied at the time doing my 'charge'—as one's daily cleaning chore was called—cleaning and polishing a corridor downstairs was my charge at the time. Mother Margaret was alone in her cell. Suddenly, as I crawled on all fours, busy with a polishing mop, I heard Mother Margaret's throaty voice above me. 'Quick, my deah, pass me the horse.' 'The horse' was Mother Margaret's own private name for the ropes of two of the big convent bells. I had learned by then to do as I was told and no questions, so I passed the horse as she asked. Mother Margaret seized the ropes and rattled out a crashing and unsynchronized version of double bells. 'Follow me, my deah,' she commanded. For some reason best known to herself, Mother had her habit tucked up around her; she was wearing over it an unkempt-looking check apron which was hitched round to one side, and I saw with horror that she had only one crutch. So instead of following her, I acted as a second crutch and supported her as she headed straight for the main reception rooms. Throwing the door open, she slithered across the floor with me and the other crutch in attendance, extended her hand to the astounded Papal Nuncio, favoured the Mother Superior and her assistants with an outraged glare, and re-marked in her loftiest county-family accents, 'Pardon me, Your Excel-lency, they don't know how to receive a church dignitary in this house.' She then seized the Nuncio's hand and kissed it with a resounding smack.

I cannot remember now, how I got Mother Margaret out of the par-lour; my chief problem at this time was how she managed to get down-stairs without me and with only one crutch. That was going to take some explaining to Mother Superior afterwards. 'But you could have hurt yourself, Mother,' I protested. 'Why didn't you send for me or wait until I came? How in the world did you get downstairs without me?' There was a twinkle in dear old Mother Margaret's eye as she told me, 'Not to make you a short answer, Shivaun, my deah, I came on me bottom.'

Mother Margaret had a remarkable memory—as old people often have—and she had a genius for telling her stories at exactly the right moment. There was the time that I got into trouble for running noisily downstairs from my cell to the basement; and for a penance, and to teach me the first rule of convent deportment, 'The sisters shall not be found running giddily through the house,' I was told by my novice mistress to climb the stairs and come down again, kneeling and saying a Hail Mary on every step—both journeys. There were over ninety steps and so over 180 Hail Marys. Mother Margaret's tea was neither hot nor strong that day, and I slopped it in the saucer too. She grumbled a bit, and then saw I had been crying, and dragged the story out of me. 'Never mind, Shi-vaun dear,' she consoled me, 'when Josephine was a novice' (Josephine was the name of my novice mistress), 'she got apples from the gardener once, tied her apron up round her waist to hide them, and hid them there. She forgot all about the apples, and when she went into chapel and let her apron down, they rolled all over the choir, and she had to crawl round and pick them up while the whole community waited to begin Vespers. For a penance she had to eat her meals alone in the middle of the refec-tory for three days, with sixteen apples lined out in front of her. But don't let on I told you, there's a good girl—and now for goodness sake, go and get me a proper cup of tea—hot and strong, and don't slop it in the saucer.'

When I left a withered flower in a vase on one of the altars, I was ordered to wear the flower on my cape for a week as a penance, but Mother Margaret insisted that I remove the wretched thing while with her. 'I can't abide fresh chrysanthemums, my dear,' she told me, 'and withered ones are quite unbearable—vulgar blowsy-looking things—take it away at once.' She knew I hated wearing it and how glad I was to be rid of it even for a little while every day.

It was rather awkward, though, when Mother Margaret insisted on doing my mending for me. My former sewing teacher had told her that 'poor Shivaun could never sew.' I had improved a little since my junior days, but Mother Margaret could never be convinced of that. The result was that before darning my stockings I had to unpick the knotted jungle of yarn that she had already worked over the holes, which were then bigger and more jagged than my heels alone could ever have made them. How I wished that she were less kindhearted, or a better darner.

I continued to look after Mother Margaret until her death about six months after I entered. She remained forthright to the end and never forgot the old county family she came from. She took as few drugs as possible—'Like to keep me faculties about me, dear,' she would say, grey with pain. But she came to depend on me to remind her of her various obligations, and I had strict orders not to feed her with a spoon when anyone else was in the room.

'Spoon-feedin' is for infants—undignified, slovenly, I don't like it,' she insisted. 'Have I said me Rosary, child?' she would ask. She had said several, I assured her. 'But have I said a Rosary for me poor father, God rest his soul?' I wasn't sure, so we would say one together. 'And now we must pray for Gerry.' Gerry was an old friend of hers—a distinguished prelate, recently appointed to an even higher ecclesiastical honour. Mother knew of the honour but evidently couldn't remember its exact nature. 'Come on, child, we'll pray for dear Gerry.' And *'De profundis clamavi,'* she began. Now the De Profundis is the prayer one normally says for a recently departed soul, and as her friend Gerry was still good for several years, I managed to persuade her that some other prayer might be more suitable, and then settled on a Te Deum instead.

The night before she died I was sitting with Mother Margaret. 'You'll pray for me, child?' she asked. 'Of course I will, Mother.' 'I'm goin' home, goin' home,' she said. I thought her mind was wandering, but she added, more or less to herself, 'I'm goin' home to the Lord, and He understands me. You know, dear,' and she smiled at me, 'the Lord is a gentleman.'

The following day Mother Margaret died.

· 3 ·

ONE OF THE SWEET THINGS about "Minding Mother Margaret" is the deep impression made on Julia by the first posh person she ever met. The Good Shepherds, like most religious orders, were divided between "choir" and "lay" members. The choir members brought a dowry to the convent and lived a life concentrating entirely on prayer and retreat—a brutally harsh life, too, before Vatican II. The dowry could be symbolic rather than financial—for Julia, her dowry was her education. The lay members brought no dowry. They took the same vows and lived in the same enclosed conditions, but they took no part in religious services. All sisters did the cleaning, cooking, sweeping, and general running of the convent, and—as in my mother's short story—they looked after the older nuns, as and when it was needed. But only choir sisters read the offices in chapel. To a secular observer it may seem like an unusually harsh and straightforward class division between middle-class and working-class entrants to the convent. Not that, in this story, "Shivaun Cunningham" seems particularly to mind.

So the surface of "Minding Mother Margaret" gives away little about the difficulties lurking beneath. But you don't have to look too hard to see shapes in the shadows. For one thing, the "school" at which "Shivaun" had been hoping to work—quite an ambition for a sixteen-year-old with no Leaving Certificate—would in actuality have been a Magdalene orphanage. Although the story complains about having missed out on the experience in the orphanage, I'm glad that my mother was spared it; glad that she took as little part in the activities of the Magdalene asylums as possible. The brutal discipline of the convent is conveyed in the story about the 180 Hail Marys, and going up and down steps on her knees, and the passing mention of the tears it caused her. The short story also discreetly notes the rivalries and animosities that beset convent life. If two nuns came to hate each other, as could all too easily happen in an enclosed community, the resulting battle could be lifelong—all day, every day, until the death of one of the parties. The same could happen with bullying. In institutions with no external supervision and no possibility of redress, appeal, or intervention, bullying had the potential to be a lethal problem.

"Minding Mother Margaret" contains another clue, perhaps an even more important one, about the difficulties facing the young postulant. The story describes an eighty-two-year-old nun at the end of her life; and what is her main topic of conversation? The ball she attended just before she entered the religious life, and the man she met there. So her most vivid memories involve not the convent but the life outside it, before it. The young nun, just after going into the convent, meets an old nun whose thoughts turn mostly to the time when she was still free. "Minding Mother Margaret," which looks like a character sketch about a snobbish but lovable old dear, carries its real emotional charge as a study of regret. If this story from around 1960 represents anything about Julia's state of mind in 1937, it is that her mind turned, before too long, to the question of what she was giving up in joining the Sisters of the Good Shepherd. A big part of the work a postulant undertakes is an internal scrutiny of her vocation: how much she believes in it herself. She tests her own thoughts and feelings and beliefs. This initial internal scrutiny is as important to the postulant as the external pressures and tests she undergoes. Christianity is a religion of works and also of self-examination, a test of the concordance between the self and the world and beliefs. In the course of scrutinizing her own feelings, Julia came to suspect that she did not have a genuine vocation. She had chosen the monastic life out of pride—spiritual pride—and a desire to help her family. The inner calling was missing. She was being propelled not by a summons from God but by the realities of poverty and peasant life.

Julia had been in New Ross at the Good Shepherd convent for nearly a year, and was on the point of taking her vows and becoming a novitiate nun, when she became ill. The symptoms were diagnosed as appendicitis, and she was taken by ambulance to Mater Misericordiae Hospital in Dublin. Her appendix was removed successfully, but the infection had been quite advanced, and the mother superior at the convent, on medical advice, allowed Julia to go home to rest and recuperate before returning to the order and preparing to take her vows.

My aunt Peggie described Julia's triumphant return to Mayo. "She came home wearing her long black postulant's dress, with the white collar and the little cape, white cuffs and the little short veil. She was wonderful, my father and mother went proudly with her everywhere, sat beside her in church, all the neighbors came to visit and brought presents, she was taken out to places." Julia was the focus of all attention and praise. That in itself may have caused things to stir inside her. As I have said, her big complaint about her childhood was the feeling that she was ignored. Now that she was lionized and made the focus of her parents' love, home had never seemed more appealing. At the same time, she allowed herself to admit to herself just how crushing the weight of the convent actually was. The discipline was too heavy, the lack of private life too oppressive; most of all, perhaps, she quite simply missed the world. So as she was being praised and loved for her decision to give up the world, she was coming to realize that she could not do it, and that all her parents' happiness for her was based on a lie.

Julia thought this over, and came to a second decision, one far more difficult than the first. She decided she could not go back to the convent. But she also did not feel that she had sufficient strength to tell her parents directly. This was a character trait I know well, not least because I inherited it. She couldn't bear to give them the bad news, to break their hearts and face the consequences. So she wrote to the mother superior, and told her. As Peggie remembers: "When Julia had been home a short time, she didn't want to go back and was afraid to tell my parents. So she wrote to the superior, who then wrote to my parents saying this. I actually saw the superior's letter. I don't know if it was best to leave it around for the family to find it, but anyway. The superior was very nice. She said, 'She's very young, she's little more than a child, and it's only to be expected. She feels she made the wrong decision. It may be she'll change later. It would be wiser for her not to go on with it.' A very sensible letter. But my parents were absolutely thunderstruck."

The whole point of being a postulant was that you were on trial as a nun: you were supposed to be giving your vocation a test, and at the same time you were being assessed for suitability as a member of the order. It was understood that the life did not suit everybody; going in as a postulant was no guarantee that you would turn out to have a vocation. Failure was not supposed to be a catastrophe. It was not even supposed to be failure. But that was not how people behaved in practice, and it was not how Julia was treated. Pat and Molly Gunnigan were well-meaning people. Yet they were country people in an intensely conformist culture, one that placed an extremely high premium on questions of family status and religious respectability. Ireland in the decades after its independence was in some respects all too like Afghanistan under the Taliban. In this world, one of the worst things you could be was a spoiled priest or an ex-nun. Just as the priest and nun had a high status, there was nothing lower or less admirable than someone who had failed in the religious life. It was a practical failure but also a deeper, more staining, more intimate shame. This may have had something to do with sex: nuns and priests were supposed to have renounced the flesh, so to have failed in the religious life was to have been overcome by sexual impulses. But whatever the source of the shame, the shame was real. Discredit was brought on everyone associated with the failure. It was a public humiliation for the family. To make this point apparent to Julia, who in herself was the family disgrace, was an imperative; apart from anything else, it was important to make sure that nothing like this ever happened again. As for the ex-nun herself, the reversal of status went beyond humiliation into some exalted state of degradation and shame. Pat and Molly did not so much turn on Julia as behave as if she had died.

It wasn't that Julia's parents refused to take her in—they couldn't do that—but they refused to accept her. She was the focus of local gossip. She was a walking scandal. "Julia went from being the absolute favorite and pet-ted, almost, child. She became barely spoken to, barely mentioned," Peggie told me. "I remember on one occasion Noreen and Julia had gone out to post a letter. Now, the postbox was out near the school. My father was *extremely* strict with all of us. We were never allowed to go out in the evening. We were never allowed to eat out. He would only have allowed Julia out to post the letter, not for any other reason, and he was watching the clock, to see that it didn't take longer than it should. He turned to my mother with a sneer and said, 'Where's the ex-nun now?' And more than anything else it was the way he said it that stuck in my mind."

As I have said, family memories differ about Julia's early childhood and whether she had been as ignored as she subsequently felt herself to have been. But there is no disagreement about the terrible blankness with which she was treated after she left the Good Shepherds. Her parents made her feel as if she were a disgrace. They did everything they could to reinforce this sense of worthlessness. There was one especially acute point of humiliation. As Peggie tells it:

"She had no clothes to wear. Remember the time in Ireland. I barely ap-preciated it, but there was *no* money. Farm produce just didn't sell. We were *miserably* poor. Fortunately we had enough to eat as we'd grow our own vegetables. We kept hens, so we had eggs, my father shot the occasional rabbit or pigeon, but honestly, we had no money. We wore hand-me-down clothes and Julia had no clothes, so she was wearing the postulant's dress. I remember cutting off the thing and making it into a short skirt, leaving off the veil and the white collar. But she was having to go 'round in what everyone could recognize was this black postulant's dress."

This—not being helped to find something else to wear—was a delib-erate piece of public shaming that Julia never forgot or forgave. I've said that there was a hardness to my mother. It was not that she couldn't be kind and gentle and loving; but she could not bear, even momentarily, to be weak. She would not be a supplicant; she would not admit to needing anything or anyone. This was the last time when my mother allowed herself to ask for something, and allowed herself to be rejected; from now on, she was the one who did the rejecting. It would very often be a pre-emptive rejection: she would turn people away before she gave them a chance to turn her away. From that, I can see how much of a wound she sustained in going home and being spurned—shunned, even. She would not ask for help or for love.

I think all of this was due to what happened to her when she left the convent. When she initially went home, she was treated as a star. For perhaps the first time, she felt she had her parents' love and attention. She may even have entertained for a moment the idea that she was loved not for what she had done, or what she had become, but for who she was. Perhaps, after all, she was loved for herself. But when she put that possibility to the test, her hopes were crushed in the most direct way imaginable. She realized that her worst suspicions were true and that she genuinely wasn't loved for herself. The high point of her parents' love and attention turned to the low point. At some level, this was the defining emotional event of Julia's life.

I realize, writing this, that it involves a version of my mother whom I never knew. The young woman who went home after a difficult childhood, looking for a sign or gesture that would make her feel that everything had after all been all right, who went home looking for love, and exposed herself to rejection by doing so: I never met her. The willingness to give people, especially people she loved, a second chance, and also the desperation, and that degree of willingness to accept pain and face rejection, were, by the time I knew her, alien. By then, she did her rejecting first. She was not reluctant to turn her back, and when she did so, it stayed turned. But because I knew her after this first rejection—which may have been the shaping experience of her life, her frantic attempt to prove that her parents loved her, and her discovery that they didn't—I know how completely she shut down that side of her personality, I know how much it must have cost her to leave the convent and go home as a supplicant for love or forgiveness. I don't believe she ever sought human forgiveness again.

There were other psychological consequences. My mother had a life-long and extreme touchiness about what people said behind one another's back. She dreaded scandal. It was a real thing to her, a physical force; it was a key truth about the world that people must not know damaging things about you, because if they did, they would use them to hurt you. If they could do it they would do it. This conviction was born of her encounters with the Ireland of "squinting windows," at the time of her return to Mayo in 1938.

To the younger members of the family, it wasn't really clear what was happening. These things were not spoken of, even in private. One minute Julia was the family heroine; then she was the family disgrace. They felt sympathy, but they also found her unreachable. Even in this plight, Julia was not an easy person to help. And the fact she never told me any of this is a sign of that. Telling me the story would in a way have been asking for my sympathy; and Julia would not, would never, do that. But of all the things I wish my mother had told me, I wish most that she had told me about this. I wish it because I wish she could have shared fully and honestly the story with at least one person who would have been entirely on her side. I don't think she ever did that. I wish she had had the chance to tell me the whole story, start to finish, and to see how outraged it made me feel on her behalf. I wish she had trusted me, and herself, enough. But, I'm sorry to say, to wish that is to wish at least partly that my mother was somebody else.

The next months were terrible for Julia. She was treated as if she did not exist. Her parents tried not to speak to her. In effect, they sent their oldest daughter to Coventry, not as a temporary rebuke but as a permanent state of disgrace. "It must have been terrible, I hate even to think of it," says Peggie now. The younger children were bewildered and didn't know what to say or how to behave. It was not clear what Julia was going to do. She had no qualifications and there was no work. This was late 1938, and agricultural Mayo was in deep depression. One idea was that Julia might train as a nurse; that required money, since in those days in Ireland, nurses had to pay for their own training. But the family had no money. This is not a figure of speech: during difficult times when there was no market for produce, the Gunnigans had no cash at all, either coming into the house or going out of it, and lived purely on the produce of the farm. So Julia was in an impasse. But then Father Tim, Pat's brother, located some funds to pay for a nursing course at Richmond Hospital in Dublin. It is not obvious where he found the cash; he may have raised it from parishioners.

Early in 1939, not long after her eighteenth birthday, Julia went to Dublin and to Richmond Hospital. This institution, which no longer exists, was known as the more Protestant of Dublin's two main hospitals. That may well have been why Father Tim chose it as the place for Julia to do her training, as a way of putting slightly more distance between her and the family; there would have been a slightly lower chance of Julia's meeting people she had known at home if they came to Dublin for medical treatment. (Though, as it happened, when Pat had his appendix out, the operation was performed at Richmond rather than the Catholic Mater Misericordiae.) The fact that my mother was a trained nurse is, for me, not the least amazing of the secrets she kept. She never once, not by implication or suggestion, or by betraying unexpected glimpses of knowledge, gave so much as a hint of this. She was a very good nurse in a domestic context, mind you; it was one of the occasions on which she gave her best and fullest attention. But I must admit to being shocked that there was a whole area of professional expertise and experience about which she never let on. She vaguely allowed one to understand that she had spent some time at university in Dublin, and implied that this had been at Trinity. Even as a covering-up lie, as a covering-up nimbus of falsehood, this was an odd thing to say, since Trinity was the college with Anglo-Irish Protestant associations—it was the place attended by "Horse Protestants," as she used to call them, quoting Brendan Behan. (Asked to explain what he meant by "Horse Protestant," Behan said, "Why, a Protestant on a horse.") The Catholic college was University College Dublin. As to why my mother projected that particular smokescreen, I don't know, unless it had started as a way of saying snap to my father—who went to Trinity College, Melbourne—and then had stuck. Or perhaps it dated to a time when my mother was trying to make herself seem less Irish, and claiming to have been at Trinity was a (highly Irish) way of doing so. But I suspect that the answer is that the medical faculty at Richmond was affiliated to Trinity, and so the sense in which my mother attended Trinity had to do with the nursing training that she kept secret.

Julia was at Richmond for two years, through 1939 and 1940. She trained there and then began working as a nurse. She would go home for Christmas and occasional holidays. The only youthful experiences with boys that she described to me date from this period, when parental supervision was fractionally less complete. One concerned a young man who had a liking for her and would sometimes give the Gunnigans a salmon he had caught illegally. One day he took her out on a boat in Clew Bay. This was a big adventure for Julia, not least because she could not swim, then or later, and was terrified of the water. As she was dragging her hand in the water and looking at the eddies, a basking shark surfaced nearby. As my mother put it, "I had conniptions." The boy slapped the water with an oar to make the shark go away.

These visits home were popular with the younger Gunnigans. "I used to love her coming home," Peggie remembers. "She always brought unexpected things. For example, she brought me my first sparklers. She brought baked beans, which I'd never had before. And she brought tinned sardines, which I'd never had, and I thought they were wonderful." Once, over the New Year, long after the younger children had gone to bed, Julia went outside for a walk and saw that the aurora borealis was making one of its very rare appearances in the skies over Mayo. She knew that this was something they might never get a chance to see again, so she went upstairs, woke the children, and made them go look at the dancing colors in the night sky. She told them that most people went through their lives without seeing the northern lights.

At the same time, however, these visits home were an ordeal. Julia had not been forgiven by her parents, and it was increasingly clear that she never would be. She was still the family disgrace. "You must remember,

Julia was not talked about," Peggie says. "She was brushed under the carpet. When she came home, sure, we were very friendly, obviously, and she was very friendly, because she was very fond of us and we were very fond of her. But my parents didn't acknowledge her."

Julia, feeling herself cut off and ignored, then did one of the things she would come to do best. She cut her parents and family off. After the Christmas holidays of 1940, with their exhausting and demoralizing mixture of sibling intimacy and parental estrangement, she returned to Dublin and quit her job at Richmond Hospital. She checked out of her lodgings, leaving no point of contact and no forwarding address, and no one in the family had any communication with her for the next two and a half years. "Nobody knew where she was," says Peggie. "Again it was whispered about but not spoken about."

This is one point where I wish I were writing a novel instead of a memoir. The reason is that there are moments in the story where I know almost nothing about what my mother did and what happened to her. I have made every effort to track down what Julia was doing in 1941 and 1942 and 1943, and haven't been able to do so. I don't think she stayed in Dublin, because Dublin is not the easiest city of the world in which to disappear. I suspect, though, that she stayed nearby, perhaps under a changed name, because that is where she was found, two and a half years later, when her uncle Bill, husband of her mother's sister Nora, bumped into her in a department store. He asked her to come for a coffee at Bewley's. After visibly thinking it over for a moment, she agreed. She thawed out as they talked, and when Bill begged her to write to her mother, telling her she was all right, she said she would.

By now Julia was working in a sanatorium treating tuberculosis patients. The disease was rife in Ireland; in the words of the health minister Noel Browne, the man who did as much as anyone to eradicate it (and who contracted it himself), the illness was "nearly endemic." As Greta Jones explains in her superb book on the subject, *"Captain of All These Men of Death,"* since the late nineteenth century the incidence and mortality rate of TB had declined around most of the world—but not in Ireland, where it had risen. TB is an illness of urbanization and development, which closely tracks a population's movement from the country into crowded towns. This was the pattern in Ireland. A slow decline in the incidence of the disease through the early decades of the century had begun to reverse in the 1940s. In 1938 it killed 3,216 Irish people, the lowest number recorded since 1922. By 1942, however, the death rate had reached 4,347. Part of the cruelty of the disease was its capriciousness and unpredictability. The apparently ill could recover quickly and live for decades; the apparently strong could suddenly die. The illness seemed to have a malicious will of its own.

In response to the spread of TB, sanatoria had opened across Europe. Here, after an initial period of bed rest, patients were encouraged to spend as much time as possible sitting in the open air. Beds were wheeled out onto verandahs; the verandah immediately outside the ward was a distinctive feature of sanatorium architecture. The "cure" of sitting outside was pursued year-round; the consumptive sitting in the open air, heavily wrapped up against the elements, was a pervasive feature of the sanatorium. Today there is controversy about whether this treatment did any good, as distinct from the undeniably beneficial effects of separating infectious tuberculosis patients from the rest of the community. At the time, though, the fresh-air sanatorium was the unquestioned treatment of choice. Even so, statistics were discouraging, especially the Irish statistics. The National Hospital for Consumptives at Newcastle, County Wicklow, did a five-year follow-up study on patients it had discharged in 1937, 1938, and 1947. The death rates were respectively 41.31, 36.27, and 46 percent. That means that some four out of every ten surviving patients died within five years. Effective drugs to cure the disease did not arrive until around the early 1950s. Until then, treatment for tuberculosis patients included the advice to avoid stimulation in the form of "exciting broadcasts or thrilling novels." It is hard not to conclude that, apart from providing good ventilation, the sanatoria did almost nothing for patients.

From the nurse's point of view, the sanatorium was not an enviable place to work. As Greta Jones writes, "Medical staff working in sanatoria had a high incidence of the disease, a fact which, together with the often depressing nature of the work, and the distance between sanatoria and the main centres of population, made sanatorium nursing one of the less popular vocations." But that word, "vocation," hints at one reason Julia may have wanted to work with tubercular patients. She sought good work, work that was spiritually demanding, partly as a way of punishing herself, and partly as a way of showing that although she had failed as a nun, she was after all a good person.

For Julia, too, the fact that the sanatorium was cut off and geographically isolated made it a good place to hide. By the middle of 1943, when she made contact with her family again, she was working in the tuberculosis sanatorium at Newcastle in County Wicklow. And then the thing dreaded by medical staff in sanatoria, the thing that happened all too often, happened to her. In the autumn of the year, Julia came down with TB.

If she had not been working in a sanatorium already, she might not have been able to find a bed in one. Space was limited, and treatment was not always available. As it was, however, the nurse became a patient in her own place of work. She was able to experience the one compensation that sanatoria had to offer their patients, which was this: in terms of class, gender, and religious denomination, they were among the most mixed places in the conformist, would-be monocultural Ireland of the 1940s. The patients tended to be young, as tuberculosis was to a large extent a disease of the young. Apart from that, sanatoria had all sorts: Protestants as well as Catholics, middle-class professionals as well as the working class, city dwellers as well as peasants, men as well as women. And it was on the wards, recovering from tuberculosis, that Julia met the first love of her life, someone who was different from her in all respects—Protestant, middle-class, urban, and male.

Nicholas Royle had been in Newcastle for some time when he and Julia met. Indeed, they may have known each other already as nurse and patient before Julia became ill. Not much is known about him in the Gunnigan family, other than his religious affiliation and that his family was said to be "very well-to-do." This is another of those moments when I wish I were writing a novel, so that I could give full weight to the importance of Nicholas Royle in my mother's life. There is only one photograph of him that I know of; it shows a skinny young man with a long

Irish face, sitting beside what is presumably a sanatorium deck chair. The only family member who met Nicholas was my mother's aunt Nora (whose husband, Bill, had spotted Julia in Dublin and prompted her to resume contact with her parents). Nora said that Nicholas was "madly in love" with my mother. They spent many of the long hours of convalescence—or perhaps, given how little the patients seem to have been helped by the treatment, that should be "convalescence"—talking. By the time Julia was well enough to leave the hospital, they were engaged to be married. Nicholas gave Julia a silver claddagh ring. The ring, depicting a pair of clasped hands, is a Celtic love token that has now become something of a cliché, but it was much less of one in 1943. It was the first piece of jewelry Julia had owned.

She was discharged from the sanatorium in time for the Christmas holidays. A photograph taken of her just after she got home shows her

shiningly happy. Nicholas was growing steadily better and stronger through his convalescence, and they were to be married in the spring. Julia never seemed happier than she did that Christmas; the family remembers her as "radiant." But then a telegram arrived at Lurgan. It was from Nicholas Royle's sister, and it carried the news that his condition had deteriorated suddenly and he had died.

"Julia was utterly devastated," remembers Peggie. "She was in floods of tears, desperate, depressed, and of course, she couldn't talk about it in front of my parents. They didn't want to know."

My mother never mentioned Nicholas Royle afterward, not once. His role in her life was oddly like that of Michael Furey in James Joyce's immortal short story "The Dead"——the lost love whose absence resonates through the life of his lover for years after, all the more so for its being silent and secret. As the song has it:

They say no two were ever wed
But one had a sorrow that was never said.

It makes me wonder whether he was the great love of her life, or whether he was the first great chance of happiness, the great compensation after her family's devastating rejection—and so his death was a double disaster, in that it seemed to confirm and intensify that earlier catastrophe. Julia must have felt that she'd gotten away from home; she must have felt a justified pride at having succeeded in being able to set up in life on her own. I'm sure she would at some level have felt that meeting Nicholas and falling in love and becoming engaged were a reward for the hardships she had experienced at home. It was an acceptance to ease the hurt of her parents' very final rejection. She would also have taken it as a sign that God wasn't quite so cross with her after all; that He was going to allow her a happy ending. And then her fiancé's death—well, where I would see a catastrophic piece of bad luck, it can only have seemed a heavy and unarguable judgment. God was showing her that the important thing was not what she wanted but what He wanted.

Julia could not face going back to work in Dublin after Nicholas's death. She was not in perfect health herself; she was depressed and in shock. Since recovering TB patients were specifically told to avoid shock, there were grounds for concern about her physical well-being. So she stayed at home in Mayo, in the terrible atmosphere of her parents' disapproval, and grieved. She spent a few months at Lurgan, mourning Nicholas and asking herself what she should do with her life. And then she chose to do what might seem about the least sensible, least logical, least likely thing. To understand her choice you have to see that it was how my mother made the tragic early death of Nicholas have meaning. If his death was just something that had happened, just a piece of bad luck to add to all the other bad things that had happened, that would be too much to bear. If it was a judgment from God, a sign of His will, it was cruel, harsh, petulant—but at least it meant something. So Julia had a choice. She could see Nicholas's death as meaningless—sad, tragic, devastating, and full of consequences for her, but finally, as a token of how the

Julia just before joining the Presentation Sisters.

Universe was arranged, meaningless. Or she could see it as a sign of a higher order—and pay the price, which was to accept that God had a plan for her. She chose the latter path, which seemed to her the path of meaning. When the family heard her decision they were astonished. For my part, though, I'm not astonished. Her choice makes sense to me, because it was the only way she could make sense of the world and of what had happened to her. In the spring of 1944, Julia announced her intention to become a nun. She was to become a postulant again and join the convent of the Presentation Sisters in Tuam, about thirty miles from Lurgan, just over the border in County Galway. The family reaction was "general rejoicing and cries of relief all around."

SISTER EUCHARIA

· I ·

I T IS DIFFICULT to comprehend the full extent of the submission
demanded of its members by a religious order such as the Presentation Sisters, in the years before Vatican II.

I am aware that some people don't see the changes brought about by
Vatican II as having been reforms. All I would say to them is that they are
lucky they never expressed that view within earshot of my mother. Her
extensive direct experience of the world of the old Church was that it
was, in terms of how nuns in particular were treated, a scandal. "You
sometimes get people saying they are nostalgic for the old days," she once
told me. "Particularly English Catholics who never experienced what it
was really like. *They have no idea.*"

Two things stand out in all accounts of life in the world of the convent
before the reforms of Vatican II. The first is the sheer extent, variety, and
magnitude of the restrictions on the nuns. Julia had already lived through
the first stage of this, as a postulant with the Good Shepherds. It is probably fair to say that the first six months of her time as a Presentation sister did not come as too much of a surprise. She knew that all property
was held in common and that she was no longer allowed to say "my" in

relation to anything. The postulant mistress would talk about "our" cell and "our" crucifix to make the point that nobody owned anything, and that all possessions (and later "offices," or jobs) were rotated to prevent any sense of ownership from developing. Julia knew about the day divided into installments. She knew that she would have to kneel to ask for a blessing from any priest she saw. She knew about the weekly "chapter of faults," when she would have to kneel in front of the community and confess her lapses. She knew that she would have to kneel when reprimanded by a supervisor. She knew that the penances were performed at mealtime and might involve such mortifications as having to kiss the feet of all the professed nuns. She knew that she would not be allowed to swing her arms or move rapidly. She knew that she would not be allowed to look up, when walking or outside or at mealtime; she would have to keep "custody of the eyes." She knew that she would regularly have to perform an "act of self-conquest" in doing things she found difficult or repellent, and that she would regularly and routinely have to mortify herself by seeking out all possible opportunities to experience shame, humiliation, and self-abasement. She knew that these were holy states, because they emptied out the self, and the emptier you were of self, the more room there was for God. She knew that she could not speak at mealtime, or eat with anyone besides other members of the community. She knew that it was her duty as a nun to die as an ego, as a self. She knew that she would have to wear a complicated set of basically medieval clothes for the rest of her life, that her undergarments, like the rest of her, would be washed only once a week. She knew that she would be forced to sit, stand, and walk in a particular way, and to keep to that way for the rest of her life. She knew that for the rest of her life, "recreation" would mean the hour a day when she was allowed to talk to other nuns. She knew that she was explicitly forbidden to make friends and that if she found herself liking another nun it was her duty to avoid her. She knew that all her letters would be read and that she would never again have privacy. She knew that, throughout her novitiate, her faults would be pointed out to her, energetically and on a daily basis. In the words of Karen Armstrong, who lived in an enclosed order in the 1960s, these reprimands were "a daily occurrence in the noviceship. A tiny incident could reveal so many of your faults, faults that you'd never dreamt you possessed until an unguarded word or action revealed them all." In Armstrong's view, "it had unfortunately become customary to train young nuns by making them excruciatingly aware of their failings. This meant that most of us lived in a state of . . . acute anxiety and preoccupation with ourselves." Julia knew that for many hours of every day she would have to preserve silence. She knew that she would have to give up all her old tastes and habits and cultivate a permanent and permanently sustained attitude of renunciation to all her former pleasures, indeed, to everything connected to her former self. She knew that she would have to experience, in the words of Monica Baldwin, who left an enclosed order in 1941 and described her experiences in *I Leap Over the Wall,* "the absolute subjection, day by day, hour by hour, minute by minute, of one's free will to the exigencies of the Rule."

Julia knew all that. She had been most of the way through a postulancy once already. It helped that this time she was closer to her family. Tuam was not far from Aghamore, and two of her sisters, Peggie and Dilly, were being educated there by the Sisters of Mercy. On free days they were allowed to visit their postulant sister, which helped Julia feel less cut off than she had as a Good Shepherd. (Later, her youngest sister, Jane, was to be one of her pupils at the convent school in Tuam.) The postulancy with the Presentation Sisters lasted six months, and she finished it with the sense that, this time, she was sure of her vocation. After the six months, a postulant "took the veil" and became a novice. Postulants wore a white veil—"veil" here in its technical sense, for which I am indebted to Elizabeth Kuhns's history of nun's clothing, *The Habit*:

> "Habit" refers to the ensemble of clothing and accessories that make up religious dress. It can also mean specifically the robelike tunic or dress that is the main garment worn over the body. The "veil" is the long cloth worn on the top of the head, extending down the back. Some veils are designed to be pulled forward over the face, and other veils are designed as thin linings to wear beneath heavier veils. The veil is usually attached

to a cap underneath, or "coif," which is a close-fitting cloth headpiece that conforms to the shape of the skull and often ties under the chin. A "wimple" or "guimpe" is the fabric piece that covers the neck and chest, and sometimes extends over the chin. A "bandeau" is the piece that stretches across the forehead, often attached at the ears behind the veil. A "scapular" is a long apronlike garment that is worn over the tunic and extends down both the front and back of the tunic. A "cincture" is a belt worn around the waist of the tunic, and a "Rosary" is a string of prayer beads and other objects attached to the cincture and worn at the side. A "cappa," cape or mantle, refers to a cloak worn over the tunic.

In the Presentation Sisters, the tunic was made of heavy black serge, falling in folds, with long sleeves. The wimple and bandeau were of white linen, the cincture of black leather. The ceremony during which these clothes were first put on was modeled on the marriage service; during it, a nun became married to Christ. After their final vows, the Presentation Sisters wore wedding rings on their right hands to announce their rela-

In the back row, Mary (then Sister Emmanuel), Pat, Molly,
Julia (from that day, Sister Eucharia); in the front row,
Noreen, Dilly, Peggie, Jane, Bernie.

tionship with Christ. After the service, the new novice, accepted into the order by her new sisters, was allowed to mix with her family.

Julia's whole family came to her clothing ceremony, and there is a photograph of the occasion; it was the last time all the Gunnigans were together. Pat and Molly look proud, and everybody looks happy, except perhaps Julia herself, who looks anxious. She is not the only "clothed" novice in the picture: her sister Mary had just passed through her postulancy as a Sister of Mercy, also in Tuam. Julia stayed in Tuam for the next stage of her training, at the central novitiate of the Presentation Sisters. She and her younger siblings found the thought of separation hard. Julia Immaculata Gunnigan was now to be known as Sister Eucharia.

The name Eucharia refers to the Eucharist. Julia chose it to point to the central attraction of the religious life for her: the closeness that this life brought one to Christ. The daily celebration of the Eucharist was, for a believing Catholic, a daily encounter with the magic of the Incarnation. The changing of wafer and wine into the body and blood of Christ was a miracle, and Julia lived through, experienced, that miracle every day. That was the center of her faith, and the center of the consolation the convent brought her. Allied to it was the amount of prayer, several hours daily, in which the nuns engaged. This, too, was an encounter with the divine: a strenuous one, in which days and months and even years could pass without a glimpse of contact with God; but it was an effort Julia was more than willing to make, a path she was committed to taking. These and the consequent austerities were not the hardest thing about the life she encountered as a novice. She knew that at the end of the novitiate she would take the three great vows of poverty, chastity, and obedience. For Julia, the hardest thing about being a nun was the finality of the submission in the third vow, that of obedience.

The aim of religious training is, in a sense, death. It is the death of the would-be religious's former self. Obedience is crucial to the process of killing off that old self. It is through obedience that you learn to ignore your own impulses and wishes, your habits and tastes and desires, and to replace them with the external commands of the order. Through that process, the monk or nun becomes free; the idea is that in giving up your conditioned former self, which in most of us is at least half the product of socially imprinted needs and wishes, you attain the freedom to serve God—in this view, the only real freedom there is. That sounds fine. This isn't a line of thought you hear much about in the contemporary world, given that it would bring the whole modern edifice of commerce, the media, and public life to an immediate halt. Which is perhaps one of the most appealing, or arresting, or at any rate *different,* things about it. So even the most disobedient and secular of us can see the appeal, if not to ourselves, then at least to somebody else, of this line of renunciation.

The trouble—for many people, my mother among them—came with the effort to put this attitude into practice in the actual institutions of the Church. There, and especially in the religious orders, the sacred duty of obedience meant absolute, unquestioning submission to every order of a superior, extending to every aspect of life, however apparently trivial. And "unquestioning" not only meant not asking questions out loud but also involved a complete internal submission. Your own common sense and intelligence were specifically forbidden from being engaged, let alone anything as debased as your own wishes or preferences. The less you agreed with what you had been told to do, the better, since it showed how effectively you were emptying out your self; the more obviously stupid and wrong and self-contradictory what you had been told to do, the better, too. The order of a superior was a direct expression of the Will of God. This was not a metaphor, it was the literal truth. God spoke through one's superiors in the order. Monica Baldwin:

> As a result, the more complete one's submission to that of the Superior . . . the more perfectly one's will is united to the Will of God.
>
> I once consulted the famous Dominican, Father Bede Jarret, about this matter of submission.
>
> He was a man of deep humour, profound learning and wide experience. I told him about an order which had just been given to me by a Superior and which had struck me as being neither wise nor just.
>
> 'I can submit my *will* sufficiently to do the thing I've been told to do,' I explained to him, 'but as for forcing my *mind* . . .'

He said: 'I once took that same problem to my Novice Master. He told me to re-read "The Charge of the Light Brigade". The idea, you see, is that you do what you're told, no matter how certain you feel that someone has blundered. To ride fearlessly into the jaws of death without reasoning why adds splendour to your obedience.'

'Even,' I persisted, 'if you feel convinced that what you've been told to do is sheerest lunacy?'

He smiled.

'Ah, but don't you see?—that's just where the heroism comes in.'

This is not, of course, a commonsense view; indeed, the whole point of it is that it is the exact opposite of common sense. It's fair to say that Julia struggled with the idea. Gradually over time, and increasingly, doing something she knew to be stupid and wrong just because she was told to, and because she was supposed to take a particular lesson in the stupidity and pointlessness of it, began—to use an expression of hers—to "stick in her craw." It might be something someone like Julia could do now and then, but to ask her to make it a way of life was to ask something against her deepest nature. Of course, from the perspective of the tradition, as it had evolved, the fact that it was against her deepest nature made it all the more important that she should submit.

The main trouble caused by the vow of obedience lay, however, in the future. Julia passed through her two-year novitiate, if not with ease, then at least with her fundamental conviction of her own vocation intact. At the end of the two years, Julia made her three great vows. She lay face-down on the floor as her mother superior covered her with a funeral pall, and announced that the person she had been was now dead. When the pall was taken off, the light was blinding. It was supposed to feel like death and rebirth, and it did. Sister Eucharia was now a Presentation sister, a professed nun. It was late 1946, and she was about to turn twenty-six.

The Presentation Sisters had a decentralized system, in which separate convents had charge of their own affairs. The convent at Tuam, to which Sister Eucharia belonged, was attached to a school. The first thing Julia did on completing her novitiate was to take the final exams required to award her the Leaving Certificate. After that she was able to teach in the school, and she did, quickly coming to specialize in English. If prayer and the Eucharist were the best things about the spiritual life of the convent for Julia, the best thing about its practical life was teaching. She loved teaching, being a teacher, and loved the contact with her pupils. It was a direct engagement, which she hadn't had much of in her life, face-to-face and committed to a shared purpose. She found that she had a gift for making her subjects interesting and making her pupils interested; she had an arena in which her natural liveliness, vividness, and humor could be expressed without getting her into trouble. Perhaps that more than anything was the core of my mother's love of teaching; it was the first thing she did in which she was allowed to express herself.

It slowly became clear, however, that this was not enough. In the same year that Julia became a professed nun, her sister Peggie had entered the Presentation Sisters. She was at Castleconnell in Tipperary, in a branch of the order that specialized in missionary work. "I had done my Leaving Cert and, I'd imagine, for much the same reasons that Julia had gone to New Ross originally—we'd got all these things about the heroism of going on missions. This was a missionary branch of the Presentation order, and I had romantic ideas about India, where they had their mission." This seems to have made Julia wonder whether she had done the right thing by abandoning her earlier longing to go on the missions. If she stayed with the Presentation Sisters in Tuam, she would in all probability spend the rest of her life there, living in the same convent and teaching in the same school. That began to feel as if it was not what she wanted. Not, of course, that what Sister Eucharia wanted was in any way relevant; but perhaps her dissatisfaction might be taken as a sense that she was not, after all, doing the Will of God?

"Julia was in Tuam and we wrote to each other," says Peggie. "Remember, your letters were censored. Your letters were all opened and read. In both directions. Julia was beginning to get discontented and sorry that she hadn't joined a missionary order." So she thought about it, and prayed about it, and became convinced that her vocation was after all in

Sister Eucharia on the MV Caledonia.

missionary work. By now, after an annual renewal of her vows, at the end of her third year and as the Presentation Sisters' rule dictated, she had taken her final vows. Her status as a nun was irrevocable. But her exact vocation was not. "So in 1948," Peggie recounts, "Julia got permission from the bishop and the superior general to transfer to Castleconnell, because she wanted to go to India. And very shortly after, she went to India." This was no small feat of will and effort. Nuns hardly ever changed from one branch of the order to another; but once Julia decided to do something, it was not easy to stop her. It was late 1948 when she transferred to Castleconnell, and early 1949 when she boarded the MV *Caledonia* and traveled to her new post at Church Park, a school run by the Presentation Sisters in Madras.

· 2 ·

I SOMETIMES THINK that my mother's years in Madras were the great adventure of her life. As was rarely the case with her childhood, she did talk about the time she spent at Church Park. It was never a connected narrative; she dealt in specific memories and specific stories. She didn't give me any sort of rundown or overview of what she did in India. But at least some of what I know about her years in India I know directly from her.

Madras is one of those cities that gets a bad press from guidebooks and casual visitors. (Since 1997, for postcolonial and pro-Tamil reasons, the city is officially known as Chennai, though I will use the old name here, to keep things simple.) Kipling, for instance, didn't miss a chance to say how dull he found it. A guidebook says that "most travelers stay just long enough to book a ticket for somewhere else." This is partly because the city has no obvious central magnet for the casual visitor. The location on the Indian Ocean is mercantile and convenient rather than spectacular. The marina, a seafront promenade, is pleasant for a stroll and some people-watching, but nothing extraordinary. The old fort, built when the city was founded by the British in 1639, is worth a look, but one old colonial fort is very much like another old colonial fort. The city teems, but not as unforgettably as Calcutta teems, and thrives, but not as postmodernly as Bangalore of the laptops, and is the center of a film industry, but not as amusingly (for foreigners) as Bombay. The old church where Clive of India married and so did Elihu Yale, he of the eponymous American university, which is interesting, but not that interesting. Some of the world's greatest temple architecture is just down the road at Mammalapuram, so why would anyone linger in Madras?

Yet Madras is one of those places that gets its hooks into people, and you are more likely to hear praise of it from residents who have lived there for a decade than from travelers who stayed for a weekend. Julia loved Madras. She had never been out of Ireland, and the most exotic place she had been was O'Connell Street in Dublin. She had never seen a black person. In Madras, people weren't just black; their skins were luminous Tamil mahogany black. Madras was different. That was what Julia loved about it, the idea and experience of difference. Postcolonial Ireland was a state that emphasized its sameness, its monocultural agrarian Gaelic Catholicism, in the embrace of de Valera's fantasy about its being an "island of saints and scholars." You could have any color you liked as long as it was green. India was every color. For one thing, the Dravidian Tamils of Madras are a minority ethnically distinct from the majority population of northern India. The city had a significant Muslim population, as well as a scattering of Buddhists, a few Parsis, the odd Jain, some vociferous Marxists, angry Hindu supremacists, pacifist Gandhian advocates of nonviolence, noble members of the new governing Congress Party, and corrupt ones, as well as voices arguing for Tamil separatism. And there was also the fact that Ireland, in the aftermath of its breakaway from Britain, was keen not to talk about class and difference, whereas the caste system in India made class a daily, all-consuming, self-evidently central fact of life. To Julia, for all the troubles caused by caste, it at least did not seem hypocritical. Like almost everything else about Madras, it was energizing.

Almost everything. There were two problems with the work of the Church in Madras, apart from the usual difficulties of convent life. One was that 1949 was not a good time for a Christian missionary to arrive in India. The country had gained its independence, and been partitioned from Pakistan, in August 1947. The missionary movements—of which there were a huge variety all over the subcontinent—were out of kilter with the postcolonialist development of the country. India was undergoing a strong Hindu revival and an upsurge in national pride; charitable works were welcome, but missionary intervention in the religious life of the nation was not. "The way things are going," Julia wrote in a letter home, "none of us are likely to be very long in India, as the country has less and less use for missionaries and the Christian message." Today, new foreign missionaries are not allowed into India, and all the nuns working at the Presentation convent in Madras are Indian-born.

This does not mean that Christianity in itself was an alien presence in Madras. Christianity has been present in southern India for centuries. There is a long tradition, and even some evidence, that the apostle Saint Thomas

Sister Eucharia on the banks of the Ganges.

traveled to India in A.D. 52, less than two decades after Christ's death, and was martyred near Madras in A.D. 72. "They're very snooty about it in Madras," my mother told me. "They like to say to people like the Goans, '*We're* Saint Thomas's Christians. *You're* Saint Francis *Xavier's* Christians. We're *much* older Christians than you.'" There are still some Thomas Christian churches in Madras, which follow the Syrian rite that the saint is said to have brought to India. So Christianity was already established by the time Portuguese Jesuits arrived in Kerala in the sixteenth century, and Catholicism was in turn established by the time the British arrived and built Fort St. George, the outpost that was eventually to turn into the city of Madras. The British brought Protestantism, and St. Mary's Church, consecrated in 1680, is the oldest Anglican church in Asia. Although foreign missionaries were about to have some difficult years in India, Christianity had traditions and roots around Madras; the local population was and is roughly five percent Christian. The Presentation convent was not working in a vacuum.

The political context was one major difficulty about Madras when Julia arrived there. The other was more straightforward: the climate. Madras has a truly horrible climate. The humidity is high year-round.

Throughout the summer months the temperature climbs into the hundreds. From my own childhood in the Far East, I remember the summer as a time when you looked not at the temperature forecast—which was always in the nineties—but at the predicted humidity. The hardest days to get through were those when the temperature and the humidity were both in the nineties; you would feel drained and exhausted by the heat. Madras is hotter than that, and more humid, and the hot months go on longer, building up unbearably until they are interrupted by the monsoon. "A beautifully enervating atmosphere like a warm bath," is the description in one account. All this contributed to Madras's reputation for being sleepy, boring, something of a backwater—which was how it had been regarded in colonial times.

Everyone found it hot. But not everyone had to wear a full nun's habit, with its "underwear designed by ascetics in the fourteenth century" (Monica Baldwin's vivid phrase). This, physically, was the hardest thing about Madras for Julia. She described it in an autobiographical short story, "My Hair and Me," that was broadcast on the BBC in 1961:

> I wore on my head, in addition to my now cropped hair, a cap, a bandeau—which is a box-like arrangement of a stiffened rubber material known as a plyalin—a pair of starched bands which secured the guimpe that covered one's chest, a smallish inner veil, or domino as it was called, and a full length outer veil—five pieces of clothing in all.
>
> Now, even if convent custom allowed one to have long hair, the heat of India made it impossible for me at least. Different people perspire in different ways and in varied amounts, I believe. I seemed to produce most of my perspiration under my veil. The sweat trickled down my face under the bandeau, it ran down my shoulders and back under the veils, it collected behind my ears and on my neck. So very soon after I arrived in India, I got the scissors and cut my already cropped hair as close to the scalp as I could get. Even then I perspired. There were nights in the hot season when my pillow was soaked through before midnight and the discomfort was so great that time after time I got up, put my head under

the tap and washed it, then climbed back into bed—wet but fairly cool—
and so got to sleep at last. I became accustomed to the heat in time but
my head went on perspiring and so my hair was never allowed to grow
more than a quarter of an inch or so on my scalp.

The nuns had a special dispensation from the fixed regime of the order
and were allowed a daily tepid bath. Tepid water, as my mother insisted
and as all old tropical hands know, is much more cooling than either hot
or cold. During the gradual buildup of heat, all she could think about was
the two months of high summer when the nuns went to work at the
boarding school they ran at Kodaikanal in the Palani Hills, almost three
hundred miles away. The altitude there was seven thousand feet, and the
relief at getting out of Madras was exquisite. As her letters make clear, Julia
deeply looked forward to Kodai. "I am longing for a lungful of cold air, a
mouthful of real cold water, and the feel of a blanket over me at night."

The emphasis of the Presentation Sisters was on education. In Madras
they had founded what was in effect the campus of Church Park, with a
convent where the nuns lived and several schools, one of them also an or-

Church Park.

phanage for Anglo-Indians, another a teacher-training college. This was an important educational institution for Madras. (It still is; in addition to the teacher-training college, Church Park now has three schools, two of which operate in English and one in Tamil.)

The Presentation Sisters' mission had been established to address the needs of Anglo-Indians—a term that should be glossed. Anglo-Indians are the offspring of mixed marriages, or at any rate sexual liaisons, between Europeans and the local population. Church Park was founded, to quote my mother, to look after the "illegitimate children of British Tommies and Tamil coolie-women." Just to complicate things more, the Anglo-Indian community of Madras was to a considerable extent of Portuguese origin, since many of the first European-Indian children in Madras were born to the early waves of Portuguese colonists; and it was their children who in turn often were the women with whom British colonists had children. Portuguese surnames were common in the Anglo-Indian community of Madras.

The status of Anglo-Indians in India is a delicate subject. In some respects they were at this point in India's history recipients of a double dose of prejudice. For the Raj, half-Indian children were, to use the terrible phrase of the time, "fourteen annas to the rupee"—in other words, given that a rupee was supposed to be sixteen annas, they were not quite genuine, not quite the real thing. Their very presence was a reminder of the scandalous and unspeakable sexual exploitation of the ruled by the rulers. At the same time, for many Hindus, the Anglo-Indians carried the taint and corruption of the West—the sense of caste contamination brought by the outsider—without the protection of belonging to the colonial overclass. Some of the distaste for the British was transferred to the Anglo-Indians, about whom it could be more safely expressed. A recent study of Anglo-Indian identity lists some stereotypes: "vulgar, conceited, ill-bred, lacking intelligence, promiscuous (if women) and work-shy (if men), more British than the British themselves, relics of and nostalgic for the Raj." The Anglo-Indian community was by definition hybridized, and Julia took a particular interest in that. The very idea of a mixed or hybridized identity—of coming from more than one place, of having something complicated about who you were and where you were from—appealed to her. She was also stirred by the idea that the Anglo-Indian community had about it a sense of shame or embarrassment. Julia knew about that. She felt a deep connection with the stigmatized.

By the time she went to work there, however, Church Park had drifted away from its origins as a school for the poor and had become an institution increasingly attended by the Indian elite. The school's high standards were one reason for this; education in English was another. The school for the children of Tommies and coolie-women was rapidly becoming an institution for the aspiring, achieving, new Indian middle class. From a charitable point of view, this might have represented something of a shift of emphasis, but the students attending Church Park were a teacher's dream, and Julia quickly found herself happier in her work than she ever had been. Her main subject was English, with a little history on the side (and very occasionally, when illness or personnel difficulties required, her least favorite subject, mathematics). Her talent and abilities were soon well known. The single possession she kept from her time in India was the Abinaschandra Medal that she was awarded by the University of Calcutta in 1951. I have no idea what it is or what it was

awarded for or why the University of Calcutta was recognizing my mother's contribution to education in Madras, but it must have meant a lot to her, because in the masses of papers and things she left behind after her death, it is the single thing—the only thing—that bears her real name, Julia I. Gunnigan.

That medal is part of how I know her Indian years were a triumph. The rest of how I know is because she told me. But this knowledge was not imparted directly. She gave hints and she told stories and she let you fill in the gaps—dared you to, enticed you to. And at the same time, it was impossible to ask questions. In 1979 my mother went back to Madras and visited Church Park. A few days after she arrived home from that trip, she came into my bedroom and gave me some copies of the school magazine. Two of them had articles about her, one of them praising the work she had done in general terms, another with a piece by a former student at the school describing a conversation with Sister Eucharia and the sister's great air of saintliness and wisdom and understanding. It spoke about how brilliant and charismatic a teacher Sister Eucharia had been, and how the girl writing the piece, now a woman in her fifties, had never forgotten her.

"I was Sister Eucharia," my mother told me. It was the only time she spoke the name to me.

I was astonished by the magazines. They were the first physical evidence I had seen of my mother's decade in Madras. I put them in a place on my bookshelves where I knew I'd be able to find them. And then the next time I looked, a couple of weeks later, they weren't there. I asked my mother what had happened to them.

"I threw them away," she said. "You didn't seem interested."

I daresay I was a highly annoying adolescent, with a big repertoire of ways to make my parents feel unappreciated. But I do think this was an outrageous thing for my mother to have said. The real reason she removed the magazines had nothing to do with how interested I did or didn't seem. It was, instead, that she did not want me to look so closely at the articles that I began noticing dates or details that might make me ask questions about her life story. But given an open-goal opportunity to accompany her gesture with a rebuke, she took it; she couldn't forgo a chance to tell me off for not giving her enough attention.

My mother told me—or rather, allowed it to emerge, over years of hints and half-told anecdotes—that she ran the school, or teacher-training college, as in some versions of her stories it seemed to be. She was young to have this job, and was proud of it. She was in touch with her family again, and was a heroine again, too. In many of her stories she had authority. Once she told me about a young woman who came to her with a problem. As they were talking, my mother suddenly said—she didn't know why, the words just came out—"How long have you been pregnant?" All the young woman could say was, "How did you know?" "And the truth is," Julia told me, "I don't know how I knew, I just did." But then, as she knew but I didn't, she was a trained nurse. The woman had been seeing a young man whom her family had forbidden her to see. My mother was able to arrange for her to go away for a few months, and presumably—though she didn't say—the baby was adopted. So she had power and responsibility and, I know from those magazines but also because I just do, an aura.

More than any specific anecdote, there was somehow in my mother's memories and stories a sense of India, of its physical realities—heat and dust, obviously, humidity and crowds, dhotis and ceiling fans, punkah-wallahs (who operate fans) and long-distance trains, unripe papaya used to induce abortions (there was a famous court case about that), mongooses used to hunt snakes, the crowded hot classroom of girls trying not to giggle, the relieving airiness of church and cathedral, the Dravidian snobberies of being older Christians than Western Europeans, glasses of cool yogurt, mangoes so ripe the only way to eat them was improperly, naked in the bath, biryanis cooked with a topping of gold leaf on wedding days, pork vindaloos from Christian Goa, *chota* for "half" and *burra* for "big" (*burra peg* meant a double whiskey), the way you would live for the merest breath of breeze. These were the incidental details of which my mother spoke, and it was these she seemed to have loved and missed the most about India. And that would be all I know about her time at Church Park, were it not for a batch of letters given to me by my aunt Peggie, with which I can fill in the gaps. I know some of my mother's life story through research, and some through what she told me years afterward, and some by having lived through it with her and seen things from my own perspective. But this is the only part of my mother's life story that I know through the words she used herself, at the time she lived through it.

· 3 ·

T HE FIRST LETTER that survives dates from March 1953. Julia had
by now done an undergraduate degree by correspondence from
the University of London—one of the many things she never
told me, since her policy was to let it be understood that her degree was
from Trinity College Dublin. She was teaching English at the Presentation
convent. The letter, to her sister Bernie, is too boring to quote at length,
but it does show the uncertainty Julia was in about her future. It was in the
nature of things that missionary nuns went where they were told, and Julia
did not know when she would next be back in her homeland. "I don't expect to go to Ireland this year," she tells Bernie. "Later on they will probably transfer me to Castle Connell and Bernie it is better this way. The work
in C.C. for the next year or two would be pure slavery with very little co-
operation or sympathy or help financial or otherwise from anyone. I am
not a bit sorry to be missing all that. I expect to do B.T. (H. Dip.) here in
July, the course lasts until March and after that I don't know where I'll be
posted." The course Julia was planning to take was a bachelorate in teaching, equivalent to a second B.A. degree. All through her time in India, Julia
was adding qualifications to her résumé as she rose in seniority in the order.

The next letter is to her sister Peggie, who was now Sister Jarlath—
that being the patron saint of the Tuam diocese. Peggie, who had been
Julia's inspiration for switching to a missionary branch of the Presentation
Sisters, had drawn what felt to her like a short straw and was teaching at
the Presentation convent in Matlock, Derbyshire, in England. She was
deeply unhappy, though Julia didn't know this.

Sister Jarlath,
Presentation Convent,
Matlock,
Derbs.
England

Presentation Convent
Royapuram
Madras
31 iii 1953

My dearest Peggie,

This will hardly ever reach you in time for Easter, nevertheless you
have my loving wishes for a happy joyful feast with an abundance too of
that Peace which was our Lord's gift to the Apostles. I shall not forget you
in my distractions and I count on a remembrance in your orisons!

I suppose the sight of my writing nearly brought on an attack of the
wallipations—well, I promised to write regularly—but, mind you, I expect
a reply. We close today for Easter and re-open next Tuesday. During the
week, I plan to do a fair amount of sewing. If I have time I shall make a
few guimpettes for you and for Mother Victoire but please don't expect
works of art. My old needlework teacher (Sister Alphonsus) maintains to
this day that 'poor Julia could never sew'. [Sewing was a big deal in the
other branch of the Presentation Sisters; it was the activity with which
the nuns were supposed to fill their recreation time.]

After Easter we have just about five weeks' school and then the summer holidays. We close on May 8th. It is very hot in Madras just now.

The papers say we have not had such weather for sixty years in March. On Saturday the temperature was 105.1. It is hard to realise that it is just daffodil and primrose time at home now. One loses track of the seasons here and quite often I find myself pausing to think what month we are in. We have had a very busy term between one thing and another. First we had a concert for the Public on March 14th. Each class gave a poem on Nano Nagle with a musical accompaniment (we did the latter for Mother General and she loved it—the melodies are picked to suit the story and it is very effective) we had, too, a dumb show which we put together when I was in Calcutta—it is very funny and everyone likes it.

On the 19th we set out for the 'Croke Park' of Madras. NO, we were not going to a football match but to the Consecration of three Indian Bishops in an open air ceremony at a Pontifical High Mass which began at 5 pm and was not over until 8. There were twenty eight Bishops and Archbishops including the three Bishops-elect and the three who consecrated them. There were at least 500 nuns of every color, race and style of habit. The entire congregation numbered 50,000, almost entirely Catholic since no others were admitted except a very few by special invitation. Normally the Indians are noisy and restless but that vast crowd was silent devout and reverent throughout the entire long ceremony. The altar and dais on which the Bishops sat was decorated in gold and red satin with the arms of the consecrating Prelates and the new Bishops across the top and behind the altar a kind of sunburst effect, each ray representing one of the gifts of the Holy Ghost. It was a very wonderful ceremony and Heaven felt near that evening in pagan India.

Now I have no more room so I must stop. If I get a reply I shall write. If now—well, that's your look out!! Fondest love to you.

Your loving

Julia

It's hard to express how strange it felt transcribing this letter fifty-one years after it was written. My mother with her ink pen at her desk in the Madras convent, me at my iBook in my converted loft in London, watch-

My dearest Peggie,

...yesterday. Actually, when Therese got back to Mylapore after she wrote me on Monday. Your letter was there, but she didn't bring it in until yesterday. Poor thing, she had a very nasty accident about three weeks ago — she fell out of a moving car — no bones were broken but she was badly shaken and bruised and no wonder. She has been an angel to me ever since she came back from England. I don't know what I should have done without her. I gave her your address yesterday and she took your address to write to you. If you chance to

reply to her, please tell her how grateful you are for all she is doing for me. I told her yesterday about having written to Mother Generalate and she (Miss J.) says that if I don't get a reply within, say, the next fortnight, I should make copies of all the correspondence, so far, i.e. my letters to Rome, to the General etc and send them all, together with a covering letter asking for immediate action, to the Internuncio in Delhi — what do you think? I am sorry to be filling up this letter with all my own woes. I was delighted to read that you are keeping so well — I was afraid something had happened when I hadn't heard last week — see how you have spoiled me!" Thank God the

parcels arrived alright. How were the raffia hats? They should be pretty crushed after the way I parcelled them, but being a natural fibre, I imagine they will come alright if they are put flat under a weight for a while. So you pronounce the Indian covers as suitable! Well, that's fine and, do please take those you want for your own use at once — no need to wait until I come — they are very hard wearing and the colours are fast too. Did the towels arrive? Are they of any use to you at all? I hope you are using them if they are worth using. We have a holiday here today — it is Ghandi's birthday + a public festival (after Dussehra, I mean) sleep. I was awake last night until after 3 a.m. and awake again this morning at 5 so I must catch up! The college tea finishes at the

Mrs. V. Geraghty,
134, Finborough Street
London, S.W.1.
England

ing planes heading for Heathrow. About the only familiar thing in the letter is my mother's habit of covering every available scrap of the blue airmail form with writing—so much so that there were times, after she filled up the main body of the letter, when I would struggle to find the continuation, written sideways along the edge of the form, or across the top, and often across the salutation and address, or along the folded-over gummed flap. But the person who wrote the letter—that person I never met. My mother did not stop believing in God, yet the intense devotion and explicit piety she expresses to Peggie here is something I never encountered. I'm glad to meet it, because it makes the time she spent in the convent more explicable to me. Though I have never felt anything resembling her religious feelings, it is clear that they were, to her, very real. Peggie was the person to whom she expressed this feeling most, no doubt because she felt her sister was, as a fellow missionary Presentation sister, the person most likely to understand.

Over the next few years, Julia's letters to Peggie sometimes refer to one T. Leetch or Tommy Leetch—an odd-looking, not-quite-Irish name, which was Julia's coded way of writing about herself. The code was necessary since, again, letters were not private. "I haven't had any further news of Tommy Leetch," she told Peggie in October. "I imagine that he'll get the job eventually but it may take a few years. I hear he is keen on it himself. Let us pray hard for him and for God's Will. You might get a chance to put in a word for him sometime." The letter refers to "plans," a shorthand way of discussing Julia's hopes that she might be promoted or transferred home or posted to Matlock to be with Peggie.

Julia's letters are necessarily short on details about her life—since she wasn't permitted to talk about that—but are instead full of requests for news from home. One exception is the following, after Julia had had a big piece of news: Jane, her youngest sister and her goddaughter, had entered the novitiate of the Columban Sisters. She was the fourth Gunnigan daughter to become a nun. This is Julia's letter of congratulation and consolation. It is one of the few times she went into detail about her Indian life. She was allowed to do so because she was describing a training camp for her teaching course, not life in the convent.

Mr and Mrs P. Gunnigan
Lurgan
Kilkelly
Co. Mayo
Ireland

Presentation Convent,
Church Park,
Madras-6
18 x 1953

My dearest Mammy, Daddy, Dillie and John,

Thanks very much, Dillie, for your letter received while I was in camp and, Mammy, for yours received yesterday. Indeed I would have written sooner but I was just waiting to get this air letter. I have been thinking of you very much every day since October 3rd. You have made a tremendous sacrifice every one of you, Mammy, Daddy, Dillie and John in letting Jane go, and for all eternity God will reward you for it and indeed you will have great joy in this life too as a blessing for what you have done. And we will all be together in heaven very soon—soon no matter how long we live. . . .

Now to tell you about the Camp.* Well we left here at about 6.15 on Monday morning 28th September. The 60 education students assembled at the College and we left Madras about 7.45 a.m. We had about 15 miles in the train and then down through a village and 'across country' to the Camp. There was no road—just a track through the fields which reminded me a bit of the short cut to Mount View from the Church in Aghamore except of course you must substitute palms (very tall ones like this ⊤⊤⊤) for furze bushes and sand for a grassy path and rice and millet fields for oats and barley and of course very cross buffaloes for just

---

*This was a compulsory part of the teacher-training course, in which Julia and two other nuns went off to train with their fifty-seven Indian fellow students. Bear in mind, when assessing the level of culture shock, that Julia was not allowed to eat with anyone who was not a professed nun, and had to obtain a highly unusual special dispensation to take part in the course.

middling cross cows. The walk was about one and a half miles and all the little children ran for their lives when they saw the white 'Kary ass three' (that's their word for a nun but it's not spelt correctly).*

Well we got to the camping site about 9 a.m. There were eleven tents altogether—nine of these were set aside for the students—and one of the nine was given to us —the three sisters. Each tent was shaped like this ⌒⌒ and was about 8ft square inside with sloping 'walls' so that only in the middle could Sister Dominic and I, who are rather tall, stand up straight. Our tent had been tarred on the outside to make the canvas waterproof with the result that the heat was almost unbearable when the tar warmed up towards mid-day. At night though it was quite cool—so we stayed out of it as much as we could during the day. The 60 of us were divided into squads and each day we had different work to do—one day cooking, another serving, another in charge of clearing up, etc etc. Besides that we had 5 regular classes each day—and talk about work, well, we got up at 5.15 a.m. and we went to bed between 10.15 and 10.30 and for the 17 hours in between we never stopped going for one minute. Thank God it only lasted 10 days—though even that was too long. There was one big shed, about as big as a big hay shed, divided into 4 by 4ft high walls and with a concrete floor. There we had our meals—on the floor Indian fashion in our _bare feet_!!! One of the instructresses was an English woman D.G. [_Deo gratia,_ or thank God] so she and I shared ordinary food for the 10 days as the students were having red-hot dishes. But of course we sat on the ground in our bare feet like the others (yes we did without stockings during camp!). On the last night a special Indian dish was served—Birryani (awful spelling). And we had to eat with our fingers—the Indians always do and they manage very tidily but you should have seen me try to get the rice into my mouth. I was sitting beside the lecturers and when they didn't ask for a spoon and fork how could I? We had meetings of Parliament several times and actually passed a Bill!

Then in the middle of the week according to rule there was a general election and to my great surprise they made me Prime Minister—and I

*The Tamil word for nun is _kanniyastiri._

was the only 'foreigner' among the students. We had Visitors Day on Saturday 3rd—the day Jane entered—and we had big-wigs from the department of education and the Corporation etc out to see the place as well as our College Principal and Senior Members of the staff. In all there were between 80 and 100 visitors and my duty was to make a speech—welcome them and tell them about the Camp. As one of our old nuns said once when telling me a story 'the perspiration was going up my back instead of down with fright' only it wasn't perspiration it was sweat! Anyhow I prepared the speech—brief and to the point mind you. They all said it was very nice and that they heard every word. Then the students gave a little concert for the visitors and after that (at about 5.30 p.m.) the Principal very kindly lent the six Catholic students the College car to take us to the station (a different road from the way we walked—about like the new road to the bog at home) and we came in to Madras to get Mass the next morning. The nuns had great welcome for the three of us—you know, only for their prayers and how good they were to us we would never have got through the camp. Reverend Mother sent us out bread and butter and coffee essence and tea (we couldn't get these things there) and they were all so worried about us and the old nuns prayed so much for us. Anyhow we told them all we could about the Camp that night and the next morning we left straight after Mass and returned to the Campers—we were there by 8.30 a.m. The remaining days were taken up with the usual class work plus tests on all we had done in Camp—learning how to put up a flag staff, make knots, bandages, collect nature specimens, hand work, needle work, a map of the area plus map reading, folk singing and dancing! No! I am _NOT_ going to tell you what I did. I mentioned squads at the beginning, well in our squad there were Catholics, Protestants (of 3 different kinds) and a Hindu. There were an Irishwoman, a Goan, an Anglo Indian, a Madrassi, and _two_ other Indian races. It was the most mixed squad in the whole camp site _and_ it was the squad that got on best together, worked best and had most fun. Everyone was amazed.

You know it was an awful experience for us nuns but it was grand there were three of us (in case you are curious our squad tent was next to ours and we did all our work in the squad tent as it was slightly bigger and had not been tarred and so was cooler). We used to laugh and when things got really bad I used to sing at the top of my voice—well not quite but almost! We came back on Wed 7th and are having holidays until 22nd. Next Monday 26th our 3 weeks teaching practice begins and goes on until Nov. 17th. Please pray for me during that time. Half our exams depend on how we do in this teaching—so then I'll write soon again. Fondest love to each of you my dearests and thanks again for everything. Did Noreen come down to see Jane before she left? Love again Julia

I like the way she compares exotic Indian detail with things at home—the view like the view from Mount View, the buffaloes in place of cows. Was she happy? It's hard to tell—but she doesn't seem unhappy. And busyness is a great panacea.

Before long, Julia got the news that she had earned her B.T. with distinction. That was a good moment, but it also marked the high point of her happiness at Church Park. A wholly unexpected piece of news came that made Julia confused and uncertain, and led her to feel some of the underlying unhappiness that had been growing in her at the convent. The news was that Peggie was no longer a nun. She had left the Presentation Sisters and was living in Dublin.

Peggie says that she had never been content in the order. "When I joined, instead of being sent to India, which I'd rather hoped, I was sent to teach at a boarding school in Matlock, and I hated and detested it." The dissatisfaction grew over the years, and reached a climax in 1953. This is how Peggie describes what happened:

"It was very difficult leaving and I was entirely on my own. I had made final vows and I'd been seven and a bit years there. I taught for a year in Matlock and then I didn't do my postgraduate diploma, and they decided that I ought to do my diploma, that the school inspectors expected it. I was sent to Newcastle for a year and I was very relieved. The mother superior in Matlock had been my novice mistress. She was a woman that I was in awe of. I still have nightmares—I literally still have nightmares—about her. So to get away to Newcastle was wonderful. But I had this terrible trapped feeling, which is difficult to explain. I had made my final vows, I had burnt my boats. Any chance of leaving was gone, so it appeared to me. I'd never heard of anyone who had made final vows leaving."

This is no exaggeration. It was extremely difficult for a nun who had made final vows to leave a religious order. The authorities made it as close to impossible as they could. The tactics at the Church's disposal included outright refusal, which would leave the religious with no choice besides staying put in bitter misery or excommunication. For people whose whole lives were within the Church, that was—to use an overused but accurate word—unthinkable. It would leave the ex-religious with no structure, nowhere to turn, and in particular, since the ex-nun or ex-priest would usually come from a religious family, no family support. On the way to that final sanction, though, the Church had an especially terrible weapon, one it would deploy without compunction: delay. Priests or nuns applying for a final dispensation—the magnificently titled Indult of Secularization, which had to come from the Congregation of Religious at the Vatican—would be stalled by their confessor, their immediate superior, the higher authorities of their order, and then by Rome itself. And all through this process they would be told that their vocation was undergoing a test and they would be invited to reconsider. They would be told to pray and meditate, to ask God for guidance. If they found the waiting a strain, they might be told that this was a sign that God did not want them to leave. They would be told that although they might have lost trust in God, He had not lost trust in them. The danger and strangeness of the secular world would be stressed, implicitly and explicitly. The magnitude of the choice they were attempting to make would be all too clear, along with the unlikeliness that their wish would be granted; and all the while the delay would stretch. The act of leaving was made to seem impossible. But Peggie, and others like her, came to feel that their lives in the convent were even less possible. That desperation brought with it a kind of strength.

"I was actually miserably unhappy," Peggie remembers. "But in Newcastle I was in a college atmosphere, I could go and read in the library, there were other nuns from other orders who were great fun. I used to look at them and listen to them and they obviously hadn't the same awe and fear of the superiors that I had. It was different. I was in Newcastle, it was the nineteenth of November 1953, and I suddenly, out of the blue, thought, 'I'm not trapped. I can leave. And I'm going to investigate the mechanism by which I leave.' I went to the confessor there and talked to him. Fortunately he was an absolutely lovely, humane person. He said, 'Can you come to the parlor privately and talk to me,' so I did. He asked me how old I was, what age I was when I went in. I'd been eighteen and he said, 'You couldn't really have known what you were doing.' He said, 'The first thing you must do, you must write to your superior and say this. And then you must apply to the Sacred Congregation of Religious in Rome and ask for a dispensation.' So I went through all that and I did

Peggie after leaving the convent.

it. It seemed like utter hell at the time, and that nothing else in my whole life could be like it again. But I did it and I left. I left in January '54. I was twenty-six, just barely twenty-six, my birthday's in December. And I felt very sorry for Julia. You see, I was never able fully to explain to Julia why I had done this. Julia must have been utterly puzzled. Also, my own life was so complex at the time that I stopped writing to Julia for a time. I found it difficult to manage anything except my own immediate life."

With the arrival of this unexpected and very unwelcome piece of news, the dissatisfaction Julia felt with her life in the convent came out in the way that sort of unhappiness often does: as anger. She was furious with Peggie. She could not think straight about her. She thought what she had done was outrageous. Julia wrote to Peggie, a bitter, intemperate letter, the only one from these years that I don't have in my possession, since Peggie kept neither it nor a grudge.

The letters for the next couple of years don't give much away. At home, the main event was the lung cancer that weakened and then eventually took the life of Patrick Gunnigan, in September 1956. There is no mention of grief or a sense of loss about her father's death in Julia's letters that I have, but that probably reflects the fact I have only some of the letters she wrote home. I suspect she was deeply upset by his death.

What there is instead of grief is a tremendous amount of Julia's badgering her sister Bernie for help getting hold of stockings—which she needs for occasional work-related trips outside the convent, it seems—and sheet music for the concerts she has to put on. Most of the music is sentimental and Irish. My mother was absolutely tone-deaf, so I feel the pain of the audiences who sat through the ensuing concerts. None of these arrangements was made easier by the fact that "at the moment we are not allowed to send a halfpenny out of the country." (Nuns had no money, not even a stipend, but Julia would have been allowed to draw on convent funds for expenses, and may have been able to squirrel away small amounts for emergency use.) She has hopes that she might be home in either 1959 or 1960. By then it would have been a decade since she had seen her family. One lively moment in her letters is an encounter with the festival of Diwali: "The monsoon has broken here and so we're having plenty of rain—torrential downpours at times. It is also approaching the big Hindu festival of Deepavali—which is celebrated with crackers and fireworks—the explosives are going off almost ceaselessly these days—the louder the noise the more fervent the celebration, evidently."

In the summer of 1957, Julia took her M.A. in English, again by correspondence from the University of London. There was a reason she needed the additional qualification: she had been made principal of the teacher-training college at Church Park. But there was a problem. As Julia rose in the hierarchy of the order, she grew increasingly unhappy, or increasingly aware of her own unhappiness. The two matters that pressed most heavily on her were "common life"—the total lack of private space and private property—and obedience. Years later, she explained to me that the sheer institutional weight of the Church began to oppress her. The further she rose in the hierarchy the more she felt it. As a junior nun, she was so insignificant and powerless that the sense of her own insignificance and powerlessness made the weight bearing down on her easier to tolerate. As she began to have power and responsibility herself, the

Sister Eucharia as principal of the training school.

weight on her, paradoxically, began to seem all the heavier. Once she was running her own part of Church Park, the burden was so crushing that at times she felt she could not breathe. The hierarchy was run by and for men, and women were less than nothing to it. The hard thing was not just to endlessly take orders and defer to men who were less intelligent, less serious, who cared less and knew less than she, and who took the credit for things she did; it was the fact that these practices were structurally built into the Church. They weren't accidents, they were the fundamental institutional realities of her world. At a meeting in Calcutta, after some particularly stupid and arbitrary imposition, Sister Eucharia lost her temper, slapped the table, and announced, "This is a man's Church!"

There was now, though, by virtue of the very same seniority, a crack in the edifice of obedience and common life. In Julia's capacity as principal, for the first time since she entered the order, she had the chance of opening her own letters. As a result, she got back in touch with Peggie after a lapse of four years. By now Peggie had qualified as a teacher, thanks to their uncle Bill. "He used to know the professor of education at UCD [University College Dublin], he used to play golf with him. He asked, Was there any way at that late stage I could get into the course in Dublin and finish it? And he arranged for it and he paid my fee. And that was wonderful. It made a huge difference. It meant that when I did want to teach I was absolutely fully qualified in all respects." Peggie had gone to teach math at a London polytechnic, and had met and fallen in love with a sculptor from Dublin, Vincent Geraghty. They were married in December 1955, and more than fifty years later are married still, and living at Nenagh in County Tipperary.

The marriage had an important consequence for Julia: it meant that she could write to a Mrs. V. Geraghty, and no one would know she was in touch with her sister. Added to this was the fact that, as principal of a school, she had contacts outside the convent, made through her work, to whom Peggie could write in return. The next letter is Julia's first uncensored letter in thirteen years. As is immediately clear, it differs completely from those before, in that it frankly discusses her own feelings and is open about her situation in the convent.

Mrs V Geraghty
134 Tachbrook Street
London SW1
England

Presentation Convent
Church Park
Madras-6
11 xii 1957

My dearest Peggie,

I can imagine you hesitating to open this letter; in fact it wouldn't surprise me if you returned it without reading it but I hope you won't do that. I am really sorry, Peggie, for writing to you in the tone I did last time. I know I shouldn't have and I regret it—I hope you will forgive me and put it down to the fact that I was at an extremely low ebb mentally, physically and nervously when I wrote. And I assure you it won't happen again. So now I hope we are the same good friends and favourite sisters to each other that we always were.

I hope you and Vincent are well and I am very glad that you are so happy. Vincent is wise to be doing some study—you mentioned in your letter that he is. Are you teaching in the same place all the time? Bernie mentioned when she wrote that you live near your work.

As for me, I have just returned from Calcutta after doing M.A. I found it very hard indeed and a great strain, especially as I was tired out after the year's work here. I hope I will get through—the results won't be out until about March. Anyhow I wouldn't like to have to go through it again—I am not as young as I used to be!

There isn't much news here. Our annual retreat begins on Friday 13th. We are having an Indian S.J. this time [an Indian Jesuit priest]. We

have a new Reverend Mother since September—Mother Magdalen—
she was here when I came out in 1949. Then we had Mother Laurence
(you met her in Castle Connell in 1952)—she was *AWFUL*, Peggie, I will
never forget what we went through. Mother Magdalen isn't so bad but
absolutely absorbed in herself and her own diseases and in all the work
she did in her day. No one knows when exactly that day was, as she has
spent most of her life in bed looking after herself!

You know you had great courage to do what you did a few years ago.
I wish I had as much. I cannot do anything before 1959—the year my ten
years in India are up. Please pray much for me, and do, like a darling,
write. I hardly ever hear from home. Maybe it is just as well.

By the way I have a certain raffia hat for you—if you are still interested. But I don't know how to send it to you. I must see if there will be
anyone I know and can trust going home this year. Of course it may not
be much use to you in London—just let me know. I would send you a
nice kind of gauze scarf instead—if you would like that better. That is all
for now. I will hardly write again before Christmas, so I will wish you and
Vincent now a very happy Christmas and every blessing in the New Year
and always. Now do please write to me and don't mention any of this to
the others.

I hope you are not too mad with me, though goodness knows you
have every reason to be. Bye bye now, my dearest.

Ever your loving

Julia xxxx

Peggie wrote back, and the sisters resumed regular contact. This made
an enormous difference to Julia. Her sense of relief at being able to open
up to someone is strong in the next letter.

3 i 58

My dearest Peggie,

Thank you very much for your letter which I was delighted to get and
for the snaps you sent. I think you are looking simply wonderful. Being

thinner suits you—and slacks do too! and also happiness! I showed the pictures to a few of the sisters and all agreed on how lovely you look in them. I think Vincent is grand!!

I am delighted to hear you are so happy, Peggie—I wish I could say the same for myself. I don't know what to do. I made up my mind to leave in 1959, as there will be someone to replace me in College then, but I have been debating since—should I go ahead and ask for a dispensation before I go home or should I have a holiday at home first. It would be easier for me just to go but it might not be so hard on them at home if I had been home on a holiday—they needn't make it public that I had left—I suppose you know what I mean. Please tell me what you think when you write. And please destroy this letter, Peggie, especially if Mammy is going to visit you—she always reads letters and if she heard of this she would make an awful fuss and that wouldn't help things. Then, I know I am not getting any younger, but at least I can earn my living—do you think could I by any chance get a post in the school or college you are in? The fact that I have teaching experience in India might be a help? Is it a government school? If it is, my certificates would have to be checked in India—if it is under private management, that might not be necessary, especially since you are on the staff. Could you, by any chance, enquire if I could get a post there in 1959? or anywhere in London? My subject is English and I am M.A. and B.T. And I could stay with you until I got settled in? I would probably try to get a flat by myself. I have some friends who would help me. I realise, of course, that they will be furious at home and will absolutely renounce me, but if I can count on your friendship, then I can manage to carry on. I won't tell them at home until it is all done— don't you think that is better? When you write and give me your opinion, I shall begin putting a few clothes together. Of course I can't get much here—I would have to wait to get woolens—coat etc in England. That's why I thought that if I went home for a holiday first, I could use the money I would get there to buy clothes—it is a big problem, Peggie, and it is at the back of my mind, night and day.

I was wondering if I could ask you to send me a _good_ corset—bra and corset, combined with a side fastening. I have £3 here which I could send you *but* are the Marshalls reliable? I have heard of people offering to bring things out to India and never delivering them.* If you think they are to be trusted, and if you think you could afford to get me a good corset by putting the balance to the £3 I send you, will you please enquire at a shop and tell me what measurements I should send you. If I am getting clothes—I must have a proper fit and for that I will need a corset. And there is this, too, Peggie. If I leave I will have people to help me but naturally I would rather be a bit independent, so I won't be a burden to you. Please write and tell me honestly what you think. I will write an ordinary letter in a day or two. Reply, when it reaches you, but just to be sure, when talking of my problems refer to me as T. Leetch—just in case anything happens, but I don't think your letter will be read. Don't, I beg you, wait until the Marshalls are coming to write—I cannot leave in 1958— no-one to replace me. Will you help me if I do? Talk it over with Vincent. He looks nice. With much love to you both Julia

Although this letter starts out by pretending to ask advice about what to do, it is clear that Julia had already made up her mind. She is going to leave the order and is thinking hard about how she is going to live once she gets out. For Julia, that meant worry—lots of worry. This was, and was to become, a dominant feature of her personality, and it is one that has a thorough airing in the letters as she lets her mind play over what life will be like on the outside. It is also clear that the worry is a useful thing for Julia, in that it gives her mind something to do with itself rather than face the blank magnitude of the change of life in front of her.

The stuff about corsets might seem frivolous or off-key, but it touches on one of Julia's most traumatic memories. The emphasis on clothes, which runs through all these letters, can be directly attributed to her experiences in leaving the postulancy in 1938. Her parents' refusal to let her wear anything other than the habit she came home in was just about the single worst thing they did to her. No wonder she worries so much over

---

*The Marshalls were a brother and a sister from a well-off Catholic family in Madras who were traveling around Europe; Peggie knew them through friends. Julia was right to be skeptical about them, since they never gave her the corset.

what she is to wear. She kept returning to this worry in the letters to Peggie. It shows how deeply she was scarred by what had happened when she left the convent before. It also made a very useful focus for displacement anxiety, and for general fussing.

As for the passage about her mother's reading her letters, this at least indicates that Julia's version of her mother was not something she made up later in life. Not everyone in the family saw Molly Gunnigan as Julia did, but Julia was at least sincere in her view of her, and her fear of her mother's nosiness and capacity for making trouble is a recurring theme. A few letters later she returned to the subject: "Please, I beg you keep my letters under lock and key, or better still, destroy them, if Mammy is going to visit you. I know, for a fact, that she will ferret out and read everything and the fuss she will make will do us no good." Whenever she heard that Peggie had been in touch with their mother, she continued the theme. "I had a letter from Mammy yesterday. She mentioned that you had invited her over for Whitsun and that she would love to go and might go too. _Please_, Peggie, keep my letters out of her hands. She will only start writing to Mother General etc etc and the result will be just extra bitterness and heartbreak. I am finding all this a great strain."

It is obvious as soon as one opens it that there is something odd about the next letter, written less than a week after her request for a corset. The handwriting is twice the usual size, the gaps between the lines are one and a half times the normal size, and the message reverts to the pretense that all is well.

9 i 58

My dearest Peggie,

Thank you very much for your letter for Christmas with snaps enclosed. You look wonderfully well, thank God, and so happy. I was delighted to hear all your news, though indeed some of it was sad—I hope you will have better health now. You should do exactly what the doctor tells you—that is always the wisest course.

I showed your photos to some of the Sisters—those who know you and who would be interested and not merely curious—all agree that you look lovely and all send you their love. Mother St John will be writing to you if you haven't already heard from her—I gave her your address.

I haven't heard from home since Christmas though they all wrote then. I didn't put pen to paper to anyone except Mammy so I suppose they'll pay me out next year and I won't get a line!!

I expect you have heard all the news there is. What do you and Vincent think of T. Leetch's plans? I am interested to hear what you think should be done. I hope you'll find time to write soon. It was such a joy to get your last letter. I am sorry this is so short—I have an awful lot to do and am racing to get this out on the evening's post.

I hope you will escape colds and 'flu' this winter and also your Vincent. With much love to you both. Don't forget me—I always remember you.

Your loving

Julia xx

That was a dummy letter. The remark about people being "interested and not merely curious" is a crack directed at whoever Julia is aware might censor it. I don't know why she was so sure this letter was being read. But the anxiety about surveillance never left Julia. Later she refers to the need to write a "code letter," which is what this one was. As she had decided to leave the order anyway, her fears over discovery seem remarkably vivid. One is tempted to ask, What was she frightened of, that they might kick her out? But that is to underestimate the effect of her previous experience of leaving the Good Shepherds twenty years before. That sense of being the center of scandal had been the most scarring experience of her life. It was the main thing she dreaded about leaving the order, and it was why she clung to secrecy as hard as she did.

The only person Julia completely trusted in Madras was her former tutor on the teacher-training course, a Miss Forrester, who joined with Peggie in arguing that Julia should leave the convent sooner rather than later. "She is afraid the strain of waiting may be too much for me," Julia reported to Peggie. Both Peggie and Miss Forrester also thought that Julia should leave before she told the rest of her family of her intentions. "I am glad you agree that I should not go home first—I rather dreaded that," Julia wrote to Peggie. "As it is, I hope to be out and in London when the news reaches them. They will have to accept the 'fait accompli.' "

Julia relied on Peggie for detailed advice about how to leave the Presentation Sisters.

31 i 1958

What I want to know, Peggie darling, is how long did it take you to get the dispensation once you actually wrote to Rome? Did you only do that after you went to Pickering for Christmas? I know you discussed the whole thing with a priest in Denham. Would it be against your conscience to tell me what you said to him? I think you told me at the time, or someone did, that a priest wrote to Mother General saying you should be let go. I wish I could get a priest to do that for me. Because I am longer in than you are, it may be harder for me than it was for you. Anything you can tell me I will be grateful for.

I thought of saying: (1) I have wanted to go several times but allowed myself to be talked into staying in religion (which is true and they know it) on account of the position at home (2) Now my father is dead, and the family settled I have decided to go as I find I cannot bear the burden of the religious life especially common life and obedience (3) the strain is so great that my health will not stand much more worry and tension (this is true) (4) I have waited this long in order to pay back in work whatever expenses were incurred in my education, passage to and from India, etc. Is that enough, Peggie? Write and tell me what you think, either to me, direct, or to the address given on the first page, but, I _beg_ you, write soon. That is all for now. I hope you and Vincent are well. How I wish the next year or 18 months were over. Then I will laugh again.

I'm not sure that her father's death and the family's being "settled"— which I think means the girls had all left home, one way or another— actually had much bearing on Julia's decision to leave the convent. I think it had more to do with the depth of her misery, and the fact that her sisters Peggie and then Mary had left their orders, and neither of them had died of shame. She was miserable; it was doable; and if she left now, there was a chance, albeit a small one, that she could plausibly think about having a family of her own. The late thirties is a common age for nuns to leave religious orders, and that is the primary reason.

As she began to imagine the process of leaving in detail, Julia thought of herself differently. She came to be aware of the fact that instead of being primarily a nun, she would from now on be primarily a woman. She would have to think of herself, and project herself, otherwise. I don't think Julia was ever completely indifferent to her appearance, but it was, obviously, another matter when she was the only person who ever saw her out of her habit. One of the most moving and entertaining aspects of the convent letters is Julia's viewing herself as a woman for the first time in almost a decade and a half.

You said you would love to know how I am looking. Well, as you saw by photographs last year I put on a lot of weight, far too much, with the result that I had a bad spell of boils and high blood pressure—not too good at my age which is not yet the high b.p. age, believe me. [She had turned thirty-seven the previous month.] Well, I was advised by doctors to cut down to as near eliminated point as possible both starches and sugars. This I have done and the result is that in the last 6 months I have lost roughly 36 pounds and am still losing—but I needed to and I feel and look better. Judging from photographs I have seen of Noreen and Mary, I think I can safely say I look younger than either. I am generally taken to be in my twenties so that my being Principal of a College causes no little surprise. My skin continues to be as it used to be but of course my color is not good. In fact one of my nicknames is 'the most beautiful nun in India—who has got all the brains too'!!! But really it is vanity to repeat that and when I get into ordinary clothes a lot of the age-hiding drapery will go and I suppose wrinkles will appear from nowhere—I haven't any now, but they will come I'm sure! You won't be forced to introduce me to your friends as your grand-aunt, though!

Nuns were not supposed to pay attention to their own bodies, so such self-assessment and measurement was in itself no small rebellion. And then there was the always pressing matter of clothes, as reflected in the following letter, a classic example of my mother at her best and her worst. It also shows that although Julia felt confident, now that she was principal, that her own letters would go unread, she was still worried about the possibility that Peggie's letters might be intercepted.

18 iii 1958

My dearest Peggie,

Your letter was very consoling, Peggie, I am very grateful indeed for all the interest you are taking. At present I cannot make any definite plans, but I *may* be in a position to get things moving in May. The latest news we have here is that Mother General is coming to India 'soon'. In my opinion 'soon' means next October or November when the weather is somewhat cool. She will never expose herself to India as it will be for the next 7 months. However if she comes I will tell her, and failing that I will write.

As regards the clothes I will get there: I have already been advised not to have warm clothes—like a coat or suit—made here as they are never done properly. They tell me to stick to blouses and cotton dresses and maybe a few heavier dresses of some kind of woolen materials and even skirts—I mean warm ones—are a risk as they are made so badly—I will have to get some money and buy them as soon as I arrive there. A woman whom I have confided in, and who has been to England and back several times, said that rather than have warm clothes made here (I mean coats etc) she would willingly wrap herself in a blanket and buy there! But I will try to have some decent cotton dresses and maybe hand-loom skirts and blouses and a knitted jumper and cardigan. Should I get pyjamas or nightdresses made? I mean I would like to have got as many of these things as possible, underwear too, in order not to be a burden—they won't be over generous with the cash I am sure when I am going and I will need what they give me to get warm things.

I was glad to hear your news that you may be expecting a baby. Now, like a good girl, look after yourself and don't worry about me—because worry is very hard at a time like this, and please let me know if it is definite. Wouldn't it be grand if I was there to look after you!

Now, to answer your questions: my skin is dry (sun of India, you know). I believe that Pond's have a cream called 'Dry Skinfood with Lanolin' which would be good for it—unfortunately it cannot be got here now and there is a complete ban on imports so if you could send me a little of that, Peggie, it might boost up my morale a little. My eyebrows could certainly do with a little tidying up and I do have a *few* whiskers on my upper lip. I think it is very kind of you to think of all this. If you do send lipstick etc c/o Miss Oliver I shall be very grateful. I would like, too, a few pieces of *either* Knight's Castile or Gibbs Superfatted Soap. I always feel that a good toilet soap is very important for the skin and I haven't had one lately. Pack everything in one box—Miss Forrester will bring them. I *do* worry about my appearance but I worry more about getting a job and earning my living! My general health is not too bad. I have lost 3 *stone* [more than forty pounds] since July but I was overweight and am the better for it. I am very tired though and inclined to tears. I tried to take Vitamins last year but they seemed to make the boils worse. Maybe if you sent some English preparation (in pill form, as you say) it might agree with me. Before I finish—please don't use the address of Mrs Balakrishnan again—they are leaving Madras and the house will be empty. I will give you another address as soon as I can. In the meantime you might write by Miss Forrester. If she is in Madras when she returns to India, I may ask you to send the letters to her, but if so it wouldn't be for long. I'll be writing again in a day or two. I wonder what happened to your last letter? Thanks once again, my dearest, for everything. I hope this will reach you in time to get in touch with Miss Forrester. God's love and bless you and Vincent. Your loving sister Julia

It was lucky that Peggie understood the degree of worry and self-absorption involved in leaving the convent, since anyone else might legitimately have minded the fact that the world-altering news about her pregnancy was fitted in between concerns with clothes and skin cream. Julia was well aware of how much she was asking of her sister. "Are you sick and tired of me, Peggie? I am, of myself, at any rate." But she had no choice, since she had no one else to turn to. And Peggie more than anyone else could identify with that. She was the only person in a position to help Julia, and so she helped her, not least by renting a room for her in the downstairs flat, so that Julia would have somewhere to live when she came to London.*

By now it was clear that Julia had irrevocably decided to leave and go to London. All that was left was to breathe deeply, summon her reserves of courage, and actually set the process in motion.

28 vi 1958

My dearest Peggie,

I delayed writing to you until today so that I would have some definite news for you—well, I have just been down at the Post Office to send, by Registered Mail (air mail of course) the letter to Mother General with the formal application to the Congregation of Religious enclosed. I can tell you it took me some time to get these two epistles written, but it is a relief now to have them off my hands. I hope everything will go well, but in a way I suppose that whatever happens cannot be much worse than the suspense of waiting for it!

I have posted to you today by registered parcel my old woolen dressing-gown; old as it is, it is still in good condition and very warm and I am sure I will be glad of it next winter. It is looking rather bedraggled as I left it out in the sun in Madras to air a few years ago, and it got faded in parts. So when it reaches you will you please like a dear have it dyed navy blue for me—I shall be very grateful if you have this done before I get home as I am afraid seeing it again as it is now would be a constant reminder of things I would rather forget! Incidentally, I meant to take my name off it but I forgot—will you do that, too, like an angel. There are whitish acid

---

*The previous inhabitant, a young woman named Vi, went home to British Guyana and married future president Forbes Burnham.

stains on the sleeve which won't dye properly—but that doesn't matter. The parcel should reach you by the end of August, I imagine; maybe I'll be there just as soon myself, but I don't think that is very likely—it is up to M. General now and I imagine she will want me to stay until the end of November—more so as she is supposed to be coming out in October.

I return to Madras tomorrow so by the time this reaches you, I will be back in Church Park and hard at work—which will help the months to go quickly.

Are you keeping well, Peggy dearest? I hope you are seeing the doctor regularly and following his instructions carefully. Have you thought of names yet? Mum seemed to enjoy her visit to London. It is just as well that you didn't say anything to her. Have you ever heard anything further from P. Marshall? Is there any chance at all of my getting that parcel out of her? Please let me know about this when you write. Would you like me to try to bring my sheets and towels with me? They are in quite good condition and might be a help to you. I can bring one rug across my arms—have you got blankets? I'll bring a hot water bottle too. I am a *cold* creature you know. Is the flat heated or do you have a fire?

Much love to Vincent and your dear self and do please write soon. I am *dreading* M. General's letter. Love again

Julia

My mother's bossiness here is, I think, outrageous. Peggie was living in a tiny flat, pregnant, with a husband in full-time education; she had already arranged a room for Julia, and was all-round indispensable to her future plans—and her reward was to be asked to dye a dressing gown because it wasn't a sufficiently consistent blue. Here as elsewhere, I want to say, "Mum, give her a break." But I can't pretend that the peremptoriness and self-absorption were not in character; in particular, they were a characteristic reaction to the stress she was under as she waited for a response from the mother general. The month between that letter and the next was perhaps the longest of Julia's life.

25 vii 1958
as from c/o Miss Forrester
School for the Deaf
Mylapore, Madras-4

My dearest Peggie,

I wrote to you just before I left Kodai telling you that I had written to Mother General and I promised I would let you know as soon as I heard from her. Well, I thought her reply would NEVER come and I didn't know what to think or do. Anyhow, when I got in from supervising teaching practice yesterday evening, I found her letter in my place in the chapel! Knowing of old that M. General writes a barbed pen dipped in acid ink, I decided that before reading what she had to say, I would have a night's sleep—which I had!! And I read the letter this morning. It was very brief—just two pages of a sixpenny air letter. She said she had received my letter and my formal application to the Sacred Congregation of Religious and before forwarding it to Rome she had to consult her Council (and *that* means that my decision is known in Madras as one of her Council lives here). From the tone of my letter to her and to Rome, they are all agreed that my decision is final and that I am not open to persuasion and so she has sent my letter to Rome—it went on the 22nd July. 'When and how you leave I will inform you by letter,' she says, 'when I get the decision of Rome on your application.' I was hoping she would realise that trying to talk me round was a waste of time, and, thank God, she has seen that. So now, Peggie, I am much nearer to getting things fixed. I don't know how things will go, but it is quite possible that I *may* be with you in September. Of course, I may still have to wait until the year's out. But if I am free to go in September—I mean if the dispensation has come, it will suit me O.K. as the students will have finished their practical exams and I will have got them through their theory syllabus and all they will need will be revision classes until November and it won't be too difficult to get someone to take that much.

Now *please*, *please*, Peggie, do write at once. Send a letter to me direct to Church Park (just to allay suspicion) and in it ask me have I heard from M. General, and when do I hope to get away and ask what clothes I have got (if any) etc. Let it be in answer to my last letter from Kodai. It need not be long just so as I hear from you—I don't want them to suspect that I am getting letters by another route. Note Miss Forrester's address is School for the Deaf _not_ School for the Blind as I told you by mistake the last time.

Now, Peggie, if I go to London in the religious dress (as I probably will since my passport is made out for Sister Eucharia) I suppose I will be met by one of the Sisters—maybe Mother General herself—and taken to a Convent to change—perhaps to Hammersmith. Now, I am sure you won't want to meet any of our Community and I don't blame you, so if I am being met, I will fix it that when I have changed I will go by taxi, myself, to your flat. Now, will you please tell me how to direct the taxi man to find the place—Tachbrook Street may be a difficult place to get at and I have no idea of where to find it. Is there any way I could phone you or Vincent once I arrive in London? Then, don't forget to tell me, will it be enough if I just bring my rug across my arm—if I fly it won't be easy to pack blankets. What about sheets and towels? _About_ what money would I need to get a reasonably complete set of clothes in London—including a good warm overcoat _and_ a suit? Please let me know when you write.

And Peggie, darling, how are you keeping yourself? I am very worried about you in case this extra load of anxiety about me just now would have a bad effect on you. Are you having regular check-ups? If by chance this letter has to follow you home—for goodness' sake keep it out of Mammy's hands! I will write again as soon as I have any news for you. Will it be inconvenient for you and Vincent if I arrive in London in September? Now, do please write me _two_ letters at once—one to Church Park and one to Miss Forrester's address. The latter is due back in Madras from Delhi today—so there may be a letter from you waiting for me at the address. Don't forget to put J. Gunnigan on letters sent to her not Sister E.

Fondest love to you and Vincent and God bless you for everything.

Write, please write soon

Julia

The fussing over details, the tremendous sense of displaced emotional force in her worries—now, this is my mother. She is gradually turning into the person I knew. The streak of ruthlessness in her is there, too. The sense of isolation, of living in the world but being cut off from it, is also strong. Yet it wasn't long before Julia returned to the all-important subject of clothes.

29 vii 1958

If I manage to get work, then I could have some of my earnings saved for the January sales that you spoke of. Thank God I have you to advise me on what to buy etc. I was quite staggered to read the winter costume of slacks—boots—furlined jacket etc. that you say I will need. But, Peggie, surely if I am teaching I won't be allowed to dress up like that going to school?—and wouldn't it be just looking for trouble in the way of catching chills etc. to wear such a warm outfit out of school hours and then to change into skirts, stockings, shoes etc from 8 a.m. to 4 p.m. each day? Do, please, tell me the answer to that one!! It strikes me that it is just as well that I have lost a good deal of weight if I have to venture forth in slacks!—God preserve me from the skin-tight variety!

Now, Peggie, darling, about the bra. It is quite impossible to get one to fit me here. I wonder would you be an angel and make another attempt to get one out to me. Do you remember I sent you a duchess set to Matlock once? [A duchess set consists of linen tablecloths or doilies.] I stitched each piece of it between the pages of a newspaper. Now, if you were to get some nice bulky paper like, say, the *Sunday Express*, and flatten out the bra between the middle pages and then tack them together and then parcel it up the usual way one does a newspaper and address it to Miss *J.* Michael, Church Park Training College, Cathedral P.O. Madras-6—it will come to me. Don't put your own name on any part of it. I have two students called Michael in the College—neither of them has the initial 'J' so I will know that a paper addressed to J. is for me. And please, Peggie, send it *Air Mail*. I know it will cost more, but if it comes by sea, it will take ages and I might not be here when it arrives. If you can do that, it will mean a lot to me as I am getting a little knitting done for London and having a bra will mean I can get a good fit. The size now is 35″ (not 36″) and I imagine the cup should be medium size and the deeper fitting the bra is the better. I have seen Twilfit ads in English magazines here and they seem to have the kind that would suit me the best. I hate worrying you like this Peggie, and indeed I wouldn't bother you, if there was anyone else I could turn to. Miss Forrester looked at my hair yesterday evening. [She was the first person to see Julia's hair since she entered the convent in 1944.] She said to tell you, it was growing very nicely and the really extraordinary part of it is that it has a bit of a wave and a curl in it now—I used to have curls as a small child but they grew out and *now* in my *latter* years they are back again—I can't understand it! Has your scientific mind any explanation to offer?

Oh, Peggie, I almost forgot to tell you. Poor Nancy Lyons is now in Church Park and quite definitely a mental case. She is having shock treatment from a psychiatrist here in Madras. She was fine in Kodai at the end of May—went back to Themi and has gradually gone off since then. She has all sorts of hallucinations, thinks she killed a woman and I believe has said that there is insanity in her family—did you ever hear that before? It would break your heart to see her. She has a haunted look in her eyes. She was asking for you in Kodai and actually got your address from me to write to you. I am very sorry for her. Love again to you and Vincent.

Some of this is like a nun's version of *The Great Escape.* Some of it is like *Black Narcissus,* Michael Powell and Emeric Pressburger's steamy film about repressed sex, madness, and nuns in the Himalayas in the forties.

5 viii 1958

My next big problem—in fact the biggest one of all just now—is my passport. It is made out for *Sister Eucharia Gunnigan* and is valid until 18 vii 1959. The passport gives my profession as Religious and has, of course, a photo of me in the religious habit—I don't mind that last as they rarely look at the photo, but I would like if it is at all possible to get a new passport *now* instead of next year and to get it made out to Julia I. Gunnigan omitting my religious name. I wonder do they issue passports at the office of the Irish High Commissioner in London? Could you find that out for me, Peggie? You could explain why I want the passport changed now. It is due to be done next year in any case, but I think it is better to have it done now. You see then they could give me the dispensation here (or at least in Bombay) and I could go home in ordinary clothes. If I went in ordinary clothes with a passport made out for Sister Eucharia and my profession down as religious they might think I was a spy or something. There will probably be a form to fill in—please get it and send it to me and find out if I should send my passport to you or what should be done.

Anxiety about passports and identification was to play a significant role in Julia's life from now on. For the moment she kept the religious passport, on the grounds that changing it would take too much time and might cause difficulties of its own.

The procedure for leaving the Presentation Sisters was that the "instrument" would be issued by the Congregation of Religious in Rome, and passed on to Julia through her order. By the end of August, she had still heard nothing from her mother superior. She was by now seriously antsy.

26 viii 1958

Well, Peggie, since I heard from Mother General on July 24th there hasn't been another word. I told you, I think, that she was having treatment and there was a possibility of an operation—well, she had the op. (gall bladder removed and stones from bile duct) on August 22nd in Derby and the latest news is that the doctor has said she is not to come to India until after Xmas—she was to come in September, you know. In a way I am glad as I half expected her to keep me waiting until she came out herself. As things are now, it looks as if Sister de Sales will have to go home as she is not responding to treatment and they *might* decide to send me home with her. Then my going home from here could be managed without too much publicity. In fact I am *thinking* of making this suggestion to Mother General when I write: as I know they are worried here about getting de Sales home. Anyhow, as usual, we will have to wait and see. As you said, M. General likes long dramatic pauses.

As far as I am concerned, I have *not* told my Rev. Mother here in Church Park—I daren't mention it as she is an APPALLING talker and it would be the gossip of the nation if she knew. I haven't told a soul in any of the convents here except for Sister de Chantal (Bridget Cummins that *was*—you probably know her from Castle Connell.) She is doing her training here in the College and she is a rock of sense, God bless her. She has knitted a very nice jumper and cardigan for me and she will never open her mouth. She is the only one who knows. Let the General tell them if and when she wants them to know. She will be able to insist on them keeping quiet about it—I cannot. And if it becomes public that I am going, there will be a great to do. I know that.

More weeks passed, and still Julia heard nothing. Acting on advice from her friend Miss Forrester, she took copies of all the correspondence so far—her letter to her mother superior, her letter to Rome, and so on—and sent it to the papal internuncio in New Delhi, with a cover letter asking for "immediate action." There was a hint of threat in that. Sister Eucharia was, as a principal of one of the Indian Church's highest-profile educational institutions, a fairly prominent figure. If she chose to walk out and make a big fuss in doing so, there would be a considerable scandal. The letter to the internuncio was sent on the second of October. Four days later Julia had her reply.

6 x 58

My dearest Peggie,

This is it!! Thanks be to God! I think my letter must have produced results. Anyhow, Rev. Mother came over this morning to say (this is the _first_ time she has referred to the matter) that the papers have already come from Rome and are actually in Madras. (I thought as much, you know.) She has been to the Archbishop about them and I must say she was very nice about the whole thing. The final decision, which is just as I would like it to be is that I leave here on the night plane to Delhi on Thursday October 30th. I have meetings in Delhi for the four days following, and I am very glad I am attending them as they have been pressing me to do so. Then I leave Delhi by an Air India International Flight and arrive in London at 5 p.m. on the next Wednesday. That means I will be at the air-terminal in the City about 6 or 6.30—I will find that out later or you can enquire there. Now I haven't heard yet if any of the sisters will meet me—I hope _not_. In that case, could Vincent take me to some waiting rooms—say at a Railway station—where I could change. I would rather not go to your flat in the Religious dress. Think about it and let me know. Then you promised to borrow a coat for me—that would have to be brought to wherever I change. And, Peggie darling, I will need a nightdress that night—please buy one for me as I am not bringing any home with me—those I have are worn out. Do, please, write as soon as you get this. I will send a 'formal' letter to you from C.P. tomorrow. Must rush now to catch the post. I have just got notice of Government Inspection—on the 27th and 28th—so that will keep me occupied up to

The letter breaks off and is not signed. She must have gotten most of the way through, then had to hide it when someone came into the room, and either sealed it on the spot or forgotten that it was unfinished, and sealed it later.

Julia had spent, by this time, fifteen years in convents. She had been crushed, suffocated, by her experience of life in the Church. And yet the first thing she says when given her freedom to leave is "Thanks be to God!" The easy term for moments like this is "ironic." That implies that they have two different meanings, one to the person speaking and a different one to others. In this context, Julia's thanking God would seem to be missing the large point that her devotion to God is what got her into this predicament in the first place. Yet I think that she was perfectly aware of what she was saying, and that she knew very well how it sounded, and that she knew also that Peggie of all people would understand. The problem was not with God—she never stopped believing in Him—but with the Church and the choices she had, she felt, been forced to make. I find a certain comfort in that. If she had spent a decade and a half in convents, giving a huge part of her life away, with nothing in return, the story of my mother's youth would be sad to the point of desolation. And it is still pretty sad. But the fact is that she loved God, felt a direct and personal love of Him. The sense of contact with God she experienced, especially through prayer and the Eucharist, was a real feeling and a real comfort. Thank God indeed, because otherwise the story of Julia's first thirty-eight years would be too sad to bear.

14 x 58

Now, Peggie darling, the next thing is—when am I to tell them at home? You can have no idea (though indeed I know well that you *can*) of how the thought of it is torturing me. Could you write and do it for me? I am afraid of Mammy collapsing or something. My idea is that they should keep it as private as possible for their own sakes. I am so long gone from home and I have written to so few people that it doesn't really matter much and the best thing for them is to talk as little about it as possible. Please tell me what you think I should do or if you can do anything. But don't upset or worry yourself, Peggie. I wish they knew at home; I see your wisdom now in insisting that I shouldn't say anything until the deed was done. I hope they will be more likely to accept a fait accompli— though I doubt it. You wonder how I am looking—well pretty worn out I'm afraid. All this has taken a lot out of me but I suppose I'll pick up quickly with you. I can never tell you how grateful I am for all you have done for me, Peggie. I appreciate every bit of it more than I can say. I hope I'll be able to do something for you in return. When do you expect to go into hospital? I am glad you are feeling so well—that is very reassuring. Don't worry about anything, you and the baby will be all right, D.V. [*Deo volente*, God willing].

Thank you very much for promising to have some night wear ready for me. As you say, pyjamas are much warmer and I'll probably be glad of whatever warmth I can muster up! Please thank Una, too, for taking me to her hairdresser. My hair has grown quite a bit so he will have something to work on. But I wouldn't like any *extreme* type of hair style. I'll be glad to have someone to help me decide, since you won't be there, yourself. . . .

You mentioned in your last letter that I might try to get some temporary work in one of the stores during the Xmas season. I would like it, if it was possible, to get into a *book shop*—the only type of merchandise I know anything about. Anyhow, we will see. I can't think of anything else now, Peggie. Please will you drop me a line as soon as you get this and tell me what I should do about telling them at home—my God! I get sick when I just think of it. That alone is what has kept me here so long—fear of facing the upheaval. That is all for now. Please look after yourself. Fondest love to you and Vincent. God bless you Peggie

Your loving

Julia

Julia thought long and hard over what to tell her mother and the rest of the family at home. The subject tormented her: Should she give them some notice, or just let them face the shock cold? In the end she decided there was no way of making her mother less aghast and angry. So she did what came naturally, and wrote the following letter, avoiding all mention of the subject.

Mrs M. Gunnigan

Lurgan

Kilkelly

Co. Mayo

Ireland

Presentation Convent,

Church Park,

Madras-6

28 x 58

The caption on the back reads: "The plane I left
Madras on, to travel to Bombay en route
to London and the rest of my life."

My dearest Mammy,

Thank you very much for your letter yesterday. I am glad to hear you are all well at home and that young Pat is getting on so nicely. God bless him. [Pat was her brother John's firstborn child.]

We have just finished our two days of Government inspection here and before that, on Saturday, we had a Commission here all morning going into the type of training given; so with all that and lots of other work besides, I am quite addled just now. We have had a lot of rain, but the weather is still very stuffy and humid—that means, of course, that there is more rain coming.

There must be great speculation all over the world as to who will be the next Holy Father. [Pope Pius XII had died on October 9. He was succeeded by Pope John XXIII, who convened Vatican II.] It will not be easy to find anyone with the qualifications to fill the shoes of our greatly loved Pope Pius XII. As you said, he really seemed closer to us than any other

Pope has been, and especially so for you at home who can get broadcasts from Vatican Radio without any great difficulty.

I was very sorry indeed to read in your letter that Dillie's baby is giving her a lot of trouble. Is he a strong child? Could it be that there is something wrong and that he is in pain? What does Mary Teresa think? [Mary Teresa was, and still is, John's wife.] Is Dillie happy otherwise? I hope she is; for goodness knows she deserves to be.

That is all for now. I am rushing to get this out on this evening's post, and if I don't hurry I'll be late. Fondest love to all at home. Please pray for me.

Your loving

Julia

That was the last letter Julia sent from the convent. By the time Molly Gunnigan received it, her daughter was no longer in India and no longer a nun. The silence Julia kept about her real plans is a truly magnificent act of passive aggression. The next day she signed the form releasing her from her vows, gave back her wedding ring, and Sister Eucharia became Julia Immaculata Gunnigan again. She left the convent without saying goodbye to anybody—as she had been ordered to do, her last act of obedience to the order—and took a flight to Bombay and then a connection to London. She had been in the Presentation Sisters for fourteen years and was weeks away from her thirty-eighth birthday. She was dressed as the nun she no longer was, traveling with a passport made out in a name that was no longer hers. She was carrying a suitcase containing the underwear, blanket, and towels about which she had corresponded with Peggie. She had no other possessions, apart from ten pounds she'd been given for traveling expenses.

COLONIAL BOY

❀

· I ·

M Y FATHER, BILL LANCHESTER, was born in Cape Town on July 31, 1926.

The experience of being loved by someone tells you a great deal about that person, almost as much as loving them does, but differently. Love has many different textures. W. H. Auden said—it was one of his most beautiful ideas—that when you love people you are seeing them as they really are. This was in contradiction to Sigmund Freud, who argued that love is always an overvaluation—that when we love people we project our own feelings and needs onto them and see them for something larger, more wonderful, more amazing, more worthy of love, than they truly are. Auden said that was wrong: on the contrary, when we love, we are seeing people as they really are, and it is this reality with which we fall in love. So to really know people, you must love them.

True, I think—I hope. Conversely, you learn a lot about people by knowing what it is like to have them love you. I know something profound about my parents by knowing the way in which the texture of their love varied. My mother's love was fierce, with a desperate edge; it was not that far removed from anger, from need. Her love had in it a fear of the world, and rage at the world, too. There was no question that she would die for me, or kill for me; and the idea that she might have to do something that extreme had crossed her mind. There was a ruthlessness to her love, a ferocity.

My father's love was not like that. His love was calming and encompassing. It wasn't that it was impersonal—it was deeply personal—but it did make me feel that it was somehow bigger than both of us. I did not feel that he loved me in defiance of the world, or in the teeth of it; instead he made me feel that the world was a place where I could move around and still be guarded and looked over by love. When I was frightened as a child (which was often), no one and nothing calmed me as quickly and thoroughly as the presence of my father. It was a function not of what he did or said but of his own sense of calmness, based on a deep conviction that everything was going to be okay. I now know that this coexisted with all sorts of anxieties and disappointments and that things were far from easy for my father, who was, in some senses, hiding from the world; but I didn't know or guess that as a boy, and I'm glad I didn't. He must have been deeply loved and made to feel safe as a child, and he knew how to pass that feeling on.

I can't be sure, but I don't think he learned that from his father. I never knew my grandfather Jack Lanchester, who died before I was born, but I know that my father did not feel him to be an easy or an especially warm man. Jack—christened John but always known as Jack—was born at home in Bridge Row, in the town of St. Helens, in Auckland, Yorkshire, on September 15, 1888. He was the third of five children born to Thomas Lanchester and Elizabeth Beaston (who was known as Anne). If for no other reason, Jack would be an important figure in my life because I derive my claim to British citizenship through him. His birth certificate—which I must produce to prove I am British, because I and both my parents were born abroad—identifies Thomas Lanchester, Jack's father, as a "Colliery Labourer." On the basis of this, I have in some moods, and usually during arguments about politics, been known to claim that I am descended from generations of coal miners. But that's not quite true. My great-grandfather Thomas was indeed working as a coal miner when his third child was born, but he had not always been one. The family business was a pub, which Thomas inherited after his own father's relatively early death. Thomas already had a weakness for alcohol, and owning the pub made it worse. Before long he was drinking his own business. (Which is surprisingly rare in his trade: publicans tend to be very careful about how much they drink—they have to be.) He became destitute, and had to work in the coal mines to support his family. Even though he was forced to sell the lease on the pub, in a classic example of an addict's self-ruinous cunning, he never sold the freehold; as long as he still owned the deed, he could always use it to get booze on credit. This does not sound like a regime calculated to ensure a long and healthy life, and it wasn't: Thomas Lanchester died at the age of thirty-seven. Because he died broke he ended up in a pauper's grave, and he is the only one of my immediate ancestors not buried at Manfield in North Yorkshire. His son Jack stayed angry with him for the whole of his life.

Children of alcoholics are often preoccupied with questions of control. They grow up with a deep sense of life's potential for chaos and instability, and seek to establish a countervailing space of order and rationality over which they have full command. That was Jack Lanchester. The way he sought to establish control was by earning money, the money to buy the freedom to live as he wanted to live—which meant not being at risk from anyone else's whims or accidents or decisions. This was the main thing my father used to say about his father: that he had a deep conviction that money is freedom. This belief was the driving force in Jack's life; it was coupled with a burning, and understandable, wish to get as far away as possible from what Auden—another Yorkshire-born expatriate—called "the enormous bat-shadow of Home." These two drives—for control in the form of money, and to get as far away from England as possible—would have a huge effect on my father's life. In that sense his grandfather's actions had a dominating impact on large areas of his life. Some of the most important things that happen to people may happen before they are born.

My father wrote a short summary of Jack's life when he was retiring in 1979 and had to take legal advice to work out his own nationality, tax, and residency status. That and two short obituary clippings are how I know some dates and the overall shape of my grandfather's life. (The clippings are from the *South China Morning Post*, the paper of record in Hong Kong, and from *The Gatooma Mail*, the paper of record in the small Rhodesian town where Jack lived for several years. Am I the only one who feels a kind of romance for these English-language papers from all over the world? *The Times of India*, the *South China Morning Post*, *The Sydney Morning Herald*, the *Singapore Times*, *The Gatooma Mail*. The titles make me see a man in a green eyeshade, frowning over a proof sheet as a fan moves the hot tropical air, with no cooling effect, while the classified-ad manager, just back from lunch and not sober, bangs through the waist-high gate that separates business from editorial.)

In 1910, after the death of his father, Jack, who had a degree in English from Newcastle University, went to South Africa to work as a teacher at the Observatory School in Cape Town. He was twenty-two. His intention was to immigrate permanently; he was sick of England. He joined the South African Defence Force as a reservist in 1912, with the idea of minimizing his obligation and maximizing his freedom of movement in the event of war. A piece of family advice that was passed down to me from him goes as follows: If you're going to be conscripted, it's a good idea to join up as a part-timer first so you learn the ropes and (one hopes) have a bit of a say in where you are sent and what you are made to do. To me, the interesting thing about that advice is not so much what it says as the implied assumption that wars are things that come along every now and then in a man's life, and it's wise to have a plan for when they do. Not many people my age in the West have that view, which would once have been not just common but sensible.

Despite or because of his scheme, Jack never saw any action in World War I, which barely touched South Africa, though there was fighting against the Germans in South-West Africa. The war years passed peacefully for him, with the steady accumulation of money, which had been his entire purpose in going to South Africa. His plan as a teacher was not to be a teacher at all. While he worked at the school, he saved as much money as he could, with the idea of putting himself through college to become a dentist. He attended night classes to learn the rudiments of dentistry and get a jump on the university course he was going to take when he had saved enough money.

After eight years of this, Jack's employers at the Observatory School got wind of what he was doing, and having determined that his mind was on other than his work and his pupils, they gave him an ultimatum: Be a teacher or a dentist. They were sure he would have to choose the former. But by then, thanks to his energetic saving, Jack had raised just enough money to say, Okay, fine, in that case I'll be a dentist. He quit his job and won a place at Guy's Hospital in London. This moment of pure "Fuck you" was one of the great occasions of his life.

Jack spent three years at his studies in London, and after qualifying as a dentist he returned to South Africa. He set out traveling to look for a place where he could establish a practice, and found one in what was then Southern Rhodesia, in the small midlands town of Gatooma, about a hundred miles from the capital, Salisbury. This was 1921. Gatooma was small and sleepy and, because of its tobacco plantations, prosperous. (It's less so now. I went to visit Zimbabwe with my father in 1980, just after the end of the civil war. As chance would have it, the man sitting next to us on the Air Zimbabwe flight to Harare had been to Gatooma. "I know Gatooma," he said. "It's a one-horse town." Then, with impeccable comic timing, he added: "The horse died.") A year or two later, while on a train to Cape Town, Jack met a lively young Lancastrian teacher with the magnificent period name Dora Higginbotham. She was impressed by how handsome he was; Jack's good looks were always much remarked on. Photographs show him as well dressed, handsome in a dated style—though it has to be said that these good looks don't really come across in photos, as old-time good looks often don't.* I'm not sure that Jack put

---

*Maud Gonne, "the most beautiful woman in Europe," seems very plain in almost every photograph. You hardly ever see an old photo in which someone who's famous for being beautiful actually looks beautiful. I sometimes wonder if this phenomenon has to do with historical shifts in the idea of beauty, or with people's relative ease in front of the camera, or with exposure times requiring people to hold poses for uncomfortable periods. To complicate things, and in very broad terms, men in old films, say from the 1930s, who are supposed to be good-looking still seem good-looking (Clark Gable, Errol Flynn), whereas the women look, at best, on the pretty side of odd. Why?

Jack

Lannie

the famous good looks to much use, as he didn't have much charm or an easy manner or much interest in the company of women. He was a man's man and seems to have been one of those men on whom handsomeness is rather wasted. To give him credit, though, he immediately took to Dora, who was lively and pretty and fun. They had acquaintances in common, and although they parted at the end of the train trip, they were both sure they would meet again.

Dora was my grandmother, Gran to me, but otherwise generally known as Lannie. As to what she was doing in South Africa in the first place, the short answer is I don't know, which is odd in a way, because Lannie is the only one of my four grandparents whom I knew personally—and also odd because she is the one who kept the family papers relating to this time. Indeed, the trunk full of papers was hers. It's a camphor-wood chest, bought, I would bet, in one of the furniture shops in Wanchai sometime in the 1930s. It is lined with the *Evening Standard* for the day of King George VI's death in 1953. That is a very Lannie touch. It was practical-minded to line the trunk with something, so she might as well do it with a bit of newspaper that would seem interesting years later. Practical but not just practical, and alert to a point of potential interest and entertainment: that was Lannie. But there is next to nothing about Lannie herself in the trunk, and nothing at all about her life before she met Jack, and she never spoke to me about it, so I don't know how she came to be in South Africa.

In any case, Jack and Lannie fell in love. He proposed and she accepted, and they were married at St. Thomas Church in Rondebosch, Cape Town, on October 15, 1924. The trunk contains a clipping from the *Cape Times*: "The bride looked charming in a sleeveless gown of white [marocain], draped with silk lace, and carried a sheaf of pink carnations." There is a photograph of my grandmother in that outfit, with a held-for-the-camera smile that had much less wattage than her real one. On the back of the photo she's written: "Wore my wedding frock *back to front!!!* And didn't know it!" They honeymooned in the Cape Province, and her "travelling frock was of a yellow crepe de chine, with cloak of beige colour marocain and hat to match."

Lannie gave up her teaching job, and went to live in Gatooma with Jack. In about a year's time, she was pregnant. As she came close to term, she set off down to the Cape to have her baby. She almost left things too late, since July was the depth of winter in southern Africa, and the road from Gatooma to Salisbury was subject to flooding; it became impassable only a few hours after she got through. But she made it, and arrived in Cape Town in time to give birth to a boy in the small hours of July 31, 1926. The boy was christened George William. I always called him Dad or Pop or variants thereof—Dadsky, Popsky, Popskianovich—and everyone else called him Bill. He was never, not once, called George. In his childhood, I see by looking through the trunk of papers, he was known as Billy to his parents. When he was a few weeks old, Lannie and Billy traveled up to Gatooma, which is where they lived for about the next six years.

My father's childhood was of a kind that has now, I think, more or less vanished from the world. He lived in the colonial bubble. In one sense the Lanchesters' life in Gatooma was typical for a well-peopled, thickly neighbored small town; the family had a cook and a houseboy, as a black male adult servant was known, and also an African wet nurse who first suckled Bill and then became his nanny. She and her children were his closest companions, and when he spent time with anyone he spent it mainly with them. Dad's childhood, while it had its peopled side, was also profoundly lonely—a colonial loneliness, marked by comfort, relative affluence, and safe, well-supported isolation. His African friends were inevitably at a psychic distance, maintained by both sides; if he had any European friends of the same age during these years, he never mentioned them to me. Nonetheless, he loved Africa. When I spent a month in Zimbabwe with him in 1980, he seemed much more at home there than he ever did during his relatively brief time in England.

By 1932 or so, Jack had become fed up with Gatooma and had raised enough money for part two of his plan for financial independence. He was accepted for a doctoral degree program in dentistry at Northwestern University in Chicago, whose dentistry school was considered one of the best in the world. Jack was then about the age I am now, and had a son of six where I have boys of eight and three. I have to say I don't feel much empathy with his desire to go away and leave his family for the better part of three years, just so he could obtain a qualification that would perhaps enable him to make more money. Jack seems to have been unable to see the happiness that was right in front of him, right in front of his nose. His childhood had damaged him to the extent that he couldn't feel happy, and he needed more than anything else to feel that he was in control. Control and happiness and independence were all the same thing, and they all meant the same thing: money.

Jack put himself through the degree program, using his savings from Gatooma, and working nights as an elevator operator in a hotel. It seems an odd thing for a family man in his forties to be doing, and perhaps an indication of his restless unhappiness and the extent to which the idea of independence had become reified: it wasn't enough to be a respected, comfortable, secure professional in a small Rhodesian town. That wasn't real independence, because real independence meant money. Money didn't symbolize or facilitate independence, it *was* independence, in and of itself.

While Jack was in Chicago, Billy and Lannie went to stay with relatives in her hometown in Lancashire. It was during their stay there that the big bad thing happened. Bill was diagnosed as having a "tubercular hip," a condition that occurs in children when tuberculosis bacilli travel in the blood supply and affect the joints. Today it is treated by chemotherapy; in the twenties and thirties, it was treated by the use of plaster casts and braces, to prevent joints from fusing, and by rest. It was often fatal, and always extremely painful. Children spent up to three years immobilized on their backs in bed. Bill and Lannie returned to Gatooma, on the advice of doctors who said that the climate there would be much better for his condition. In Gatooma he spent six months in bed and another six months with his leg in a brace. At age eight, he was not too young to be frightened. He deeply felt first the pain and later the boredom and enforced solitariness of the condition. In later life Bill was to think that this period permanently marked him, and gave him a shunt toward dreaminess, fantasy, a feeling of unworthiness, and isolation.

I know this story from things my grandmother and my mother told me, and from papers in the camphor-wood chest. My father never mentioned any of it, except to say he had worn a leg brace for some time. Indeed, he never said that he had had TB, and I didn't know it until I began looking through his papers and found the short autobiography I mentioned earlier (the one he wrote for the purpose of—of all bathetic reasons—clarifying his tax status). To have had one parent who had TB and never bothered to tell me about it might be called an accident, but to have had two qualifies as—well, I'm not sure I can complete that aphorism in a suitably Wildean way. Let's just say my mother and father tended not to blurt things out. When at age thirteen or so I had a TB test at school and it turned out negative, my parents took an unexplained but keen interest in the fact. No wonder.

Both Bill and Lannie felt that this period of sickness exacerbated his bookish, dreamy insistence on living inside his own head—something he did as much as anyone I've known. That's one of the things I have to stress in describing my father. This gentle, soft-spoken, intelligent man, short-ish and roundish and well dressed and friendly, a listener and a calm-seeming grown-up of quiet humor, good-natured and straightforward in manner and externally so conformist, was one of the dreamiest, most inward people I have known, one whom reality affected only when it intruded on his inner world by force. He was capable of extraordinary feats of not noticing—and whereas this is so often a passive-aggressive act, a wish to deny the existence of someone or something, with him it was a testament to how far within his own world he was living. His gentleness and kindness and good manners were related to that, as if he had worked out the rules of human interaction only by close study, and had learned the importance of certain sorts of conduct without gaining any real sense of how normal give-and-take, the ordinary rough texture of daily interactions, actually works. It wasn't life as an only child in an especially solitary version of the colonial bubble that made him like that—God knows enough people emerged from a similar background as more or less the diametric opposite. But in his case, it helped. It's possible to have a childhood as isolated as that today, but it's only just possible, and perhaps only if your parents are a bit dotty, or home-schoolers or religious freaks, or people doing good in the third world. My father took up residence in his own head in a way that would have been excellent preparation for a career as a writer or an academic, but that didn't, as it turned out, serve him all that well in the life he lived. I caught a glimpse of what he must have been like in childhood when his mother, my grandmother, took me out to the shops or gave me pocket money: she used to beg me to spend it on sweets. Her great and entirely well-founded fear was that I would want to spend it on books instead—which is what, if she wasn't looking, I would do. My bookishness made her nervous because it reminded her of her otherworldly, defenseless son.

It was to this time in his life that my father dated his addiction to reading. There used somewhere to be a photo of him with his leg in a brace, sitting in the shade of an African patio, reading *Jock of the Bushveld*. The photo captured a whole set of feelings about Dad's childhood—the isolation, pain, privilege, the colonial comfort and weirdness and solitude, the sheer amount of his life he spent inside his own head. (You may think that most people live inside their own heads, but plenty of them don't. In fact, if you do think that, you're almost certainly one of the minority whose primary life is internal.) *Jock of the Bushveld*, a once popular but profoundly grim children's book about an überfaithful South African dog, was notable to me because it was the only book my grandmother gave me. I accepted it with great solemnity, then went off to check the last chapter and the ending. At the age of ten, I had a rule about not reading any story about an animal in which the animal dies at the end. *Jock of the Bushveld* looked from the cover to be that kind of book—as indeed it was. I didn't read it then, and never have.

Once Jack had his shiny new Ph.D., he joined Lannie and Bill in Gatooma. Back in Rhodesia he quickly "realized"—although this might have been part of his plan all along—that his adopted hometown was too small and too remote for the rich clientele base he now needed. In Chicago he had learned, as he put it, "millionaire's dentistry." But now he lived in a place that didn't have any millionaires. So, with the taste for travel and migration he had acquired, he went in search of a place that did have millionaires, and booked a cruise around Southeast Asia. Even at the distance of all these years, presented with only the bare facts, you can feel his itchy restlessness, the unrelenting way he was driven by a hunger for something he called "freedom." The idea was that the family would spend some time together—Jack had now been away for nearly three years—and tour the sights of Ceylon, Malaya, Singapore, Hong Kong, perhaps even Australia. At the same time, Jack's plan was to find a place with a convenient gap in the market for an ambitious high-class dentist. He found it when the ship docked in Hong Kong. A few days spent wandering around and asking questions established that the colony was temporarily without a European dentist at his level. Jack inquired, made a decision, and informed his family that they would now be living in Hong Kong.

Jack Lanchester's practice thrived in Hong Kong. In those days the colony was a deeply stuffy, socially rigid, hierarchical place; even by standards of the British Empire at the time, it was a backwater. W. H. Auden, who passed through on a war-tourist visit to China with Christopher Isherwood in 1938, wrote a poem about it; Hong Kong, he said, was "a worthy temple to the Comic Muse." Not one of his best, but it shows how inherently trivial, and how profoundly provincial, the colony seemed to a super-intelligent cosmopolitan visitor in the 1930s. When I was younger I used to resent that poem, thinking it showed a lapse in judgment by Auden to see the colony as inherently comic. Did that mean its several hundred thousand Chinese residents were comic, too? Or simply invisible? Now I think Auden's blindness to the Chinese is just a description of how that world seemed to the overwhelming majority of its European inhabitants; and as for being comic, well, he didn't have a crystal ball. I once overheard a young woman at a party in Britain in the early 1990s who had just come back from a year in Hong Kong. "What's the proportion of Chinese and Europeans?" she was asked. "About fifty-fifty," she cheerily said. Real figure: ninety-eight percent Chinese.

The chasm between the British and the Chinese in the 1930s was wide; racism was pervasive and explicit. The events that were to transform the colony into a world city—the Chinese civil war, World War II, the Communist victory in China, the economic expansion of the territories as a trading entrepôt, the 1997 handover—were all a long way off. The British by and large were there to make money, with a view to going home, or moving on, after a few years. Jack's plan fit this template to perfection: his goal was to go back to South Africa after he made his pile. He had no intention of returning to England, as far as I can tell, ever again. The only time he left the territory in the 1930s was to go on a holiday to South Africa. He rapidly built up a good-size practice, and began to earn proper money. Jack and Lannie rented a cottage on Lantao, the big island, then largely uninhabited and relatively wild, a few miles from Hong Kong; they went there for weekends and, when Jack could be persuaded to take them, holidays. Hong Kong, famous for being urban, in those days also had some genuine countryside on the outlying islands and in the New Territories, and all of the family loved the mountains and the beaches and the walking. Decades later, when Lannie bought a cottage in East Looe in Cornwall, she was to name it Lantao, after the place where she had been happiest.

The move to Hong Kong was a good idea, and a lucky break, of the kind in which you make your own luck. But like many a piece of good luck, it turned out to be a piece of bad luck. As the thirties went on, it became clear that war was imminent in the Far East, just as it was in Europe. This was not the civil war in China, which was obviously going to be won by the Nationalists just as soon as the Communists gave up their reluctance to admit that they were beaten—it was the war that would be caused by the expansionist, imperialist ambitions of Japan. You would have had to be unusually optimistic to think that this wouldn't engulf Hong Kong, and my grandfather was no fool. By the summer of 1940, it was clear what was likely to happen and—in parallel with the evacuation taking place in Great Britain, up to and during the Battle of Britain—women and children were evacuated from the colony in July 1940.

Bill and Lannie were slated to leave Hong Kong. My grandfather was marked to stay. It was virtually impossible for men to leave, and Jack had now taken on a job as official government dentist. I have no evidentiary basis for suggesting this, but part of me thinks that he might have assumed that the likeliest thing to happen was for Hong Kong to fall to the Japanese, and for him to end up in civilian internment; and the problem with that, from the financial point of view—which was how he always took his foremost opinion of things—was that he would not be able to earn any money while he was interned. The combination of internment and private practice would ruin him. If he was in government employment, however, he would collect back pay for his years in the clink after he was released, and while he would be nowhere near rich, he would be a long way ahead, in cash terms, of where he would have otherwise been. (Not to mention the important reduction in expenditures while interned . . . No, I'm pretty sure not even Jack would have considered that a bonus.) It may just be that with a war coming, he thought that steady government employment was a better bet than private practice. This is speculation. I do know that the imminence of war caused him to turn down what would have been the biggest and most astute purchase of his life. Jack rented offices in a building in Nathan Road, then and still now the main commercial artery in Kowloon, just across the harbor from Hong Kong Island. (Kowloon then as now was as lively as Hong Kong Island, but less posh. The wife of the governor gave lasting amusement and offense in the thirties with a speech that referred to "the ladies of Hong Kong and the women of Kowloon." Lannie would quote this about once a month for the rest of her life.)

At some point during 1940, the landlord of Jack's dental office approached him and offered to sell him the freehold of the entire building.* The landlord was worried about the war, and so was Jack; the amount in question would have been a serious stretch; and there was also the question of what would happen to Hong Kong after the coming war— whether it would remain a colony, or a British colony. President Roosevelt was known to be no fan of the British Empire or the colonial presence in Hong Kong, and the smart money would have been on a handover to China sooner rather than later—in which case, given that China was in a civil war and at war with Japan, what odds would you get on its acknowledging colonial-era property deals? Jack thought it over and

---

*Actually, technically, what he offered to sell him was the several-hundred-year-long lease. There was no freehold property in Hong Kong, since the entire territory in those days belonged to the British crown. I don't know who owns it now—the Chinese government, I suppose. This might sound like an esoteric point, but when negotiations over the future of the territory were opened between the British and the Chinese in the 1980s, the issue that brought both parties to the table concerned lapsing commercial leases in the New Territories.

Bill on horseback, during a holiday trip to French Indochina.

turned the deal down. Oy veh. Nathan Road is now some of the most expensive real estate on the planet. If he had done that deal, I would, instead of writing these words in longhand on an index card in South London, be sitting on my own tropical island, contemplating a trust fund the size of Andorra's gross domestic product. Too bad. Actually, though I can joke about it (as a fat tear plops down to the page and smudges my handwriting), I think Jack in later years saw this chance as the one that got away—the big break he had been offered, the ticket to ease and riches and to definitive independence, which he had let go.

So Jack the government dentist had to stay. Bill, for his part, was better off if he left. He liked school well enough—he was at the newly built

Central British School in Kowloon and reliably came at or near the head of his class in everything. That's about the only thing you can tell from his school reports, which are different from their modern equivalents. They are much terser, and about all they ever say is "very good" or "excellent," except in drawing, where Bill went from "weak" (40 percent) to "poor" (35 percent) to "poor but improved" (53 percent) to "tries but is not very good" (50 percent). Hard to imagine a much worse review than that. Five years of school reports don't reveal a single thing about what my father was like—they give absolutely no idea of his character or interests. One thing that is clear from the reports, though, is that Bill's health had greatly improved. He had hardly any days off school, according to his reports—nine days off in his first three years, and none at all in his last two. Pretty good going, and it fits with something he told me in later life, that he'd never missed a single day of work through illness, until he had a heart attack in his late forties. That's not unusual for men, who do sometimes sail through life without any illness until they suddenly drop dead. But his parents were worried, and with reason, because if the Japanese were to come, internment was the likeliest outcome, and internment would destroy the health of people more robust than Bill. Also, the general climate in Hong Kong, hot and humid and downright bad for most of the year, suited him less than the dry heat of Africa. Lannie had come down with malaria in 1936, and was suffering attacks, which were to recur every couple of years for the rest of her life. That brought home the fact that Hong Kong wasn't the healthiest place in the world. Evacuating Bill was the right thing to do.

Jack thus didn't really have a choice about staying, and for Bill to leave was self-evidently the right decision. That left open the question about what Lannie should do. She had the choice of

Lannie in summer 1940.

staying with her husband or leaving with her son; to put it slightly differently, she had the choice of which of them to abandon. To me, today, it seems obvious that she should have left with Bill; but it was less clear at the time. Lannie had a nursing qualification; and it was plain to everyone that in the event of fighting, nurses would be needed. So although the order was for a general evacuation of all women, she had specific, essential skills and it could be seen as her patriotic duty to stay. If Bill left, he would be going to boarding school, so he would be surrounded by company at all times—indeed, there were times in the normal course of things when it wasn't unknown for a child to be sent away to boarding school and not to see his parents for a year or more—whereas Jack would be isolated and on his own in hostile territory. Bill was going to safety, and Jack was going into danger, so it was her duty to stay with Jack. It was a terrible choice, a decision between abandonments.

"Duty" is one of those words that has more or less vanished from our culture. It—the word, and perhaps the thing as well—exists only in specific ghettos like the armed services. We often prefer to use "care" or "carer" for people who would once have thought that what they were doing, in, say, looking after incapacitated relatives, was a duty. I find that the notion of duty makes some burdens easier to bear. To call the act of changing someone's soiled underclothing a work of caring can make you feel as if you should be doing it because you want to do it, whereas the idea that you're doing it because it's your duty makes it more impersonal and therefore—to my mind, anyway—a lighter burden. It leaves you free to dislike what you are doing while still feeling that you are doing the right thing in doing it.

There was, however, another reason why Lannie wanted to stay. To understand it you first have to know something about what she was like. She was a much lighter spirit than Jack, which isn't to say that she was less tough, because she was one of the toughest, most indomitable people I have known. But she was lively, and liked company, and liked a laugh and a party; she was sociable and made friends easily, and kept them, too; she was thin and short and quick, birdlike, in her movements, even when I knew her at the end of her life. She had, to use the period term, plenty of "attack"; she could be flirty; she was the kind of teacher whose pupils want to stay in touch with her. She had a group of "girls" who would visit her en bloc when, later in life, she went to Hong Kong, and whom she would visit in turn, in a round of teas and lunches and, once or twice, elaborate spectacular multicourse dinners that were my first experience of full-on, high-level Cantonese cooking. (They were a bit of an ordeal, actually—I was too young to get the point.) The idea of their being "girls" was to me as a child too bizarre to be entertaining, since they were Chinese women in their fifties and older, all formidable, and all married to rich and powerful men. Lannie used to say that she knew teachers who behaved to their pupils in strict accordance with how important they thought the pupils—read: their parents—were. She said it made her laugh because these teachers usually ignored or dismissed the very same poor, ambitious Chinese girls who tended to marry the kind of men who went on to be powerful, important, and—crucial in a Hong Kong context—rich. At the dinners the men tended to be very well dressed and smiling but also rather quiet and mousy—domestically, at least, the women ran things. They were visibly and movingly fond of Lannie.

In some ways the Lanchesters' marriage was a mismatch. Jack was increasingly obsessed with money, brooding over his income and, as time went on, more and more on his investments. Lannie wanted to have a life. Her great hobby—it's even mentioned in Jack's obituaries—was amateur dramatics. The am-dram was in part her escape from Jack into company, variety, laughter, and the chance to pretend to be somebody else. This might seem a recipe for marital difficulties; perhaps that's sanctimonious. But Lannie met someone she liked in her am-dram group, and began to have an affair. The man's name was Leslie Holmes; he was a young barrister and a part-time lieutenant in the volunteer Royal Hong Kong Regiment, who was certain to be involved in the fighting when the Japanese came. She was happy, she was guilt-stricken; she was ecstatic, she was delirious with misery. It was the usual story.

How Jack found out about the affair I don't know; I think Lannie probably told him. Twelve-year-old Billy found out because one weekend on Lantao, when his parents thought he was asleep, they started arguing about whether or not to get a divorce. He overheard the conversation, and began to cry. They heard him, went into his room, and told him that they wouldn't get divorced, it was just a silly grown-up argument. I know all this because Lannie told my mother, and my mother told me. The affair is, I think, the other reason why Lannie stayed in Hong Kong. The psychology of the situation was complicated: the fact that she had already betrayed her husband may have made it harder for her to leave him. She also didn't want to leave Holmes, with whom she was still in love. It was a question of leaving behind not one man she loved, to war and imprisonment, but two; and it was that fact that tipped the scale and made Lannie decide to stay. This also made the guilt about her decision to abandon her son all the more intense.

The decision to evacuate had to be made very quickly. People were given a week's notice, and were not told where the evacuees were to be sent. The Lanchesters' decision was made: Jack and Lannie would stay, Billy would go.

In 1950, Lannie wrote an account of their parting in a gray-blue school exercise book with the title "Lest I Forget."

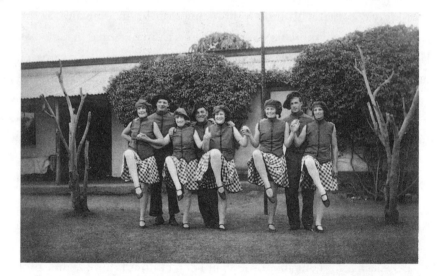

Am-dram at its finest: Lannie (third from left) in the "Gay Gatoomas."

Friday July 5th. Sad day packing off one's son (14 years old on the 31st of the month) in charge of a friend. Son complete with Penguin editions of Shakespeare's Comedies—waistbelt with compartments stocked with American dollars—lots of advice & injunctions all completely ignored and forgotten as soon as said—trunk & suitcase well stocked with clothes & books & even some bedding. Farewell from the wharf side—disappearance of son below to his camp bed (one of several hundreds it seemed in former lounge of Empress of Canada) to get down to one of the Comedies. To be told destination Manila (Philippines) & then to Australia.

Previous to departure one had to be 'collected' at the Peninsula Hotel & one sat there waiting until one's name was called. Looking back after nearly 10 years one wonders how one could have endured it & what feelings one's only child had at the moments of departure!

Home we the parents went in the pouring rain & the flat seemed curiously empty.

It was more than five years before they saw each other again. The pain in that short passage is so great I find it difficult to read. For Lannie it was so great that she couldn't bear to write her son's name.

· 2 ·

THE ATMOSPHERE on the *Empress of Canada* was anxious but excitable. Bill felt the excitement and fear of being alone and responsible for himself. The Lanchesters had a family friend, a Mrs. Braithwaite, who kept an eye on him as far as Manila, a journey of about a week. He sent what Lannie called "cheerful and amusing" letters home from Manila. He also reported that, after a great deal of careful thought, he had bought an airgun. Lannie found that funny, but it is painful, too, since it shows with some pathos how his mind was running on the idea that he might have to defend himself. The evacuees were sent to a hotel near Baguio City, a mountain holiday resort. There, final arrangements were made for some of them to go to Canada, others to Australia. When Bill was asked where he wanted to go, he said Melbourne, because friends of the Lanchesters were on holiday there and he would at least know one family on the new continent. An acquaintance of the Lanchesters, a Mrs. Barker, was also going to Melbourne, and she took over the job of keeping an eye out for him. They left Manila at the end of August 1940, among the last group of evacuees. Mrs. Barker's help was to be invaluable, in giving Bill somewhere to stay while he found, essentially by himself, a place at boarding school. For that he was carrying his Hong Kong school reports with him. The last of them, signed by his form teacher, Mr. Orr, has a large scrawl across the page: "Exams cancelled due to evacuation."

Jack transferred money to an account in Melbourne once it was certain that Bill was going to end up there. Part of it was to pay school fees; it came in handy when Bill won a place at Melbourne Grammar. This was, and is, one of the best schools in Australia, though one with an establishment and Anglo bias. Bill struggled hard to fit in—too hard, he later felt.

With the background of fantasy which I had in my mind—stories told to myself to amuse myself during immobilisation in plaster—at the back of my mind was a comparison (unflattering!) between myself as the (heroic) leader of my talented gang & myself as the usually-left-till-last follower in the real life of the concrete school playground. And the contrast can have only strengthened the feeling of hurt—hurt that the fantastic qualities which were really mine should go unappreciated.

This feeling caused by disparity was particularly strong when I first joined Melbourne Grammar—oh what a feeling of 'where do I fit in?' Curious that I should have accepted, almost as an axiom, the feeling that I must fit in *it*, & that the thought seems never to have occurred to me that perhaps the 'it' was not suitable to me—no ability to 'stand off', to 'be critical'.

Those remarks come from a notebook of 1959. Bill was being overly severe on himself—as he never stopped being. The sporty, hearty, unreflective ethos of the school no doubt didn't suit the introspective, dreamy, physically unrobust child he was; but a fourteen-year-old boy separated from his parents and everyone else he knew by thousands of miles, an indefinite stretch of time, and a world war, had no choice but to try to fit in. And there is always, for clever young people, the old standby: When all else fails, find some exams to come first in. So that is what Bill did.

No small part of the story of the Lanchesters' war years is told by the different types of paper that survive. This, from Jack's office a year after Bill had left, is the only letter on a proper letterhead.

DR JOHN LANCHESTER

L.D.S.R.C.S. (Eng.) D.D.S. (Northwestern University)

Tel 57689

32A Nathan Road

Kowloon

Hong Kong

Sept. 2/41

Dear Bill,

Your letter of August 15 arrived yesterday. You tell us that you were 1st in Division and 1st in Group and 3rd in Form. Well this is very good and I am very pleased you can hold your own 'down under'. At Central British here there wasn't much competition but I imagine there'll be some good stuff where you are now. Well don't get conceited—keep plugging steadily away and I wouldn't be surprised if you do better the next examinations. Good—keep it up!

The market has staged a sudden upturn these last few days & I am watching it. May get out if things go on rising for they will surely fall again. It's just a case of guessing the top.

I suppose we can look for a lessening of the heat now and I'll be glad. We are both very fit. Dr Shannon gave me a faculty handbook on the B.D.S. (Dentistry) of Melbourne University—get one for yourself & let me know what you think. It looks a very good training to me. Dentistry is a very good profession (I know you'll laugh at *my* saying that) but I have made a lot of mistakes which afterwards gave me a lot of headaches—I wouldn't do those mistakes again. I'd try to get into the Colonial Medical service as a dental surgeon if I had to start again.

Well Cheerio & good luck.

Yours affectionately,

Dad

This is the first letter from Jack that survives in the family papers. When I read it, it was the first time I directly heard his voice, and in some ways it lives up to the negative image I had formed of him. One of the most expressive things about it is the printed letterhead: Jack felt he had gotten somewhere in life, and he was proud of that. When I first read the letter, I thought that his recommending to Bill—gentle, dreamy, congenitally unworldly Bill—that he consider becoming a dentist shows how very little he knew his son. The tone-deafness to what Bill was like, the bad advice and the inappropriately timed pressure about careers, the immediate injunction to not get conceited, the talk about his own investments, the "Yours affectionately" instead of "Love"—all of this is Jack the money-minded dentist, an easy man not to warm to. But that is not all that can be felt in this practical letter, since you can tell, clearly tell, that Jack dearly loved his son. It's in the tone, hard to pin down but tangibly present. Some of the bad advice, I now think, came less from Jack's not knowing Bill than from his having a strong sense of what his son was like, and being very worried about it. He thought Bill had his head in the clouds (which he did), that he didn't have a clue how the world worked (which he didn't), that he was prone to fantasy and buffeted by strong feelings he didn't know how to modulate or control or express (all true). He tried to cure Bill's dreaminess by giving him practical advice, advice calculated to turn him into a practical man. Does that, can that, ever work? Probably not. But I was surprised and pleased by how strongly Jack's love for Bill comes through in these letters from the 1940s, his only writings to have survived.

The letters to Bill from the days before the fall of Hong Kong are mainly from Lannie, and they are mainly full of wittering. If you took them at face value, you would think that she had no idea what was going to happen. Except that she did: war was coming, it was only a question of when, and war would almost certainly bring internment and a longer separation. So she is consumed with worry, while pretending not to be, and thus her letters have a tone of not listening to themselves, like a nervous person talking in the hope that she will be calmed by the sound of her own voice. Lannie's habit of asking questions without question marks makes it look as if she wasn't interested in the answers; and at times, I think, she wasn't. Worry is supposed to be a positive thing or, at worst, a way of expressing love. But I wonder about that. Sometimes, reading through her letters with their inexhaustible listings of things to do, their orders and injunctions, I feel that the worry and the bossiness are mainly ways of avoiding painful feelings. The real content, I think, is: "I love you and I miss you and I don't know when I'll see you again and it hurts." That's what they're really saying; perhaps that is what Bill really needed to hear. Instead he got one big To Do list. And perhaps, too, that was easier to take: it was easier to experience feelings of irritation at maternal bossiness and remote control than it was to face the great anxious void of separation and war.

If it worked, denial would be the best thing in the world. Sometimes it does, more or less. This was not one of those times. The Japanese attack on Hong Kong began on December 8, 1941. Bill would not have known any details, other than that the fighting was fierce. I think he was prepared for the fact the defense would not, could not, be successful. It wasn't. The governor, Sir Mark Young, surrendered to the Japanese on Christmas Day. That was the last piece of news from the colony for some time. Bill did not know whether his parents were alive or dead.

The war years saw Bill's life divided in two. He lived an external life, in which he got on with the business of doing well in school and making friends. In that respect, the great blessing of his time in Australia was his virtual adoption by the family of a close friend from Melbourne Grammar, Tony Street. Tony was Bill's best friend at school, and his large extended family took Bill in when he was not at school for the duration of the war. The Streets were big Victoria farmers, a well-established and respected family whose patriarch, Brigadier G. A. Street, was serving as minister for the army in the Australian wartime government. Edna Street, the brigadier's wife and Tony's mother, treated Bill with a kindness and generosity he never forgot. The Streets were the only people who knew directly how difficult he was finding these years. Bill spent his holidays with them in Melbourne and at Eildon, the farm belonging to Mrs.

Thornthwaite ("Dook"), a cousin of the family. Dook was a crucial figure in Bill's life, taking him to her heart and, along with Edna Street, acting as the maternal presence he needed so badly.

Bill loved being included in a large, busy family. He also loved farm life. The sheer spaciousness of the landscapes was a balm. He loved the work, too: mending fences, going out with the dogs, fetching and carrying and digging and, especially, herding sheep on motorbikes. One good thing about the work is that he didn't have to do it, and was allowed to study when he wanted to. Farm life was a mixture of steady satisfying routine—particularly satisfying if you knew you weren't going to spend the rest of your life doing it—and occasional spectacular crises: floods, fires. One year he did his bit with bucket and pump to defend Eildon from a wildfire, and then joined a gang who cleared a firebreak and saved thousands of acres of farmland from destruction. Given the aching hole in the middle of Bill's life—his journal later spoke of missing a sense of affection, of missing "family love"—this was as balanced and happy a time as he could imagine.

His internal life was another story. Bill's great difficulty was that he had nowhere to put the anxiety that was consuming him about his mother and father. He had convinced himself that the way to get along was to fit in, show a stiff upper lip, and not raise any fuss. Australia was at war, and people were making all sorts of sacrifices; he did not feel his own situation counted for much in the overall scheme of things. As indeed it didn't. Yet it was his situation, and it was not easy; it had to be lived, and the way he chose to do it was by ignoring the anxiety and fear he felt. He kept no continuous diary for the war years, but there are quite a few sections of journals and notes and letters, and none of them mentions his parents. The first news of them he heard was on June 27, 1942, six months after the fall of Hong Kong, when a list of civilian internees was published in Australia, and he saw his mother's name on it. That day he sat down and wrote a letter.

Melbourne Church of England Grammar School

Cr. Orrong & Balaclava Rds.,

Caulfield.

Melbourne.

27th June 1942.

Dear Mum & Dad,

A queer coincidence occurred today—I saw the lists of the H.K. internees & then later bumped into Mrs Garton, who, being in the Red Cross, told me that it is now possible, for the first time, to write to internees. I have seen your name, mother, in the lists, thank God. But I have not seen Dad's: however, the lists have no claim to be all-inclusive.

I hope that you are both well: I am in very good health. I have even been told that I am looking fat! My school-work is going very well. The school has been shifted: the junior school are at [blanked out by censor] and we are at Grimswade (one of the prep schools). The old school [blanked out by censor].

I hope that you get this letter: I expect that I shall be now be able to get letters through fairly often. Unfortunately this letter is limited to one page.

Your loving & devoted son,

Bill

All through Bill's letters and journals, he uses words like "curious" and "strange" to denote something that causes overpowering emotion; it is the flag he flies over his biggest episodes of denial. Here he uses "queer coincidence" to describe his learning that at least one of his parents is not dead. But there is a clue to the fact of how strong his feelings were, and how hard it was for him to contact them at all: this was one of only two letters Bill wrote to his parents for the duration of the war. I was always told that this was a huge thing in the family, and that my father felt guilt over it from which he never fully recovered—but it was my mother who told me that, and she did so as part of a campaign to emotionally black-

Received Ap 21/43

Had letter from Winnie Phillips abut the 18 + one from her Philly abut the 7th or so of...

Melbourne Church of England Grammar School,
~~Domain Road, South Yarra, S.E.1.~~
Cr. Orrong & Balaclava Rds.,
Caulfield
Melbourne.
27th June 1942.

Dr & Mr Lanchester

Dear Mum & Dad,

A queer coincidence occurred today— I saw the lists of the H.K. internees & then later bumped into Mrs Garton, who, being in the Red Cross, told me that it is now possible, for the first time, to write to internees. I have seen your name, mother, in the lists, thank God. But I have not seen Dad's: however, the lists have no claim to be all-inclusive.

I hope that you are both well. I am in very good health. I have even been told that I am looking fat! My school-work is going very well. The school has been shifted: the junior forms are at   , and we are at Grimwade (one of the prep schools). The old school

I hope that you get this letter. I expect that I shall be now be able to get letters through fairly often. Unfortunately this letter is limited to one page.
Your loving & devoted son, Bill.

mail me into writing home from boarding school more often than I could be bothered to do. I was told that this meant a great deal to him, and perhaps it did; he was a great one for taking things to heart, especially anything that could be construed as a failure or weakness of his own. But adolescent boys are notoriously bad letter-writers. It also seems to me that one of the main reasons Bill wrote so scantily was that he simply didn't know what to say. You can see this in the other letter he wrote to Stanley Camp, from early 1943. At this time he still did not know whether his father had survived the fall of Hong Kong.

["read May 17 44," in Lannie's handwriting]
To Mrs J. Lanchester
Room 12
Block 5
Stanley Internment Camp
Hong Kong

From B. Lanchester
Melbourne Grammar School
South Yarra S.E. 1
Melbourne
14 February 1943

Dear Mother,

I am very well, and hope that you are.

I got my Matriculation last year, getting English, Latin, Maths I and IV, and European History. I also came top of the second class Honours in Ancient History Honours—Honours is the year that comes after Matriculation, and is equal to the first year of University. I am going back to school again this year to do Honours English, Latin, Ancient History, European History and Matriculation Chemistry and Intermediate German. Next year I will go to the University (with a scholarship, I hope) and do Medicine and Surgery. I am 5 feet 11 inches tall and weigh 147 pounds—quite grown up. Have plenty of money.

With all my love,
Your devoted son,
Billy

Bill's keenness to relieve his mother's anxiety—a reflection, perhaps, of just how anxious he was himself—is apparent in the boast that he has miraculously zoomed up to five-eleven. Since he was never in his life a fraction over five-eight, this was an odd claim to make. Perhaps it is a clue to the fact that this whole letter is an untruth; its pretense at normality is a lie. And perhaps he wanted to say something comforting because he thought he might never see his mother again, and he thought that his father might already be dead. The pain beneath what is being said comes through very clearly. But good news was not far away. A week after he wrote that letter, Bill received a Red Cross telegram—it had taken seven months to get to him, which was quick by the standards of the war—that told him his father was alive.

17 JULY 1942

BOTH HAPPY AND WELL WRITE GRANNY BULLS AUNTIE FLORRIE ERIC FITT[*] DO NOT NEGLECT YOUR EYES GOOD LUCK IN EXAMINATIONS NO NEED TO WORRY

It wasn't true; they were neither happy nor well. Bill, who wasn't stupid, would have known that. But at least his parents were alive. Over the next three years he was to receive four telegrams and four letters from them. The telegrams were sent via the Red Cross, and the letters are all on flimsy official paper, with "Stanley Civilian Internment Camp" typed across the top—not at all like Jack's proud prewar letterhead. Censorship meant that these communications couldn't say much; they consist mostly of requests that Bill do various things, such as write to them, tell friends and relatives that they have written, and look after his health. All through the war years, Bill only once received uncensored news from Stanley. It came late in 1943, when Canadian civilian internees were sent home as part of a deal with the Japanese government. Two of them wrote to Bill from the boat taking them home.

---

[*]Granny, the Bulls, Auntie Florrie, and Eric Fitt were, respectively, Lannie's mother, family friends, Bill's aunt, and another family friend, all of them in England. The idea was that Bill would transmit the news that Jack and Lannie were alive.

Form 56

STANLEY CIVILIAN INTERNMENT CAMP
HONGKONG

TO :-   FROM :-

NAME: George William Lanchester   NAME: Dora Lanchester

NATIONALITY: British   NATIONALITY: British

ADDRESS: Church of England Grammar School ADDRESS: STANLEY CIVILIAN INTERNMENT CAMP,
Balaclava Road,   HONGKONG Block 5 Room 12
Melbourne, Victoria,
AUSTRALIA

STANLEY,   30th June   1943.

We are both well but would like to get letters regularly. So far
one from you, two from Home and one from Bulls and Worralls. In a
few days you will be seventeen - Happy Birthday! Hope I am with
you for the next.
Sorry I didn't send all your books and album as they're gone now.
Managed to get a few clothes and that's all.
Try writing through the Red Cross, Geneva, it might be quicker.
Apply Government Representative, Sydney if short of funds.
Durham's Daddy has entertainted us all a few times.
Don't forget to write to our people at Home and Mrs. Bull as we
can't if we write to you. Tell them what you are doing in case we
get their letters before yours. Would love to know how you are
getting on and what your position is. We have no photographs of
you so send a snapshot when you can, as we love to see how much
you've grown. Are your eyes any better, or do you need to wear
strong glasses?
The sunshine and fresh air here keep us fit - I have quite a
girlish figure.
We both send our love.

Dora Lanchester

MS 'Gripsholm'

At sea

23.10.43

Master Lanchester:

Well here's word of your Father & Mother whom I last saw at Stanley
September 23rd 1943 and they were then both well but hungry. I hope
you are appreciating your three per day, or do you get more in Australia.

Both Father and Mother are doing splendid work in Camp and you
can justly be very proud of them.

Father was particularly anxious to know how you got on in your
Matriculation—you had better do well and I am sure you will as he is
expecting to hear good news.

Write as often as you can as all the letters sent do not arrive.

All the best to you and with the hope you will soon be a united family.

Sincerely yours

C. M. Hall

It's hard not to miss the bitterness and repressed anger in that letter ("or do you get more in Australia"—the lack of question mark makes it resemble clenched teeth). Food was, as we shall see, just about the only thing the internees ever thought about, and a month after leaving Stanley, Mr. Hall is still, clearly, suffering. He may have been one of the very many internees who never fully recovered from the experience. But "you had better do well," to a seventeen-year-old boy who hadn't seen his mother and father for three years and already had enough to worry about, does seem a little minatory. The other letter was gentler and warmer.

Motorship Gripsholm
30 October 1943

To Mr George William Lanchester
Church of England Grammar School
Melbourne

Dear Mr Lanchester,

I send you some news from your beloved parents Dr and Mrs Lanchester in Stanley Internment Camp. They were quite well when we, Repatriated People to America and Canada, left the camp on the 23rd of September 1943. Father is sometimes a professional dentist, sometimes a lye-maker for the whole camp. He renders in the way great services for soap is often lacking. Mother is helping in getting ashes from here and there. She told me to let you know that she is also *Wong* no. 2. [The Wongs were a family who had worked for Jack and Dora before the war. Decoded, this meant that she was doing a great deal of clothes-washing.] They are living in a small room in a Chinese quarter. They are longing for freedom as well as for better and more abundant food as well as all the people still in the camp. Everyone hopes to be repatriated in November according to what the Japs told them. We were believing it too, but it may not be so soon.

They received a letter from you some time ago. You were speaking about your promotion. They would like very much to know what you study now, is it matriculation? They sent you $500 HK at Christmas 1940, through the purser of your school if I remember. Did you receive them? Please write them a long letter, telling them as much as possible. They are wondering about you, you don't know how much.

Maintenant, comme Madame votre mère m'a dit que vous aimez beaucoup le français, je vous dis, dans celle langue, combien j'ai apprecié vos bons parents et combien je les ai trouvé courageux dans ce malheur que atteintant le monde. Aimez-les bien et soyez toujours leur foi et leur consolation par votre bonne conduite et une application soutenue dans vos études.

Une correspondante inconnue de vous mais que Madame votre mère connais bien sous mon nom anglais,

Sister St. Stephen

Miss. de L'Immaculate Conception, en route pour Montréal, Canada, via New York*

So Bill knew that his parents were alive and hungry and keeping busy, and that they were greatly respected for their conduct under internment, but that was about it.

A few months later, starting on January 1, 1944, he began to keep a diary. By now he was working like a demon to get into Trinity College at Melbourne University—though he wasn't yet sure what he wanted to study. He had done less well than he had hoped at the time of his matriculation, when his secret plan had been to get honors in every possible subject. Now he was studying up to eight hours a day, concentrating on British history. He regularly made lists of his own faults, chief of which was "daydreaming," and he was preoccupied with what to do with himself. He thought about joining the army, though it weighed heavily on

---

*Now, as Madame your mother told me that you like French very much, I tell you in that language how I appreciated your good parents and how brave I found them in the misfortune that is afflicting the world. Love them well and be always their faith and their consolation by your good conduct and a sustained application in your studies.

A correspondent unknown to you but whom Madame your mother knows well under my English name . . .

him that this voluntary assumption of risk would not be fair to his parents. He couldn't decide whether he should follow the "academic" or the "diplomatic" path; he had girl friends, but as yet no girlfriend. Some people in his circumstances, isolated and under stress, would have developed a new or different self—harder on the outside, tougher on the inside, more opportunistic, harder to hurt. But Bill didn't change. His clever, sweet, gentle, anxious, slightly lost dreaminess was the same as always.

Feb 26 1944

Went to pictures. *The Trojan Limits* with the Crazy Gang and *In Which We Serve*, which is a great film, perhaps the greatest I have ever seen. Thinking all evening after pictures, though not as a result of them, of joining the Indian Army instead of going to University. I would infinitely prefer to do so, but it wouldn't be fair to either Dook or Mum & Dad. Hell and damnation. And there isn't anyone I can really talk it over with.

If there had been people for Bill to talk it over with, they would probably have laughed and told him not to be so silly. Mind you, Noël Coward would have been pleased. His performance in *In Which We Serve* was so implausibly butch that after the premiere, when he walked into a room full of friends, there was a moment of embarrassed silence. The master broke the tension. "Don't worry, dear," he told the assembled company. "Mother *knows*."

A failure to detect the camp aspect of *In Which We Serve* was very much in character for Bill. My father was close to being the ideal audience for almost any play, film, or novel, because he identified so closely with the principal characters that he shared their emotions more or less without qualification. I say "close to" the ideal audience, instead of actually being the ideal audience, because this strong identification meant that works of fiction would often be too painful for him to read or watch. Anything in which bad people were rewarded over good was for him too troubling, too unsettling; anything that touched on themes of loneliness or abandonment or not fitting in. He could not, for instance, bear to watch *The Go-Between*, because "it reminded me too much of how I felt when I was

in Australia." My mother blamed this tendency on a deficient education. She would say, "He *identifies*," shake her head, and add, with a sigh,
"Melbourne."

That diagnosis was wrong. Bill's way of reading had nothing to do
with his education; it resulted from his fearing the strength of his own
feelings. This was something he might have already learned, but the experiences of the war years made it into a fundamental cast of mind. When
a letter from Lannie came in March 1944, he told his diary, *"Letter from
Mum!"*—but he didn't say what news the letter brought, or how it made
him feel; he never said anything about his absent parents. He had learned
that when anything painful, anything touching on pain, happened, he
must turn back at the sign that said "Don't Go There." Indeed, there is an
almost physical sense of a block between him and painful subjects.

When in doubt, come first in an exam. Bill won a scholarship to Melbourne University to read law and switched to history when he arrived in
late 1944. Dook, who had been advising him throughout, helped pay his
living expenses. He immersed himself in study, made some nerdy friendships, looked around for girls to go out with, and discovered with relief
that sports were not going to be as important a part of university life as
he had feared. And all the time he worried about what to do next. From
the end of the first year he was eligible for war work, but was also in a position to get a deferment if he so chose. For Bill, the question of what to
do was mainly a concern over figuring out what was right. The algebra
was complicated, because the obvious right thing—joining up to do his
part in the war—was counterbalanced by the opinion many people gave
him that voluntarily risking his life was not fair to his parents. What
would happen if they served their years of imprisonment, dreaming of
freedom and being reunited, kept alive by the thought of Bill in safety in
Australia, only to come out and find that he had gone and gotten himself
killed in the fighting? Only with the benefit of hindsight do we know the
atomic bomb was coming to put a brisk end to the war in the East. At
the time, the likeliest scenario was that the Allies would have to fight all the
way up into and through the Japanese archipelago, in actions that would
take years and cost millions of lives. The risks were not hypothetical.

Bill as a private in the Australian army.

When Bill was assessed for his fitness, he was graded B2, or not suitable for a direct combat position, on the grounds that he had "flat feet." (This may have been a doctor's gentle way of alluding to disabilities left from childhood TB.) At first this news gave him "the blues," as his journal refers to them, but then he reported that he had "been feeling less depressed than usual." It may be that the B2 rating gave him a way of volunteering to do his bit while not risking his life directly. In February 1945—having gotten the top second in his history exams at the end of his first year at Melbourne University—Bill joined up. He did his basic training, and was then sent to a camp for three months to learn Japanese, in order to serve as an interpreter. In practice, in the event of Bill's being sent anywhere near the fighting, this would have meant sitting in on interrogations. That was what most of the training focused on. But then came the dropping of the atomic bombs, and the announcement by Emperor Hirohito that "the war has developed not necessarily to Japan's advantage." Papers brought news of the liberation of Hong Kong. And in the middle of October, Bill heard from the Red Cross that Jack and Lannie were at a refugee camp in New South Wales. He was told that they would be reunited in Victoria, and he was given three weeks' leave.

· 3 ·

CHAOS: THAT WAS THE WORD Lannie used when she spoke about the fall of Hong Kong. It was an immersion in the experience of total disorder, total uncertainty.

In the run-up to the war, after Bill had left for Manila and then Melbourne, Lannie retrained as a nurse. Life was dominated by the impending war. The Japanese had conquered much of China, and it was only a question of time before they would launch a war on British or American interests. Preparations were made to defend Hong Kong along a line of fortifications in the New Territories, whose official name—not all that confidence-inspiring—was the Gin Drinkers' Line. It might have worked, too, if there had been enough troops to defend it, and that would have meant arming the Chinese population. British forces numbered about 12,000, but a recent estimate reckons that the British could without difficulty have added another 75,000 Chinese troops to their own total. The government in London chose not to do so, believing that the Chinese could not be trusted. For London, the main point was to hold on to the colony at the end of the war. If 75,000 armed and battle-hardened soldiers decided that Hong Kong was from now on going to be part of China, who would be able to stop them?

When the attack came, on December 8, 1941, the Japanese bombed Kai Tak airport, taking out the colony's air defenses, and then invaded over the border. The fighting was intense but brief. Within a few days, the defense had fallen back to Kowloon and begun a general evacuation to Hong Kong Island. Lannie, who had been based in Kowloon, was treating a stream of casualties. The British turned down an invitation to surrender on December 16. (The governor had arrived in the colony only a week before the attack. How unlucky was that? He spent most of his internment in a prison camp in Manchuria. Even less lucky were the thousands of just-trained Canadians who arrived and were pitched straight into the fighting.) There began to be stories about Japanese atrocities. My grandmother saw some of the victims, including nurses who had been raped; there were stories, which proved true, about hospital patients being bayoneted in their beds. (Some inexperienced Allied soldiers had used the hospital as a firing position. The Japanese then attacked the hospital as a military target.) The Japanese invaded the island, divided the defense into two, circled it into pockets on the Peak and out near Stanley, and shelled the defenders into submission. The fortifications where this fighting took place were a feature of my childhood; playing with friends and out walking, I would regularly come across bunkers and dugouts left over from the war. We would play cowboys and Indians, Vikings and Romans, Brits versus Germans (though never Brits versus Japanese) without having it ever occur to us that real fighting and real dying had taken place there. My most frequent and favorite family walk, around Black's Link with a view out over Aberdeen, circling back around over Happy Valley and the harbor, approached the sites of some of the fiercest fighting.

Jack and Lannie were separated during the battle. Jack went to Queen Mary Hospital on the island, where the wounded were to be treated; Lannie was put in charge of refugee accommodation in temporary quarters at the Central British School in Kowloon. On Thursday, December 11, the matron at the school took Lannie aside and "told me that the Japanese would probably enter Kowloon that evening but did not want to spread the news around in case of upsetting the younger assistant nursing sisters." (Lannie kept a fragmentary record of those days, written in barely legible pencil in a tiny pocket diary for 1942—she must have bought it in late 1941, just before the fighting began.) Later that day the nurses and staff were called together and told that "the Japanese were expected to be in Kowloon that evening—we were advised not to leave the building and it was the Governor's wish that we should stay at our posts. 'All the military and police are being withdrawn to the Island and we are abandoning you.' " Lannie called the hospital and, just before the phone lines were cut, managed to get through to tell Jack the news. "He was horrified— he said nobody had mentioned such a possibility & said 'Oh do try & come over here.' I replied that I felt I could not desert my post & that I felt I must stick to the others & take whatever they had to take—since I'd thrown in my lot with them. I added also that even if I'd wanted to come I doubted if I should be able to get there—as looters were already busy in the streets. We'd previously agreed too that it would be better for one of us to be on the mainland & the other on the Island so that at least if the worst happened one of us might be saved."

The Japanese arrived the next day. Over the following days the nurses were moved from place to place while the fighting went on; the bombing and shelling of Hong Kong Island was particularly hard to watch. There was no law, no order. Looters were everywhere. Some of them tried to pillage the school. This event is recorded in Lannie's diary as follows: "looters—chased them away." I like this for the way it makes my five-foot-three-inch grandmother, who weighed a hundred pounds sopping wet, sound like a female Clint Eastwood. And then the fighting was over, and the governor surrendered. This is her diary for the last days of the fall:

Wed. Washed clothes & had drink. Xmas Eve so different from last year. Hope all our loved ones are well. Beautiful weather warm & sunny something to be thankful for. Heard QM hospital had been bombed hope Jack is safe & well.
Thurs Xmas day. Miss Lurgan decorated hall with poinsettia—going to

have service at 11. Had carols & service & Xmas pudding & chocolate. Quite a good meal & I made coffee 24 spoonfuls for about 70 people. Voted very good & so it was. Drinks in evening. HK given ultimatum until midnight.

Frid 26th HK surrendered.

28th my birthday—46.

Tues 30th Our men came past to concentration camps—pitiful sight but they showed good spirits.

On January 23, 1942, Lannie and the other women were moved to Stanley Internment Camp, where they were to spend the rest of the war. Jack was already there waiting for her. The relief at being reunited brought a terrible sting with it, since Jack had a piece of bad news for Lannie. Leslie Holmes, her lover, had been killed in the fighting for the Peak on December 21. It must have been an appallingly hard moment for Jack, breaking this news, which can only have brought him tormentingly mixed feelings. As for Lannie, her diary says simply, "Heard about Leslie." That's all she says about Leslie Holmes—the fact that she uses his first name is the only hint, if one can call it that, of her strength of feeling. All through the story of my family, the things that were felt most strongly are precisely the things that were never said.

The Japanese occupation of Hong Kong was violently miserable—so much so that it became a focus of controversy even inside the Japanese army. The colony degenerated into anarchy. In some respects, one of the best places to be was Stanley Internment Camp—though that was a deeply relative benefit. The camp, a former school with barracks buildings around it, was home to two thousand internees during the war. Soldiers, who were held in the military prison at Sham Shui Po, had an even harder time of it. The big problem was lack of food. The internees' diet consisted almost entirely of rice, often in the form of congee, or rice gruel. Many of them died; many others had their health broken and never recovered. Jack was among the latter. The death rate among civilian internees of the Japanese in Southeast Asia during the war was at least 13,000 out of 130,000. A number at least equal to that died shortly after.

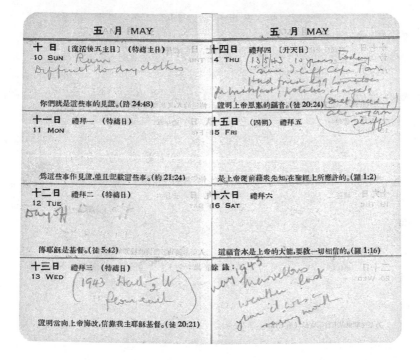

Lannie's diary of the war is mainly about food. Internees were not supposed to keep records of any kind. Although the camp was in theory self-governing—run by the British—the Japanese, especially the military police, or Kempetai, were notoriously heavy-handed captors. So Lannie had to be careful. Just how careful became apparent when prisoners associated with the British Army Aid Group were arrested by the Kempetai. The BAAG was an undercover organization dedicated to maintaining contact between internment camps and the outside world. It passed information between the camps and Hong Kong, and out into China; its mission was to smuggle news and supplies in and out of camps, and to develop and maintain escape routes into the parts of China the Japanese did not control; it had a particular brief to help Allied airmen who'd been shot down. In October 1943, the Kempetai arrested thirteen members of the BAAG, who had been betrayed by an informer. The men were tortured for information and then beheaded on Stanley beach, in sight of the internees. The fact that Lannie's diary makes no mention of these events shows how conscious she was of the risks; the leader of the men caught and killed, John Fraser, was one of her and Jack's closest friends. A Scottish lawyer, and the assistant attorney general for Hong Kong, Fraser had been a patient of Jack's before becoming a friend; his death was the worst moment of the Lanchesters' time in Stanley. His execution was something for which Lannie never forgave the Japanese. The war itself she saw as one of those things that happen between nations, not something to blame individual soldiers for. But she felt that the Japanese treated prisoners as less than fully human. That attitude reached a nadir, for Lannie, with Fraser's torture and decapitation. To the end of her life she would have no Japanese-made object in her house.

But Lannie's diary was about food not only for reasons of self-censorship. Food—or the lack of it—soon became the only thing anyone in the camp thought about. The diet was monotonous, rice and water; any extras were due to occasional gifts allowed by the Japanese, from Chinese well-wishers, or from one of only three Red Cross deliveries to reach the camp in the entire war. (One batch of parcels, sent from Britain in November 1942, arrived in March 1945.) The internees depended on luck and the decisions of others, and if the Japanese decided to let them starve, they would all rapidly die. Often the only thing with any flavor or texture would be the burnt rice stuck to the bottom of the cooking pots. Lannie tried to get hold of this whenever she could. She developed a taste for burnt rice that she never lost, and she'd always ask for it scraped off the bottom of the pan when she was staying with us.

A few things in the diary are not about food. Many of them note one-year anniversaries of her last months of freedom—especially walks and trips to Lantao. "A year ago today since Tai Mo Shan [the highest mountain in Hong Kong; Lannie must have walked up it]. What a contrast." "Climbed Shatin Gap a year ago alone. L climbed Lantao Peak one year ago." Leslie Holmes climbed Lantao Peak on the same day Lannie climbed Shatin Gap. A lover's pact? I'll climb this mountain while you climb that one, and we'll think about each other on the way up. I wonder if they looked toward each other as they stood on their respective summits.

The only mention of Bill in the diary is in a note that somebody had entered Jack and Lannie's room in the amah's (maid's) quarters and stolen Bill's watch. It was returned three months later, without explanation, by a Catholic priest, Father Murphy. The thief must have been overcome with remorse and handed it over in confession. Thieving was a very high-order crime in camp, as it is in all closed communities.

Happy memories are a problem for prisoners. They need them as a source of consolation and strength, but at the same time it's important not to let thoughts of the past become a source of gloom or despair—as Dante wrote, there can be no greater misery than to remember a time of happiness when you are in despair. In these circumstances, the combination of depression and malnutrition can quickly kill. And hope is a problem, too—perhaps even more of one. Prisoners need to think that they will one day be free; but if the hopes become too specific and too short-term, they are easily crushed. That crushing can rapidly turn to fatal depression. So prisoners learn to be very, very careful with their hopes—they ration them, nurture them, fuss over them, deny their existence, even to themselves. Hope becomes a hypersensitive plant or a private religion.

Part of what made the internment, at Stanley and elsewhere, so difficult was that no one knew how long it was going to last; in that sense, it was worse than being in prison. A prisoner serves a specific sentence, and comes up for parole at a specific date. POWs and internees didn't have that privilege: they had to wait, open-endedly, as the days stretched into months and then years. Once they had been interned for a couple of years, they knew they could be held for any length of time, certainly years more, perhaps decades more. An amphibious assault on Japan, fighting all the way up the chain of islands, would cost millions of lives and would take years. Yet at the same time, they could be repatriated at any moment; all that was needed was for the British government to cut a deal, as the Canadians had. So there was no hope, and yet there was imminent hope, hope so close you could touch it—the kind of hope that can kill.

Under these circumstances, the best advice is the simplest. At the end of *The Anatomy of Melancholy*, his multihundred-page examination of all the

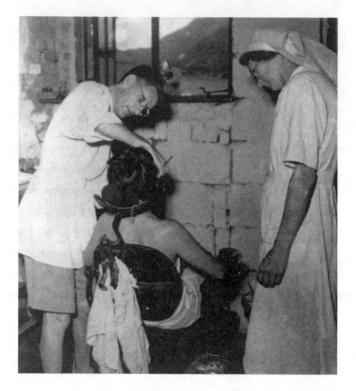

different aspects of his subject (and the least-read great book in the English language), Robert Burton gives a single clear piece of advice: "Be busy." It is good advice, and it is advice the inmates of Stanley Camp took. First there were the practical things to do, the self-organizing business of running the crowded quarters. Jack had his dentistry, though he had almost no medicine; a photograph of him, taken by the Japanese for propaganda purposes, shows him at work in crisp clean clothes in what served as his dentist's office. He did some other odd jobs—Lannie's diary mentions his running the boiler while she supervised the washing—until he found an important niche: making lye. The main source in the camp was ash; Lannie would gather ash from the cooking fires, and Jack would make it into lye, which was the closest approximation they could have to soap. Lye-making is the thing for which Jack was mainly remembered afterward by other internees from Stanley. (More so than the dentistry, whose usefulness was limited by the absence of medicines and tools.) I can't begin to say how much I admire my grandparents for the way they behaved in these hard times.

There was another thing Lannie did to keep busy. In the last days of fighting before the surrender of Hong Kong, the British hurried to collate records and documents about war crimes that had (in their view) been committed by the Japanese in the course of the fighting. John Fraser, in his capacity as assistant attorney general, had some of the paperwork with him when he went into the camp, hidden in his personal belongings. He didn't think he would be able to keep it secret indefinitely, so he asked my grandmother to hide it for him. Lannie was able to do that because the Japanese always searched the camp in the same order, so there was notice between their first arrival in the camp and the time they reached the laundry where she worked; she managed to hide the papers inside sheets that had been folded over clotheslines. In this way she secured the documents for the duration of the war.

Lannie thought about Billy all the time. His two letters were a temporary comfort, but they made her long for more, and more detailed—perhaps, more believable—news. The most useful and consoling letter she received during these years came from Dook, and arrived on July 27, 1944, about a year after it was written.

Mrs D Lanchester	from Mrs Frank Thornthwaite
British P.O.W.	Larra
Room 12 Block 5	DERRINALLUM
Stanley Internment Camp	VICTORIA
HONG KONG	AUSTRALIA
CHINA	31st July 1943

Dear Mrs Lanchester,

    I am hoping that this letter will get to you to give you news of Bill. He is very well and has just spent the day with me and, as it is his birthday, I hope it has been a happy one. He has spent most of his holidays with Mrs Street, whose son is also at the Grammar School and they have become friends. The Streets are cousins of mine.

Bill has done very well at school, passed his leaving and, at the end of this year, is doing honours. I am anxious to help him to go up to the University for a year as he is very keen to do this, but was uncertain what to take up. He thinks that he would like to do either a Law or an Arts course.

This morning we went up to interview Mr Medley, who is the Chancellor, an Englishman and a personal friend of mine. I felt that a talk to him would be a great help to Bill, as he is a most understanding person and could give him much good advice. They got on very well together and he advised Bill to go up for a year and to do either Arts or Law and try for a scholarship to one of the residential colleges. If he cannot get this I will help him with his living expenses and fees.

It will be a great pleasure to me to be able to do this as I have no family of my own and I think that your son is a grand boy and has shown such pluck and determination. Do not worry about him as I am sure he will get on. Everyone likes him. Physically he has grown a lot in this last year and looks the picture of health.

I do hope that it will not be long before you are reunited, but anyway Bill will not be required for any other work for another two years.

With best wishes,

Yours sincerely,

Mrs Frank Thornthwaite

That letter, with its concrete news and clear signs that Bill had found good friends in Australia, was a great comfort. But Lannie was thinking about children in another way, too, because her diary repeats at regular intervals the phrase "things due" with, usually a day or so later, the phrase "things occurred." It took me a while to figure this out, until I saw the regularity of the intervals at which "things occurred." That's right: Lannie was recording her periods, which means she was worried about having a baby—which in turn means she and Jack continued to have sex while in prison, there in the sweltering amah's quarters. Good for them. There's nothing like making your own entertainment. "Hope this does not portend an addition," she says, on one of her two missed periods throughout the two years of the diary. A baby would have been a disaster, and the "thank God" when her next period does come is the only expression of relief or happiness at any point during the five years of war.

So the days passed. When the Canadian citizens were released for repatriation, on September 23, 1943, there were rumors the same might happen to the British: that they would be exchanged for Japanese citizens held in Australia. These rumors gave rise to the most dangerous varieties of hope. But they didn't come true—for a reason that camp inmates sometimes speculated about darkly: because the British government wanted a British POW presence in Hong Kong at the end of the war, to facilitate reclaiming the colony for the British Empire. This was something my grandmother spoke about as a black rumor, and like not a few black rumors, it is now a matter of historical record, thanks in part to Philip Snow's book *The Fall of Hong Kong*. The Japanese would have been willing to negotiate a deal repatriating the internees, who after all were of no use to them. It was the British who wanted them there. The fact that the suffering of the prisoners and internees was all so that the flag would be promptly raised again over the colony at the end of the war—well, in a way, I'm glad my grandparents never lived to find that out.

When the war ended, the British reclaimed the colony with a brisk lack of fuss. The news of the surrender came through on August 17; there had already been stories about a "big bomb" dropped on Japan. A parachutist appeared—as recorded in Lannie's diary—on August 29, and the British flag was raised over Stanley the next day. It was all over.

On October 7, the aircraft carrier HMS *Singer*—"lend lease from America" according to Lannie's note on the back of a postcard of the ship—set sail for Manila and then Sydney. "Very pleasant trip—everybody exceedingly kind," says her diary.* Jack and Lannie were sent to a Red Cross camp sixty miles west of the city, in the direction of the Blue Mountains,

---

*Not quite everybody. The literary critic Sir Frank Kermode, who was on a ship carrying former internees to Australia, was shocked at how snobbish they seemed, and how some of the women complained about having to mix with people they had forcibly associated with in camp. He thought they made too much of a palaver about how hard a time they had had.

and there they waited while the Red Cross got in touch with Bill. They waited two weeks before hearing that they would be sent on to Melbourne, where Bill would meet them. He had been given three weeks' leave from the army. While waiting for him, they received a letter from Edna Street, the mother of Bill's friend Tony, who had done so much for their son.

Eildon

Lismore

Victoria

26 October

My dear Mrs Lanchester,

I feel you won't even feel you have time to read this, you will all be so excited to be together again. But I do want to tell you how terribly glad and thankful we all are to know you are safe and well, and not only safe and well, but actually here. There is so much to say, that it would be quite impossible to begin to say any of it in this little 'welcome back' letter, but it takes you so many good wishes, it should be over weight a dozen times.

D'you think Bill looks well? He has been such a complete brick, all through these difficult years—you'd be terribly proud of him if you knew, or rather you will be terribly proud of him when you do, as he is not very likely to mention it himself. I keep thinking of the excitement he must be feeling, *really* going to be seeing you both on Saturday. We shall meet each other soon, I hope—after your holiday at Barwon Heads, which I am sure you will enjoy.

Give my love to Bill,

Yours very sincerely,

Edna Street

A kind, warm letter. There is no way of knowing from its tone, or anything else about it, that Edna's husband, G. A. Street, had been killed in a plane crash two months before. Of all the different kinds of reticence that feature in this story, this seems to me the most admirable. The Lanchesters were going through the greatest happiness, and the greatest relief, of their lives. Edna Street's great grief would be intrusive if she let it show; it would be a form of impoliteness, of gate-crashing; so she kept it to herself. She was able to separate their joy from her pain, and even to feel some of that joy, at one of the worst times of her own life. In this story, there is reticence as shyness, as self-protection, self-concealment, and avoidance of pain, but we should not forget that some forms of reticence can come close to being a form of heroism.

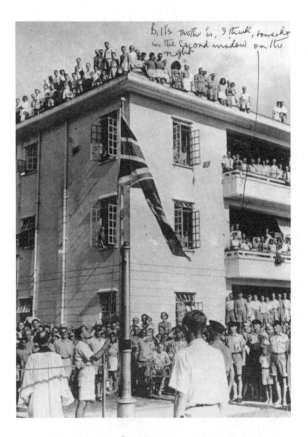

The liberation of Stanley Camp. Julia has written on the photograph: "Bill's mother is, I think, somewhere in the second window on the right."

On October 23, Lannie and Jack arrived at Melbourne, where a few days later they were met by their son, whom they had last seen as a thirteen-year-old boy, and who was now a nineteen-year-old private in the Australian army. Bill's reunion with his parents must have been one of the happiest moments of their lives.

· 4 ·

 HEN JACK AND LANNIE arrived in England in March 1946, there was a letter waiting for them.

Buckingham Palace
September 1945

The Queen and I bid you a very warm welcome home.

Through all the great trials and sufferings which you have undergone at the hands of the Japanese, you and your comrades have been constantly in our thoughts. We know from the accounts we have already received how heavy those sufferings have been. We know also that these things have been endured by you with the highest courage.

We mourn with you the deaths of so many of your gallant comrades.

With all our hearts, we hope that your return from captivity will bring you and your families a full measure of happiness, which you may long enjoy together.

George R.I.

The boat home.

That was nice of King George VI, if a bit impersonal. Another letter, from the governor of Hong Kong to Lannie, meant more.

Government House
Hong Kong
1 January 1947

Mrs Dora Lanchester

Madam,

The Government of Hong Kong would wish, if it were possible, to express to every individual concerned its high appreciation of the countless acts of courage, self-sacrifice and devotion to duty that were performed by residents of Hong Kong both in the course of the hostilities of 1941 and during the subsequent occupation of the Colony by the enemy. In very many cases lack of information prevents this recognition from being given, but, seeing that your conduct is known to me to have merited commendation, I take pleasure in expressing to you, with my personal gratitude and appreciation, the thanks and the approbation of the Government of Hong Kong.

> Mark Young
>
> Governor

Translated into English, that letter says, "Sorry." It referred to the time when troops evacuated to Hong Kong Island, and Lannie and other women were left to be overrun in Kowloon. Rather than that apology, Lannie would have preferred news about the cache of papers she had been given by John Fraser and had kept through the war, at the risk of her life and probably Jack's. She had handed them over to colonial authorities before she boarded ship for Australia. But nothing more was ever heard of them. The war-crimes trials over Hong Kong were rather muted, in line with the Japanese war-crimes trials in general. There were widespread suspicions that the Allies downplayed the matter of Japanese war crimes as a way of easing the transition from imperial to occupied rule.

Bill stayed in Australia. This seemed a natural thing to do: he had his year of service in the army to finish, and then two more years of university. And he was a young man of nearly twenty now, not a boy. His friends were in Australia; it was the place he knew best, the place that, to the end of his life, he thought of as his real home. But at the same time, it boggles my mind that after almost five and a half years of separation the Lanchesters would choose to be separated for almost three more years. I think Bill's ambivalence about the idea of going "home" to England was a big part of this.

To understand a man, you must know what the world looked like when he was twenty (said Napoleon). When my father was twenty, in 1946, he was a British citizen, because his passport said so. But he had spent only a couple of years in England, and had no memories of it. Since then he hadn't been within six thousand miles of his notional homeland. Just to recap: He was born in Africa, was raised there and in Hong Kong, was educated in Australia, had been a private in the Australian army, and spoke with an Australian accent—and yet he was, as anyone but him would have told you, British. (He would have said, I think, that he was Australian.) In the colonial world there is a Center, a Home (or a "back home")—a fixed reference point. Even if you've never been there, you know about it, can feel its presence, its gravitational pull and navigational utility: the district administrator in Malaya wondering about what's on in the West End of London, the magistrate in Senegal dreaming about arguments in Paris cafés. There is a Somewhere Else whose imprint you bear. Despite the fact that England wasn't a place where Bill felt any desire to live, in 1946 it was still in some sense the center of the world for him. In the words of a letter of Lannie's, "London is *still* the hub of the universe even if it has to be ruled by America."

Although my father's passport was in one way wrong—the ridiculous idea that "home" was thousands of miles from anywhere he had ever been—it was true that England was a psychological lodestone. You can feel connected to a place you've never been, as Irish-Americans do to Ireland, or foreign-born Tibetans do to Tibet. It's not that you are phonily nostalgic, it's a real feeling, though the place you're connecting to is a fantasy, which sometimes has things in common with the real place, but more often doesn't. To understand my father, you have to grasp the feeling that something more compelling, something more real, was happening somewhere else.

After his convalescence in England, Jack returned to Hong Kong and to a scaled-down version of his old job, topping up his finances in the last years before he was due to retire. Again, the letterhead tells a story, as he was by now living at the YMCA; Lannie stayed in Britain and found a job in London as a teacher. Jack wrote to Bill with advice on what to do next. "The last thing I want is to push you into something you don't want. I have hated dentistry like hell—and don't want you to be similarly placed. My new profession is fun to me, not work. I would like you to get work that is fun. You'll more probably be a success that way." By his "new pro-fession" Jack meant playing the stock market. There is great pathos here, given that six years before, he had been recommending the idea of be-coming a dentist to his son. Four years of internment seem to have changed his mind on that score. He is back, though, to his habit of trying to bully Bill into being sensible, showing love through the desire for his son to be different. You feel for Jack at the same time you feel the dis-ingenuousness of his efforts at pretending that he is just airing his views, no pressure, no attempt to get Bill to do what he wants, none at all.

"This is just to clarify *my* views," begins the next letter, from late June 1947:

> I know that at 21 we are sort of bogged down in the field of knowledge. I was that way as a young man. One can't put old heads on young shoul-ders I know. Everyone has to work out his own solution for no two cases are ever alike. We who have been over the course can see some of the pit-falls and I want to give you the benefit of my experience (and I think I have packed into my 59 years a good deal more than the average person). I've been places & seen & read a good deal. When one's young it's hard to sort out the grains of gold from the heaps of sand. To know where to look and, what is just as important, where not to look. Naturally, you with your sheltered position, haven't yet joined in the fray.
>
> I am just sort of entering the last phase—my working life is finished & mam is being very brave in trying to carry on as long as possible. She's aged—quite a number of grey hairs now. So I feel we have to consolidate what we have—and at the moment it is quite a bit—at least for us who both started as elementary school teachers (which isn't very high in the rungs of life's ladder). Unfortunately we are now in the post-war stage—a time of settling down & perhaps more importantly of settling up after world global wars. This post-war phase is going to be long & austere. (Just the same as after the Napoleonic Wars.) Then they had the hungry for-ties (1840s) now we are in the hungry forties again, only it is a century later—action & reaction as usual.

"Just to clarify my views" . . . I can see here what my father perceived as control-freakery and bullying. This was the aspect of Jack that made Bill unable to speak about money: his own father had used it as a means of control, so the feelings that money touched on were too painful to be raised. A nastier or more direct man than my father, or at any rate a different man, might well have replied: At the age of fifty-nine you're living on your own at a YMCA, thousands of miles away from your wife and son, and you're giving me life advice?

But this is not the letter of a bad person or an ill-wishing one. Although Jack is obviously keen to see himself as a wise man and someone who has done his fair share of living, nonetheless, the breadth of perspective is impressive. To have survived parental alcoholism and a father's descent into destitution and early death, to have qualified as a teacher, emigrated, gone to the imperial capital to qualify in a different trade,

reemigrated, married, and set up in yet another country, had a child, gone to America to retrain, gone to yet another country and set up yet again, made some money, seen a war coming and gone into government service, spent a few years in a Japanese prison camp, gone "home" to recover and then gone back out

to take up your old job at age fifty-nine—well, you would feel you were entitled to a few opinions of your own. It was very important to Jack to feel that he had lived his own life and made his own mistakes. But he was reluctant to let Bill do the same. Every parent can identify with that; even though we know in our hearts that we don't always protect our children by trying to protect them, the impulse is almost impossible to check.

Bill was finding things difficult at Melbourne University, and he let some of this slip to his father. The result was this letter:

YMCA

12 July 1947

Dear Bill,

This is a continuation of the air mail letter. Now tell me which of any of the following is bothering you.

1. Are you well mentally or physically? [Freudian slip—he means "ill," not "well."]

2. Have you any financial worries?

3. Have you got what I can only describe as post-war fever—I had it after the last war so I quite understand—It's a feeling of frustration—of not being able to get going. I was very unhappy for about 4 years. This was the time I changed over from schoolmastering (which seemed a very poor occupation to me) to dentistry.

4. Have you lost taste for study? We do temporarily but somehow I feel it is up your street and feel sure it will come back naturally.

5. Are you in the throes of a love affair? There's nothing to be ashamed of about this. We all do it including your father and it is perfectly natural right and proper but only at the *proper time*. This I can tell you from my own experience, which is pretty extensive. It's just this . . . a love affair & study just don't go together. The one is fire & the other water. One or other suffers, often both.

I tried to mix a love affair with my first college course. The result was disastrous. I just scraped through about the last on the list and the anxiety to me for the last six months preceding the final exam was terrific, for I suddenly realised that for over a year I had been dreaming—consequently hadn't done the work I should and was afraid that I might fail the exam. This atmosphere was not conducive to good work. I tried to cram which is distasteful. I made up my mind I would never try to mix study & a love affair again. This romance was broken up when I went to South Africa. (Propinquity is the be all and end all of a love affair.)

Well I'm damned if I didn't do the same thing again in South Africa. After deciding to make a try to get a degree to go along with my teaching certificate—I failed inter twice & didn't marry that girl. So I flopped again for the same reason as before.

You'll now see I speak from experience—so I want to give you the benefit of my 59 years to keep you out of the pitfalls I fell into. Unfortunately I had no father who could & would discuss this kind of thing with his son although I know he did something similar or worse than this.

When we become conscious of sex it is very difficult to steer a course away from this—you are at a co-ed institution—this has advantages but I still think co-ed university education is a mistake because of the extreme instability introduced by sex. (Thank goodness Guy's hospital didn't take woman students.)

I can't offer you much advice except one thing—it's hopeless to try & see how close one can get to the flame without burning one self—no—in this the only remedy is to get as far away as possible—the only safe course.

Dad

The reason was number 5, the love affair. Bill had finally found a girl-friend, Joan Miller. He did not love her, but she loved him—loved him, I think, for his gentleness and sweetness of nature, and for the fact that he listened to her. To a man with Bill's capacity for guilt, this made things difficult. He was worried about using her, worried about getting her pregnant, worried about the fact that he did not love her, and worried about how he was ever going to dump her; worried about why he was not in love himself, and whether he was even capable of feeling love. He also worried about whether this love affair was getting in the way of his swotting, and whether he was thereby failing to do his duty to his parents. Hence the letter to Jack. The distance—the literal physical distance—takes a toll here; it's almost impossible to write a letter like that and have it not seem heavy-handed, overbearing in its anxiety.

Bill eventually took Jack's advice, in the worst form possible. He kept the affair with Joan going until he began preparing for his exams, and then dumped her, cruelly and directly: she came in the library looking for him one day, and he looked straight through her as if she were not there. She looked back at him, at first smiling, then disbelieving, then incredulous, then devastated. She ran out of the library. When Bill came out, an hour later, she was still sitting on the steps, being comforted by a male friend whom she later married.

Bill was in a state. When he took his finals he was convinced he was a genius or a worm or both. Everyone was sure he was going to get either the top first or the next one down. He tried to answer two questions at the same time; he tried to be brilliant; he failed to read what he was being asked. In the British system, the top category of degree is called a first, roughly comparable to graduating Phi Beta Kappa. Most students get seconds, either upper (a two-one) or lower (a two-two). The next category down, a third, is usually seen as a token of underwork or worse. Bill hoped to get a first, perhaps even a good first; if things went wrong, he feared, he might get a two-one. But he got a two-two. More than thirty years later, he told me that the day the exam results were posted was the worst of his life.

YMCA

Dec 23/48

Dear Bill,

I have your cable. Well it's not so bad, considering you hesitated so in the middle of the course—I mean in summer of 1947. Of course to get a first one has to enter the thing with gusto & keep in front all the way. But you seemed hot & bothered in 1947—about something. Couldn't make up your mind whether you wanted to go on with it or abandon the course altogether.

At least you now have something to show you were at a university for 4 years. I've told you I leave here on Jan 21st for England on the Canton— so you go straight home. I've got a passage only thro' knowing someone in the know (as is always the case). You can take 50 lb of food into England. Fats, butter, bacon & meats are the things to go for—seeing you soon I hope.

Dad

I have to say I rather love Jack for that letter—for "it's not so bad" and "seeing you soon I hope." Anything more gushing, anything out of character, might not have been a comfort. And perhaps Jack was also secretly relieved: if my father had gotten a good degree, he might have been offered an academic post, and that would have meant that he would not have been going to England with Jack, who was now retiring. So his happiness at being reunited outweighed his disappointment at Bill's exam results; you have to quite like him for that. A few days later he wrote another letter of semiconsolation:

> Now don't worry about the exam results. This may be your first major disappointment but it's nothing new to us older people. We've all had this & other disappointments even where we thought we had provided for everything. 'Man proposes, God disposes.' It would be very useful of course to know where your calculations went astray for future use.
>
> No doubt you're sorry to leave your friends. We all are but there are times when one has to think of the future. It's just this inability to pull up one's roots that keeps millions trudging along on what they realise is a poor outlook—but they can't make the break.

Since these letters are the only place I ever directly encountered my grandfather, I have to record my feeling that he had reservoirs of love and warmth that he found movingly difficult to express. He is not an easy man, but not an unloving or uncaring one, either.

I think, if I had been my father, the eight-year separation from my parents—five years of war, then three of university—would have left me feeling very touchy indeed about their attempts to advise and admonish and control. Lannie intuited that Bill felt resentful, but I'm not sure that he himself was aware of it. At the end of January 1949, he left his friends and his familiar Melbourne and boarded a ship to begin his adult life in England, the country he had no memory of and no feeling for, but which was officially "home."

· 5 ·

I N THE FORTIES AND FIFTIES," my father told me, "when Australians arrived in London for the first time, it had a hell of an impact. It seemed so old, so rich, so sure of itself. Aussies going there for the first time either started to wear big hats with corks dangling around them to keep the flies away, smoking roll-ups and saying things like 'Fair dinkum, cobber,' or put on a three-piece suit and a bowler hat and became more British than the Brits."

I was in my teens when he told me that, and I didn't realize that he was talking about himself. The impact of London—still, just about, an imperial capital in early 1949—on him was twofold. Finally, he felt he was at the center of something. Admittedly, the city was exhausted, dingy, depressed, austere, rationed—knackered. In a way, though, all those qualities were more apparent to anyone who could remember it from before the war. To people who couldn't, it was still a place that expressed history, confidence, a thoroughly marinated sense of its own centrality, which was all the more powerful for being so unconscious and so unexamined. That, I think, was why Jack retired there, at the end of his travels and his labors. He was tired of bouncing around the periphery; now, past sixty, he felt something soothing about being somewhere that seemed to itself like the center of things. There were no more places to go. Lannie, not one of nature's retirees, was working part-time in a school and gave the remainder of her energies to nursing her increasingly unwell husband, who, it was apparent, had not fully recovered from Stanley Camp, and never would.

Bill's reaction to this feeling of centrality was to want to get as far away from it as possible. It was not an instantaneous decision: he knocked about for a bit, went to job interviews, and tried to convince himself and his father that it could be a good idea for him to take an advanced degree. That would require Jack's permission and, more, his financial support. But Jack was immovably resistant to the idea. He had never wavered from his view that Bill had his head in the clouds. He needed to be more firmly rooted in reality. The way to do that was to spend some time doing a proper job—something well paid, not necessarily with great room for imagination or flights of fancy, something secure, something reliable both physically and in terms of status. He did not intend for Bill to spend the rest of his life doing that same boring, repetitive job—so Lannie told my mother. The idea was for Bill to have some training in the world's dull realities. In making that plan for Bill, Jack was, he felt, passing on the main thing he had learned. The great lesson of his life, Jack felt, involved financial security, because financial security was freedom. According to Jack, Bill should do something boring but lucrative to set himself up in life and get himself inculcated in the reality principle. It was an expression of love, an attempt to harden Bill in ways in which he needed hardening; Jack would have been doing better by his son if he had steered him toward a way of life in which hardening wasn't needed. He had said that it was best to do something that was fun, the very Jack-like reason being that you're more likely to be a success that way—not, heaven forbid, because things that are more fun are more fun. But it wasn't advice he was prepared to stick to giving. Bill would do the boring job until he had found out about the reality principle, and then he could go do something more interesting. This is like the situation of those people who announce that they're going to do a well-paid job for a few years, then quit and do something more interesting—sail around the world, write screenplays, open a B&B. (These are specific examples from people I know, not hypothetical ones.) In every case I've known, when somebody says that, it doesn't happen. People find it impossible to give up the money. There seems, where money is concerned, to be no such thing as enough. In the very rare instances in which people do give up, they go off to try to make even more money. I'm told there are exceptions to this rule, but I've never met one.

We're back to the idea that money is freedom. Except it isn't, a lot of the time. I don't know whether Jack ever looked at his life and traced causal links: Search for freedom = search for money = ending up in Hong Kong = ending up in prison. If he had stayed in Rhodesia he could have had as low-key a time in World War II as he had had in World War I. To me his quest for freedom through money seems a version of the much-told story in which a hero is given a prophecy and goes to extraordinary lengths to avoid its fulfillment, only to discover that his very efforts are the thing that makes the prophecy come true. (*Appointment in Samarra. Oedipus Rex.* The ones where a king locks up his daughter.) Jack, though, certainly didn't see things in those terms, and his advice to Bill helped ensure that my father spent his whole life working at something that he hated. As a fairly direct result, I've never believed in the version of freedom that people say comes from working for a big company and being well paid. It seems to me a version of life whereby the things you are supposed to control or own end up controlling you. Many, many people are owned by their possessions. They seem not to see it that way, but that's the truth.

So Bill couldn't become an academic because his father wouldn't let him, and he couldn't go into the civil service with his colonial two-two. (He could have, if he'd gotten another degree, but again, Jack wouldn't let him do that.) Bill applied for jobs where his skills were useful, and found himself, thanks in no small part to his near-fluent Japanese, landing a job with a firm he knew well from his childhood: the Hongkong and Shanghai Banking Corporation. Or in Hong Kong parlance, the Bank. Bill was to work for it for the next thirty years, until boredom and the release from the need to pay my school fees led him to take early retirement.

HSBC is now one of the biggest and most successful banks in the world. In 1949 it was a well-run provincial company, highly conservative in its working practices. That conservatism was one reason the bank was popular with the financially adventurous, risk-loving Cantonese. Bill's choice of employer meant that my father could spend his adult life moving around the margins of the former empire, as far away from "home" as he could get. This was no accident. It was not that he hated England, just that he felt it didn't really have anything to do with him. It was cold and gray; he wasn't used to that. He was used to being a long way away from his parents, too. It was as if, having allowed Jack to make the central decision of his life—as it turned out to be—he wanted to escape, like a victim fleeing the scene of an accident.

Bill spent a few months in London training and enjoying the amenities. His journal has him rather self-consciously going to the Albert Hall with a new bank mate, John Allen (later to be my godfather) to hear Yehudi Menuhin play the Elgar and Mendelssohn violin concertos.

The Mendelssohn started well, with that lovely theme, which is however unfortunately the only meat in the whole piece: the whole piece is simply and entirely a decoration with nothing substantial under the fairy icing. The romantics have the virtue of being easy to listen to—except, as with Mendelssohn, when they do not have enough to say. Nobody would say this of Elgar: he must be one of the most idiomatic of composers. I mean one of those who have built their own private language—Elgar seems to have two main strains in him: mysticism, and also a curious streak of vulgarity—those loud, raising, trumps on the trombones, the blasts of horns and cymbals; yet this is not quite vulgarity though it is both showy and 'effective'—somehow Elgar got away with it, and this very fact makes him all the greater. Perhaps it would be fairest to say that this quality of his is not vulgarity, but the common touch, an earthiness which makes his mysticism the more valuable. (For mysticism must well from our deepest roots if it is to be healthy.)

Hmm. The next day Bill went to a movie called *The Glass Mountain,* about a married composer who falls in love with an Italian woman after being shot down in wartime. The film's main attraction for Bill was Valentina Cortese, the love interest: "Not a model beauty, but so alive it made me ache, as all things you long and yearn from your stomach for, make you ache. Ah me! Will I ever meet someone like that? The universal ache and dream." There's quite a lot of yearning going on here: I can't help feeling that twenty-two-year-old men are better-off spending their time chasing women than contemplating how nice it would be to be the kind of person who chased women.

If you think that this mind-set, introspective and high-cultural, is the wrong one to have when you're entering an externally uneventful life of office routine, you would, I believe, be dead wrong. Thousands, millions of people divide themselves between a monotonously conformist work life and a private world of intense, consoling pleasures and interests. In fact, this division of private and public is almost the norm. The trouble for Bill was not his Elgar-appreciating, Mendelssohn-critiquing side, but the unappeasable ache of a greater life being led elsewhere. It was that sense of a "universal ache and dream." This was obviously connected with his sense, left over from a colonial childhood, of having had his nose pressed against the sweetshop window of other people's more exciting lives. Perhaps it also had to do with not having a girlfriend; perhaps it was just the way he was. But he had an unshakable feeling that real life, and real drama, and big exciting things, happened only to other people; and it is not possible to be happy, or fully occupied in your own life, if you think that.

The day after Valentina Cortese moved Bill to reflect on "the universal ache and dream," he got on a boat and set sail for his new working life, back in his childhood home, Hong Kong. He began a decade and a half in which he hardly ever spent more than a year in the same place. He first spent a few months in Hong Kong, where he had more training and learned more ropes. During these months, he lived in the Mess—the communal quarters for foreign bachelors who worked for the Bank. This brought home, and reinforced, as it was intended to do, the fact that young expatriate bankers were not expected to marry. Not yet, anyway. Their first years abroad were to be occupied lashed to the wheel, working long days, including Saturdays until early afternoon; they slept and ate at the Mess; their main recreation was, as my father told me, "steaming out to get drunk every weekend." In one way it was convenient, and the lack of privacy involved in communal living was less of a problem to a generation used to boarding school and the war; as for the loss of liberty involved, well, that was just part of the deal. The mood in the Mess, a low building halfway up the Peak, tended to vary; there were large collective ups and downs. One night there was a general gloomy silence until a young banker named Sandy McCall cracked under the strain. "I just can't take it anymore!" he shouted as he jumped to his feet, picked up his plate of curry—it was curry night, the kind of old-school curry with sultanas—and smashed it against the wall. The dye in the curry was so powerful that the mark was still visible when my father left the Mess six months later.

The existence of the Mess showed that the Bank was still firmly rooted in the colonial worldview. Dad saw the funny side of that, and liked to tell stories about it. There were plenty of men around who missed the good old days, people who had worked, before the war, in places like Mukden in Manchuria, where Bill's great friend "Daddy" Soul (the universally used nickname alluded to his kindness and gentleness) had had to carry a revolver in the course of his bank duties. The Bank's training manual gives an occasional whiff of this more vivid past. One of the sample phrases, in the section on using codes for telegraphic transmission, was the sentence "The marketplace is dominated by small Manchurian bears." My father told me this when I was about ten, and it immediately became my favorite sentence—the first time I remember taking conscious, almost physical pleasure in a piece of language for its own sake. Even after Dad explained what it meant—that the market for some commodity or other was being influenced by Manchurian investors who didn't have much money and who thought prices would be going down—I still loved to think of the image, resembling something out of Tintin, of a town square overrun by small, fierce bears, knocking over trestle tables laden with food, biting people on the leg as they tried to run away, defecating on the ripped canvas awnings . . .

When Bill left Hong Kong, it was to go to Tokyo (because of his Australian army Japanese), then on to Osaka. That was one of the happiest periods of his life, and one of the most interesting, too, as Japan recovered from the war, approached the end of the Allied occupation, and began to adjust itself to various postimperial, postmilitaristic new realities. Bill loved Japanese culture; he loved the complexity and subtlety of the language, he loved judo, which he studied with a local master. (This was before color-coded belts were popularized, as a way of making the sport accessible to foreigners; Bill, when pressed, reckoned he rose to the standard of a not quite black belt.) He bought a terrifying samurai sword, which I still have in my study, in defiance of the law. (For years my mother pretended to have lost it; I found it hidden in a trunk, wrapped in blankets, after her death.) The main recreational activity was drinking. In Osaka, where the bar-and-red-light area occupied a sizable warren of indistinguishably crowded streets, tiny bars would produce matchboxes that showed their name and a little map of how to find them for a subsequent visit—if you took potluck and just wandered about, you would never make it to the same place twice. So when Bill and his friends and colleagues went out on a bar crawl, which was at least once a week, they hit on the brilliant idea of putting matchboxes in their right pocket if it was a good bar, and in their left if it was bad. Or was it the other way around? In the course of the evening, the exact details of the system would be forgotten, or sudden improvements would be thought of, such as the inside pocket if it was a very good bar, back pocket for a very bad one, top shirt pocket for otherwise uninteresting but cheap bar, hip pocket for local color . . . or no, wait, was it hip pocket for the place where we got thrown out? . . . Inevitably on the weekend mornings after these experiments, Bill would wake with a head-splitting hangover and an unusable database of mixed-up matchboxes. In any case, there were so many streets and so many small bars that nobody went to the same place twice.

Although Bill loved Japan, he was there for only a year or so. His next posting was to Malaysia, which was uneventful except for when the Bank-supplied driver pulled a knife on the Bank-supplied cook. Bill felt he had no choice but to sack him, so he went to the police station, and everyone gave statements explaining what had happened. When no one wanted to press charges, Bill wrote out a good reference for the driver, paid him his wages owed and a month in advance, all in front of the duty sergeant—he wanted a witness to his treatment of the driver, so there would be no basis for complaint or vendetta. Everyone parted on good terms. Forty-eight hours later the boiler at Bill's house exploded, demolishing the back quarter and part of the kitchen. By chance, because it happened early in the morning, nobody was killed. The boiler engineer diagnosed the problem: someone (i.e., the sacked driver) had filled the boiler with paraffin rather than diesel fuel. The police went looking for the driver, who had vanished and was never found. The one good thing that came out of the incident was that Bill made friends with the boiler engineer, a former U-boat captain who'd gone to live in the Far East at the end of the war. The man would come over and listen to Bill's new record player—mainly Wagner—and they would practice the German that Bill had begun to learn while staying with his aunt Louie, Lannie's sister, who lived in Garmisch-Partenkirchen in Bavaria.

Next he was posted to Singapore. He was rising in the Bank hierarchy; he was bored by the work but liked the pay; he liked living abroad, the mixture of the exotic and the familiar; he liked the tropics; he liked the feeling of rootlessness from moving so often, but disliked the difficulty in forming lasting relationships, especially with women, who were, in any case, in short supply in the tight expatriate world. There was a contrast between the life the men tended to live in Asia, which often involved wanting to get away for reasons that would not always have seemed respectable at home, and the restricted, rule-bound life choice available to women. This was the fifties. The regular moves gave Bill the impression his life was changing, even though at the time he knew it was really standing still.

In those days Bank employees could choose between having an annual month-long holiday or saving it up and taking three months off every three years. Bill did the latter, so he had no holiday at all between 1949 and 1952. When he went to England, he was shocked by how much older Jack seemed. Lannie was her usual lively, brisk self, but Jack was weaker and more crotchety than Bill had expected. They had moved to Chiswick, West London, and Lannie was still teaching part-time. It was a relief to spend a few weeks with Aunt Louie in Bavaria, skiing and learning German.

Louie was Lannie's younger sister. Bill and Louie got along—better, in fact, than she and Lannie did. Louie had fallen in love with and married a German, Herbert Kirchner, in the thirties, and moved to his hometown, Garmisch-Partenkirchen. When war came, Herbert was conscripted and sent to fight on the eastern front. He did not come back—but there were persistent rumors that some of the men who had not come back were still alive, dispersed throughout the Soviet gulag. Some of the rumors proved true: the last German prisoners to be released were let go by Khrushchev in 1956. Louie, like millions of other German women—except, of course, she wasn't German—had to wait for news, and chose to nurse the flame of hope that Herbert was still alive. It was this waiting, more than the actual events of the war, that dominated her life. Louie told many stories of the hardships of war, the main theme the same as that of her sister's stories: hunger. Food shortages were savage, and large parts of Germany were reduced to rubble by bombing. (There's an irony, or something, in the fact that during the war both these Lancastrian sisters were bombed by the Allies, Louie in Bavaria and Lannie in Hong Kong.)

Louie was in her late sixties by the time I got to know her, and Lannie a few years older. Louie was skinny, frail-looking but not frail, lively, which was like her sister, and neurotic, which was not; a hypochondriac; and a great one for fussing over her liver. (Instant coffee was a particular no-no. Very bad for the liver.) She had lived in Germany until the sixties and then retired to Cleveleys, near Blackpool, and near where she and Lannie had grown up. Louie was particularly fond of Bill, who in some ways served as the child she had never had; he had visited her a number of times in Garmisch. Louie was also a bit silly, or a bit of a fool. She had the tendency to blurt things out that people see in themselves as a form of shyness or innocence but that others often find indistinguishable from malice; she couldn't see the distinction between what was and what wasn't all right to say.

The interaction between Louie and Lannie was a great source of entertainment and instruction to me. I have no siblings, and have always been fascinated by all aspects of sibling dynamics. When I eventually had children, the birth of our second son made me realize how deeply I identified over our older son's anxieties and discombobulations. I found it hard to bring comfort. If a brother or sister comes, why wouldn't you have an episode of psychotic rage that lasts the rest of your life? So it was highly educative to see how completely Louie still occupied the role of the youngest in the family, even into her late seventies. Her silliness, need for and expectation of attention, and air of expecting subtly different treatment were all qualities belonging to the youngest of a big family, and were described as such by everyone who knew her. They were all, equally clearly, sources of irritation to Lannie. When Louie told stories about how grim it had been in Bavaria during the war, Lannie would ostentatiously read a book or look out the window. Once when Louie was doing her spiel at dinner I— aged about twelve, and noticing she'd gone quiet—said, "Gran, are you all right?" "I've heard it before," she told me. Louie and Lannie were an education in just how unalike close family members can be.

While he was staying in Garmisch on his 1952 holiday, Bill got news of his next posting: he was to be sent to Jakarta, the capital of Indonesia, in those days under the dictatorship of Sukarno. This, he felt in later life, was the strangest place he had ever lived, with its constant sense of chaos and menace and impending violence. It did not help that Indonesia had been colonized by the Dutch, who had a reputation for being the most brutal and racist of the colonial powers in the Far East. It was said by internees that people locked up in former Dutch colonies had the hardest time of all POWs, because the local people hated them and did nothing to help. During Bill's time in Jakarta everybody seemed to be drunk all the time, which did not help. He once saw a man come out of a bar to discover that his car had been blocked in by double-parking. The man took out a switchblade and shredded all four tires on the car blocking him in.

Then he crossed his arms, leaned back on the hood of his own car, and waited for the driver to come out so they could have a fight.

"You'd go into work, find a couple of streets roped off," Dad told me, "do your day's work, go home, turn on the World Service, and hear the news begin: 'Jakarta was in flames tonight, as . . .' "

In the bars and clubs, typical conversation involved just how many, or rather how few, men would be needed to take the city and overthrow the government. Estimates would start in the middle hundreds and gradually decrease.

"Two hundred. Properly armed and trained, two hundred."

"If I had the right men, a hundred. Radio station, airport, lock up Sukarno. Or just shoot him. Maybe even seventy-five."

"The right men—the *right* men—no more than fifty. You could do it with fifty."

And so on.

Bill lived in quarters of his own and used to like the tropical nights of Jakarta, standing on his balcony with a beer and hearing the city go about its business. His great consolation was listening to music.

Then he was back in Singapore, more senior now, as the deputy accountant—the third most important figure in the branch. He had a girlfriend or two, and a red sports car. One day he and a girlfriend had an argument. He drove home in a rage, went too fast, lost control of the car, and rolled it over into a storm drain. A concrete footbridge above the ditch stopped the car from falling in. He was held upside down by his seat belt and managed to climb out. A foot farther over and the car would have gone into the ditch and he would have been killed. A foot in the other direction and he would have hit the bridge head-on and been killed. And the luckiest thing of all was that he hadn't hit a pedestrian, because if he had, it would have taken two lives: he would have been pulled from the car and beaten to death.

He was still bored by the work, still glad to be away in the world, enjoying the feeling of independence that came in flashes between the oppressive realities of office routine. And then somehow three years had passed and he was due for leave again. He spent the holiday the same way he had spent the last one, half in London and half in Bavaria. Jack was frailer, Lannie was much the same as ever. Bill had clothes made in Savile Row, and liked that, and the fact that he could afford it; he liked being able to wander around London and feel he had a place there, and he could compare it now with other cities he'd known. Nonetheless, it was a relief to get to Germany and to its different otherness. The three months went by in a rush of European sensations—cold, culture, live music, being surrounded by white people all day. Without admitting it, he found it soothing to be back in Singapore. And then almost immediately the news came that Jack was very sick: he had pancreatic cancer and was not expected to survive.

There wasn't much Bill could do except express his love and support. There wasn't much Lannie could do, either, except nurse Jack as he grew more ill. Jack was stoical. On one of their last outings together—they had taken a bus tour of the Lake District, to visit landscapes they had both loved in their northern childhoods—he turned to Lannie and said, "I've always loved you, you know." As she later told my mother, it was the only time in his life he said anything like that to her, and it gave her a surge of happiness and reassurance that she never forgot.

Jack died on February 12, 1955. Bill was in Singapore, where he received Lannie's telegram. He wrote back.

Mrs John Lanchester
8 Sutton Lane
Chiswick
London W4

Hongkong and Shanghai Banking Corporation
PO Box No 896
Singapore
Sunday 13 Feb 1955

Dear Mother,

I got your telegram last night—they phoned it through to me—and hope you got my reply this morning: I only hope that Dad's death was a release for him. I'm sure it must be for you too, after the very heavy strain of the past months. It was no great surprise to me—thanks to your having warned me so well that it was to be expected.

I am very happy that I got to know Dad well during my leave, so that I now have a clear picture of him, less warped by the antagonism which till my leave, I am afraid, prevented me from seeing him as he was. What a good man he was in so many ways—not petty or small minded, charitable, kind, not bearing any malice. Only by a hairsbreath was he not a *very* good man: for he *was* a difficult man. But that stemmed inevitably from his childhood & his parents, & he could not help. All we can do for him now is to remember him as he was, in some ways good, in some ways bad, in all very much better than most. I have never thought much about life after death; so far as I have I think I believe in reincarnation. It would be so right, somehow, to think of him as being born again, with new possibilities for good & evil.

It must be so much more difficult and painful for you than me, for you have been through so much together. But time is the Great Healer, if you can keep your heart open to your memories of him. I am sure that your courage and commonsense, of which you have such a very great deal, will enable you to bear it.

And so do not be too sorrowful, for he would not wish it for you.

But at the moment you will need rest and a change more than anything after this long strain.

Your very loving son,

Bill

Twenty-eight is not the worst age to lose a parent. Your grief is at least the grief of a person who is whole (more or less): it's still a wound, but you suffer the wound as a grown-up and not as a child. In a perfect version of Bill's life, he would, after grieving for Jack, have felt that he had done his filial duty by him, in spending his six years of drudgery getting a thorough grounding in the reality principle. He would have felt that he had done his time. But as I said that didn't happen. Bill was increasingly oppressed by the repetitive, uninteresting, but precise and, in its way, demanding work of the Bank. The problem was that it was demanding in ways he didn't find interesting. There's nothing unusual about that. We fight for autonomy over so many areas of our lives—for decency and democracy and freedom, for suffrage, for the right to have some say over our lives, some control—and then in the central question of what we are to do with our days, with our working lives, we give all that freedom away in return for a paycheck. And are content to be bored and obedient, resentful and uninvolved and tired. This is such a standard, universally accepted feature of the modern world—that we will dislike and be bored by our work—that we have forgotten to notice that it doesn't make sense.

Bill gave away the best years of his life to a job he disliked, a job that bored him. Many years later he told me that I mustn't do that, and I have tried not to. He knew he was doing it, but couldn't stop himself. The realization gradually grew stronger toward the end of the 1950s. His journals are all about this sense of boredom and misfitting.

I have always been wary of listening to music of the Romantics: my defences were up against it. I could not properly pay attention to it, and I would dismiss a piece before hearing it. I have just realised that this was because much of it captured for me so well just the very atmosphere of vague longing, grandeur, and yearning promise of something perfect which I had for so many years and with such pain carried round unsatisfied inside me. 'Wombmusic' I would have called it if I had thought of the phrase, and that would have been accurate, not as a description of the music, but of my reaction to it. I was afraid it would upset me, and I covered my feelings by jeering mildly at it.

Tonight, though, I put on Rachmaninov's 2nd Symphony. It must have been the first time that I have listened—been able to listen—to it properly. I must before have exaggerated the emotionalism of it to excuse my dislike for it, for on listening tonight I heard instead a freshness of spirit unstaled by the world, an adventurousness, a reaffirmation of the happy possibility of greatness in the world, which suddenly brought me up short. It suddenly came to me how much the self-recriminations of guilt and loss of confidence in myself and in life have filmed me over and reduced me to dull automatism and spoilt my life. It made me realise that I have lost the expectation that life had something to offer other than disappointments and difficulties!

Romanticism can be dangerous, in that it may offer us the promise of perfection greater than we can find in life and by so doing spoil life for us by making it seem worthless in comparison: if it does that it is our own fault for abandoning the world and turning to the Dream—a return to the womb. It should rather serve us as a reaffirmation of its value, a reminder of the promise that life should hold for us. We must dive into the waters of Romanticism to refresh ourselves for the hot and dusty world, not lull ourselves to drown there.

He is so hard on himself. And there, perhaps, is the answer to why Bill stayed at the Bank doing the job he hated: He was punishing himself. For what, I don't entirely know. Perhaps the boredom and confinement of the job matched the boredom and confinement of the formative time he had spent in plaster; perhaps he felt he had to abide by his father's wishes, despite, or because of, the fact that they were a kind of punishment, an attempt to bend him into shape (just like the plaster, again); perhaps he never got over all the guilt and rage he felt during the years of separation, and was taking them out on himself; perhaps he was choosing to be in a prison, just as his parents had been in a prison. Or perhaps it was some or all of those things. Here, though, is a diary entry that directly talks about his sense of boredom.

I worked till 8 tonight. Being tired, I felt depressed. What a strain boring work is. How many people dislike office work? Surely few like it. What a waste all this earning a living is—especially earning a good living. I must save money, and buy leisure, buy the time to be myself.

I must tell Father that we are alike in this desiring leisure. (It is curious how alike we are: Father disliked his dentistry, and worked only for the money that would set him free from it; it is the same with me and my banking.) These reflections are awakened by something that happened today—Champ Jones said he was resigning and going to go on a tour of Australia to see where he would like to settle: here is a man not daunted by the fear of insecurity. I envy him his courage, and hope to be but a much paler version of his brighter purpose.

That sentiment is not, in itself, tragic. But it is tragic that Bill realized the depth of his own boredom in 1950, and kept working at the same job for another twenty-nine years.

Perhaps it was the movement and the constant reposting that kept him from acting on his feeling of stuckness. Or perhaps it was actually that sense of stuckness that he liked, and that kept him at the Bank. His next posting was to Calcutta, where he was again deputy accountant, the third most senior figure in a busy and important branch of the Bank, in one of the world's great cities. It was in Calcutta that Bill encountered his first case of criminality in the staff. A young clerk was found to have been stealing from dormant accounts—accounts whose customers had forgotten about them or died, or whatever. "The thing that was so awful about it was the scale," he told me. "Not that it was big, quite the reverse. He liked to give people Johnnie Walker Red Label whiskey. He'd hand out Benson & Hedges and he'd pat you on the back and say, 'There you go, Bill, I know you like Benson & Hedges, none of those rubbish Indian cigarettes, nothing but the best for my friends.' And that mattered so much that he stole for it and ended up going to jail. It was so sad. And most corruption that I've seen is like that. It's not people going off to buy a tropical island for themselves, it's people wanting the next lifestyle up."

The yearning for a better life—Bill was sensitive to the way this could be a tragic feeling. And he was becoming more and more conscious of the sheer artificiality of the expatriate semicolonial world, living this strange constrained life in one of the world's greatest, liveliest, most overwhelming cities. As Christmas approached, he found himself describing expat Calcutta to a friend: "Basically, a life of getting up at 8, in office by 8.45 or earlier, working till 7, home, drink, dinner, & in bed by about 10 doesn't leave time for much else at all." But Christmas was worse.

This is the 'social season'—basically a dead loss unless one really enjoys 'parties'. Am slowly getting a picture of the social scene in Calcutta: it seems to be a. a small, possibly-by-now-non-existent, group of rich, smart, (horsey?) people whose imagined style of manners and life is inspired by b. a larger group who feel that they must emphasise the difference between themselves and c. Scotsmen and cockneys who work as radar mechanics, artisans in factories, and jute mills. Groups a. and b. have strong Oxford accents, c. speak dialect; *all* wear evening dress to cocktail parties, or any other sort of party for that matter. Many, indeed most, people are badly off by normal European-in-the-East standards, and one has to be very careful, on our pay which is (relatively) good, not to give the impression of showing off—the fact that I have a car, for example, tends I think to upset people who, having done 20–30 years here, have *not* got one or have only just got one from the company. All this *matters,* terribly. It is the England of 30–40 years ago transplanted, crystallised—dead.

So why put up with it? The answer is that this life, and especially the weight of the Bank, made Bill feel safe. He never again wanted to have the experience he had had when he took a boat to a continent where he knew nobody, and had "oh what a feeling of 'Where do I fit in?' " Even if being in the Bank was a living immurement, at least he knew where, and who, he was. The stolidity of it all was what he complained about, but it was also what he liked. He was not emotionally illiterate; on the contrary, he knew his own feelings, and understood them. He understood them well enough to know that he wanted to avoid the things that upset him, at almost any cost. That was Bill in his early thirties. "What a liking I have for spaciousness," he told his journal. "Reaction against the small space my obsessions have been trying to force me into?" The reader thinks, Well, yes, probably. He also made a list of "Work Points," as he called them.

1. Narcissism. Need to be lost in drink, sex etc. Pride.
2. Self-centredness.
3. Drive for perfection—perfective self.

4. Distrust of women.

5. Need to be full always—drink, food, cigarettes etc.

6. Storytelling—imagining.

7. Oversexual interest in women.

8. *Too close to womb.*

But the list leaves out the most important item of all, "Stop being so hard on self." That was a lesson he never learned.

In 1959, Bill's triennial leave came around again, and once again he made the trip "home" to England. He stayed with Lannie, and visited relatives, and did all the things he usually did. But this time, before he went back to Asia, Lannie did something she didn't usually do, and gave a dinner party, where she introduced him to a friend she had made at Avondale, the school where she was teaching in West London. The friend, a new colleague who taught English, was about Bill's age, a lively, funny, vital Irishwoman who had spent time in India. Her name was Julie Gunnigan. At the dinner, Julie and Bill got on famously. They spoke about all sorts of things, especially poetry and writing; two particular shared enthusiasms—which I would have thought were mutually exclusive—were for Robert Graves and Lawrence Durrell. Both Bill and Julie agreed it was a pity they had met so late in his leave. He was returning to Calcutta the next week, but he promised to write her with the full title of a book of essays by Graves, which she said would help her with a class she was teaching.

B.T.J.

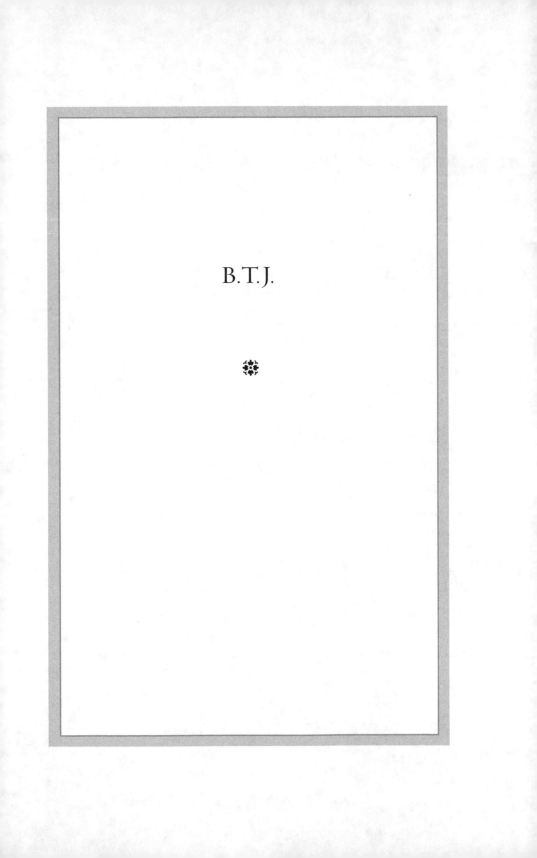

THE YEAR BETWEEN leaving the convent and meeting Bill had been eventful for Julia. On the evening of October 30, 1958, Sister Eucharia of the Presentation nuns got off Air-India Flight 107 at Heathrow, passed through Customs and Immigration, and was met by Vincent Geraghty. They took a taxi to the flat in Tachbrook Street where Peggie, eight and a bit months pregnant, was waiting for them. It was dark when they arrived, which helped ease Julia's sense of shame at entering dressed in her religious habit. She went in and embraced Peggie. And then she went into the bedroom and changed from her nun's habit into cast-offs and hand-me-downs Peggie had waiting for her. Julia Immaculata Gunnigan picked up the identity she had laid down in 1944.

The experience of leaving a religious order is overwhelming. This is still true today. In the world of the Catholic Church before Vatican II, it was even more so. But Julia did not have time to be overwhelmed. Peggie and Vincent could not support her; it was not just urgent, but essential, that she get a job. Luckily, she had her teaching qualifications and references from four people she had known in Madras, one of them the chief inspector of schools. Teachers are never paid enough, and in much of the

English-speaking world they aren't sufficiently respected; but they can, at almost all times and in almost all places, find work. The first place she looked was where Peggie was teaching, City of Westminster College. This was an institute of higher education, attached to Regent Street Polytechnic, that specialized in preuniversity courses for students who had enrolled in British schools but first needed to brush up their qualifications or their English or both. The college attracted "lots of ex-army, air force, Americans completing their education after the war, people of all colors and creeds from far-flung places," as Peggie remembers it. Julia had asked Peggie if she could find her work there, and as it happened, there was an immediate need for a qualified teacher of English as a Foreign Language, several evenings a week. So Julia found work more or less straight off the plane. Peggie remembers that she was particularly anxious to earn the money for new clothes. These were both a practical necessity and the symbolic core of the new identity she would have to construct for herself in civilian life. She bought one or two things and then, on Peggie's advice, decided to wait for the January sales.

At home in Tachbrook Street, life was dominated by the arrival of Siobhán, born in St. Thomas' Hospital on November 4, five days after Julia's arrival from Madras. Julia loved babies and was immediately devoted to her niece. In the mornings, Peggie would sometimes come downstairs and pop the baby into bed with her half-awake aunt. "Julia said she liked the noises she made," Peggie recalls. "She liked the noises babies made in the morning." It was a happy experience for Julia, but one that made her sharply aware of how late she was leaving things if she was ever to have children herself. Her thirty-eighth birthday came when Siobhán was a month old.

Because the Westminster job was part-time, Julia looked for another to supplement it. Within a few weeks, in the January term, she found a job teaching English at Pimlico School, a school full of children who had failed England's highly divisive 11-plus examination, in what was then a fairly rough working-class area. Her sole knowledge of the neighborhood was derived from the Ealing comedy *Passport to Pimlico,* which she had seen in Madras, subtitled in Hindi. (Anthony Burgess claimed to have seen Laurence Olivier's *Hamlet* dubbed into Hindi and then subtitled back into English. The subtitled "To be or not to be" soliloquy began: "Shall I live on? Or do myself in? I do not know.") The intake was not big on social graces—much less so than at Church Park—but it was, to this Irish-woman landed in a city she had never visited before, unexpectedly warm and friendly. It probably helped that the area had a significant population of Irish, who at this time still had a trace of disreputability—they were as-sumed to be manual laborers or their children, drunken and dirty and quick-breeding. That was not an assumption Julia shared. The boys queu-ing to hand over their lunch money would sometimes pause at the head of the line and demand: "Fulham or Chelsea, Mam?"—these being the two local football teams. The wrong answer would get a scowl and a sneer; the right answer would be met with: "Buy ya dinner." It was the closest thing Julia had experienced to flirting in many years.

London is, I think, a cold city, one that turns a face of inhospitable in-difference to outsiders—but I first fetched up there in 1987. My mother arrived in 1958, and she did not find it so. The atmosphere of Pimlico School was rough but friendly. She was astonished by how education did not seem to be perceived as crucial. In rural Ireland and in Madras, everyone knew that education was the all-important means of escape and life transformation. In England it was, on the contrary, important not to get above yourself. No one would ever admit it, but people were happy where they were. They were especially happy with the level of complaint and grumbling, which often seemed one of the most important plea-sures. A few of her brightest pupils at Pimlico had passed the 11-plus and been offered a place at grammar school, the academically superior type of high school, but their parents had not allowed them to go. She raised the question with one parent, who shuffled and looked shifty and embar-rassed and eventually admitted to her—perhaps the parent wouldn't have if she hadn't been Irish—"We didn't want him to think he was bet-ter than us." Education had become fused with class, and in this world parents did not necessarily want their children to have more opportunities than they had had. It was the opposite of everywhere else my mother had taught, where providing your children with more chances than you had had was seen as education's primary purpose.

The corollary of this was a great feeling of warmth and solidarity and everyone's being in things together. It was exactly what my mother needed, coming from the closed, competitive, authoritarian world of the convent: warm, friendly, rough, democratic, and indifferent to qualities of status and protocol. My mother felt that she had spent a decade holding her tongue; here nobody seemed to do that. In the convent, all impulses were repressed, and then the pain of that repression was "offered up to God." Here it was much simpler: nothing was repressed. If you felt anger or envy or greed, you shouted or gibed or gorged. Pimlico School was a liberation.

Outside the school, Julia's main friends were in the London Labour Party. The Tachbrook Street flat was owned by a young couple, the Garsides, who were active in local Labour politics. (Mair Garside went on to be deputy leader of the Greater London Council, just before it was taken over by Ken Livingstone.) Another Labour friend was Ashley Bramall, who later became head of the Inner London Education Authority. Julia joined the party; her new friends in it were kind to her, at a point in her life when she needed kindness. Her life so far had been all about roles, her identity provided by the institution she lived in; outside it, she was acutely aware of the need to make herself up; she felt as if she were nobody. These new friends didn't care who she had been, they just took her as she was now—and that, again, was a liberation and a release. She also had to learn how to behave—to interact with people directly, rather than as mediated through the hierarchies of authority and the Church. She had to learn how to go for a drink after work, how to act at a dinner party, how to pay bills, how to cook, and perhaps more than anything else how to behave with men—how to flirt, how to keep them at a distance. It wasn't that this new, habitless way of being with men didn't have rules; it had just as many as the convent had, but they were entirely different. A nun's smile is not the same thing as a pretty girl's smile, even if the nun is a pretty girl. For the first time in her life she felt free. For the first time in her life she

wore slacks. She sensed that she had left the convent just in time to feel young.

Julia was, as photos show, pretty, and looked much younger than her age. She was lively, funny, clever, and very good company. She soon got the hang of how to talk to men and began to get along especially well with a teacher at Westminster College named Tom Aitkins.* He was a colleague of Peggie's and a sort-of friend to her and Vincent.

"He was a person I half liked but didn't altogether like," says Peggie. "He was an only son, and his mother and father absolutely adored him. They were always telling you how wonderful Tom was, et cetera. Tom was good fun, I liked him. He afterward occasionally wrote columns for *The Guardian.* But when he had too much to drink, which was quite frequently, he got very aggressive and foulmouthed. And I'm *terribly* suspicious of men like that. I feel that I can't altogether trust them."

At the end of the spring term, Julia found a job as head of English at

---

*Not his real name.

the Avondale school in West London. There she met and quickly made friends with Dora Lanchester, who was teaching part-time. Julia continued to teach evening classes at Westminster and continued to get along with Tom Aitkins. "They got closer and closer and closer," is how Peggie remembers it. And then one day in the summer, no more than nine months after Julia had left the convent, she and Tom came upstairs to Peggie and Vincent's flat and announced that they had some news: They were going to marry. Peggie felt a touch of apprehension about this, based on her reservations about Tom and the relatively short period of time Julia had had to locate herself in the world outside the convent. But the happy couple, and especially Tom, were bursting with their news. "He in particular was ecstatic and went around telling everybody."

About a week later, Peggie was in her kitchen, standing at the sink, when she saw her sister come in, ashen-faced. "Julia came up looking absolutely shaken. She said, 'The most terrible thing has happened. Tom's mother rang me, and she was absolutely furious and railed at me to leave her son alone. She didn't want her son to marry anyone like me. She went on and on.' I said, 'What are you going to do, Julia?' She said she didn't know. Almost as she was saying this, Tom rang the doorbell. So the two of them went down to Julia's flat. Tom was there for quite a while, and when he left, Julia came up. She was so happy. Tom was absolutely furious with his mother. He was going to go home, he was going to move out, he was going to move into her flat. He was having no more to do with his mother until she apologized to Julia, and to him, et cetera. I was so pleased. But poor Julia. She never saw Tom again. He just disappeared off the planet."

Tom stopped going to work, moved from his flat, and left no forwarding address. He broke off all contact with Julia. In a life that had already had one devastating rejection, and one horribly cruel and abrupt termination of an engagement, this combined rejection and broken engagement left Julia spinning. And she was already spinning anyway, from the shock of leaving the convent. It left her feeling that every good thing would always go wrong and that she could rely on no one. Her first expe-

rience since leaving the order, of extending her trust, had ended in catastrophic failure and public humiliation. Three months after this, she met
my father. Peggie, Vincent, and Siobhán had moved to Norwich by then,
Peggie having taken a job in a school there, so Julia was in Tachbrook
Street on her own when she met Bill over dinner at Lannie's.

I find that I don't want to write too much about my parents'
courtship. There is often a point in memoirs where someone finds a
"cache" of letters and droolingly recounts the secrets therein. I'm not
going to do that; but I will quote a few examples suggesting how my parents fell in love. The attraction was based, I think, on the fact that Bill and
Julia found each other easier to talk to than anyone else either had ever
met. Perhaps that's one of the most common reasons for falling in love;
it certainly seems to me to be among the better ones.

Bill's first letter to Julia is a short note, giving the title of the Graves
book—*The Common Asphodel*—and complaining about the difficulty he was
having importing his new record player into Calcutta: "Bureaucrats are
having Bengali field-day." She wrote, he wrote, and they got into the
swing of things. I won't quote the correspondence at length, but I will
give a flavor of it with the second letter each of them sent to the other.
Bill described his life in Calcutta.

Your very welcome letter has been lying invitingly on my desk since 10
o'clock, but I had no chance to open it (is 'had no chance' a Bengali-ism?
I read so much of it that my command of English English, or Irish English
if you're going to be stubborn, is sensibly weakening) till now, 20 past 10
pm. I am still very busy—busier—working till 7–8 every night just keeping abreast of daily necessities, and it has not been made easier by the confident arrival on Friday of two Inspectors from HEAD OFFICE, one of whose
jobs has been to sit at my desk and ask me questions (sly, delivered with
a frank open expression and only slight hesitation, and straightforward—
'when you commit a felony do you prefer a pen, or an axe?') for two or
three hours a day. I *think* I passed, A with a few smudges, but these gentle-
men are so smooth that I shall not know for sure till judgement is deliv-

ered, in the prosaic form of a report from Head Office written when they are again, in safety, there.

Seriously I am very busy. If I am not interrupted, and have nothing that needs looking into, I can be away by 5 or 5.30, but the Accountant, whom I like very much—'feel very fond of' is more accurate as he is rather like a small boy, I should hate to hurt his feelings at all—loves to talk, particularly about Banking, and his brilliant solutions of the profound and difficult ('It's the *simple* things that are the *most* difficult') problems which can be found therein. I go into his office to ask if he agrees to my paying a bill for say £10, and come out, an hour later, with no answer but having had a long discussion (monologue, rather, and a monologue is *not* a conversation) on what we are *really* doing, as bankers. His need for somebody intelligent (somebody?) to talk to is rather pathetic—a clever man who is bored to death by doing dull work and who is driving himself, and us, round the bend by trying to convince himself that the work is difficult enough to be worth tremendous pains. A very nice— eccentric—to other people—man. He is, I think, aware of being in the grip of an obsession, and needs the solace of human contact (contact means a 'listener') and finds in me, I think, a person who listens sympathetically—does he *feel* that I am listening to the person and not to the words perhaps? A small, thin, dark man, married to an intellectually smart woman.

That letter was addressed to someone he called "Julie." Julia by now was turning into someone else. Julie was Irish, but less Irish than Julia or Sister Eucharia. She was educated. She was funny and, on her own turf, even overbearing, though shy in some public spheres. She didn't stress her own Irishness as much as Julia had done. I have thought of telling my mother's story divided into the different people she was at different times in her life: Julia, Sister Eucharia, and Julie. The latter two of these were, in their own ways, constructed or chosen identities. Sister Eucharia was a person who was partly created, and propped up by, the Church, and whose experiences were structured by it. She saw the world through an institutional prism. But Julia had a self that didn't entirely fit that grid;

her own feelings, her own wants, eventually made institutional life impossible. Sister Eucharia couldn't stand being herself anymore. She became Julia Gunnigan, who was then to become Julie Gunnigan, and then Julie Lanchester: free, married, British, a mother, an escapee.

Julie found it easy to confide in Bill. She wrote a long letter that was startlingly candid about her recent mishaps in love.

Tell me, Bill, how would you feel if you were likely to meet Jean [an old girlfriend] here and there more or less unexpectedly? I ask because I met Tom again last week at a teacher's meeting. I didn't speak to him—couldn't; but seeing him brought a lot of the old heartache back. I hoped no one else noticed anything so you can imagine how I felt when the girl who was sitting beside me asked me afterwards if I was nervous at the meeting because my hands were shaking so much—I could scarcely hold a cigarette. I don't know what to make of myself—I don't want to marry Tom—that is quite definite, I know now that it wouldn't work. I have no wish to start meeting him again but he still attracts me—even though I don't really *like* him. Do you know what I mean, Bill? Or does this sound like raving? And can you tell me why? I thought years of silence had taught me enough about myself never to be surprised by my own behaviour. I am bewildered and I don't like it.

That she felt easy in being honest with Bill didn't mean she was any sort of pushover, as her letter went on to prove.

Your description of the Accountant made him so real that I think I'd recognise him if we met. I call him Mr Hastings—don't know why. But what, please, is an 'intellectually smart' woman? I haven't any picture whatsoever of his wife. You like Hastings, I know, but what about Mrs H.? Have you ever noticed that very few men can really describe a woman as she is?—I mean in writing (same applies to women writing of men). Even Durrell himself slips up with his women folk. Justine is a little bit phony to me and I am afraid that he is going to make Clea too good to be true [characters in Durrell's *Alexandria Quartet*]. The milk of human kindness must turn sour at some time for every daughter of Eve. It's just as well for me that we are not talking now as I know you'd pull every bit of this to pieces and probably try to make me eat my words. But I have so many other things to write about that I don't want to go on for pages making a case here. And all because I cannot imagine what intellectually smart Mrs Hastings looks like or is like, I should say.

So Bill rapidly learned that he wasn't going to be allowed to get away with anything. But he wasn't put off. A key point in the correspondence came when he read, and showed that he understood, Katherine Hulme's novel *The Nun's Story,* which Julie had sent him by way of explaining life in the convent.

You will probably be surprised to get a letter from me while you still owe me one (HINT), but I picked up last night—I think I have been avoiding it—*The Nun's Story,* and I want to thank you for it. I found it very moving. It also made me feel very angry. What a waste. There must be very few people indeed who are born to that life, and can it ever be anything but a triumph of the will in those not born to it? When I say this I mean that no, or few, triumphs of the will are much good.—Why exalt one part over the other? It does seem such a pity that one should have to *shut out* so much; is The World so powerful? It is very distracting, certainly, but the life of the cloister is such an extreme one, it must make as many difficulties as it does away with. I felt so glad for that nun, when she describes herself sitting in the cafe at the end of the book—how she must have enjoyed the sensations of being in a world of *colour* once again! For there is no colour at all in the rest of the book you know—all black and white light. Perhaps that's why she loved the Congo so much.

The World may be extreme, but so's a nunnery!

You know—it only really struck me the other day—you are perhaps the only person I know that I can really talk to! This will perhaps explain, and excuse, my having talked such a lot! You may remember that I apologised for talking your head off!

The same letter then moves into a much more intimate mode, as Bill describes an unpleasant experience he had had with a flatmate who went off with a French girl whom Bill had been pursuing. It was a painful thing to talk about, an admission of feelings, but again, Julie did not let him get away with anything.

You say the whole episode would have hurt more if you were jealous. But, weren't you? And who wouldn't be in the circumstances? Perhaps only your pride was hurt. I wonder, though, if you could, by any stretch of the imagination, have brought the whole thing on yourself? You say your French girl may or may not have a brain. Very likely she had. She had to contend with a certain amount of language difficulty. And it is quite possible that she was aware of your quest for a brain and maybe scared or put off at the idea. I don't think any woman likes being dissected. We haven't got your brain to face the ordeal with, Mr Lanchester! Can't you manage to achieve a synthesis between your brain and your 'solar plexus' (what on earth is your, or anyone else's, solar plexus anyhow) and like them with both?

Leaving your friend aside a while and returning to you. Why are you 'not sure of yourself'? You are normal, intelligent, well-mannered, sociable. Why shouldn't people like you? They do. Is it that you feel they shouldn't and if they do, there is something wrong? You keep on looking for snags—of course you'll find them. People like to provide you with what they think you want to find.

One last thing about jealousy. It may be part of you—but you are bigger than it—it is only a part. And why should you be afraid of something less than you? Face it, and its cause, and don't be afraid to fight it for what you want.

You said something in your letter about writing about someone else and telling so much about yourself in the process. Well, if I thought long about all that your clinical eye must have found out about me through reading what I have written, I might panic! However, I don't mind what I tell you—it's in safe hands. It may not have occurred to you that I have done more talking than you have! Or rather, I have talked to you more freely than I have ever done to anyone else. And why should you even think of apologising for what you choose to call 'talking my head off'. My head is as firmly in position as ever it was, thank you, and I like being talked to. Neither do your letters worry me; it is not very flattering of you to think they should. I like hearing from you, though of course I realise that I have run the risk in this letter of being struck off your list of correspondents!

Not surprisingly, there is a bit of a gap in the correspondence after that. It is a psychologically acute letter, sharp to the point of merciless-ness, and one of the most striking things about it is the definiteness with which Julie takes a position on the moral high ground. It's clear in his let-ter that Bill is upset, but that doesn't prevent her from delivering a lec-ture to the effect that it is all his fault. You can see here her experience as a teller-off, and as someone used to possessing the ethical upper hand. She is not even a tiny bit shy about telling Bill he's to blame for the fact that he has been humiliatingly dumped by a girl who went off with his flatmate.

It took some time for the correspondence to resume. Julie wrote a couple of long letters—no further mention was made of this exchange— and Bill began to write back. The tone warms up, until on August 2, 1960, he has some momentous news: "I HAVE BEEN POSTED TO—HAMBURG!!" His manager inevitably tried to stop him from going, but was overruled. This was a huge deal for Bill, because for the first time he would be within easy visiting distance of England. He would be able to see his mother, and would be able to keep in touch with any friends he made while staying with her in London—such as, for instance, Julie. There is a sense, when one reads the letters, that this is the point at which they began to think seriously of each other as potential partners. With Julie in London and Bill in Calcutta, taking a break every three years, there wasn't much point in seeing the relationship as having a future in anything other than friendship and letter-writing. There is an irony: If they had been playing boyfriend-girlfriend games, they would never have reached this point of candid intimacy, which enabled their relationship to grow closer and more serious. But they started falling for each other because they could talk frankly; and then a deus ex machina entered, in the unlikely form of the Hongkong and Shanghai Bank. With Bill in Hamburg, a mere hour's flight from London, able to visit Lannie regularly, things would change. The letters between him and Julie warmed up. Bill was given a few days in London to prepare before moving to Hamburg in late October. Julie wrote to ask whether, when he came to London, he would like to see Siobhan McKenna as Pegeen in *The Playboy of the Western World*. He sent back a telegram saying, "YES YES YES."

Those few days in London went very well. Bill and Julie, to use a favorite phrase of hers, "hit it off." One of the things they spoke most about was families. At some early date in talking to my father, Julia became aware that he wanted a large family. He felt he had paid a high price for being an only child, and he liked the idea of his own children having company; liked too, perhaps, the idea of himself as a patriarch. He was explicit about it—and may have thought it was a selling point to the Catholic girl he was chatting up—that he wanted to have lots of children.

Another big topic was Julie's excitement about the stories she had written, which she had just heard were going to be broadcast on the BBC. After the breakup with Tom Aitkins, she was working on her writing for the first time. With this came an ability to see more clearly her life as it had been—to see the choices she had made and the decisions that had been forced on her. She had always wanted to write, but for obvious reasons, in the convent, had never been able to; now she started some autobiographical short stories about things that had happened to her in the convent. She had sent one to the BBC, and it had been accepted. Her first attempt, "My Hair and Me," was to be broadcast on the radio, and she had been asked to read it herself. My mother was on the way to becoming a writer. She couldn't use her own name, of course—word would get back to the family, or to the convent, or to the school, or something. So for the purposes of becoming a writer, Julia Gunnigan became Shivaun Cunningham. The pseudonym was my mother's way of reducing the psychological exposure involved in writing, and a way of reducing any embarrassment to her family from people saying that they had heard her on the radio, and why wasn't she still in the convent? And it was also a passive-aggressive way of marking her own territory. By now her own life story was one of her very few possessions; she created Shivaun Cunningham as a way of having first claim to it. She owed nothing to anyone, not even her name. The day of the reading was the most exciting of her life.

· 2 ·

JULIE WAS, for the first time in years, genuinely happy. Her letters
burn with a sense of possibility and new life. And Bill was happy,
too. He loved Hamburg, where "the view down towards the
city from the nearer bridge on a cold crisp night with a cold horrid little
wind ruffling the water, and the brilliantly sharp neon signs, makes me
glad to be alive—it's so hard, cold, clear, and sharp." He loved the lakes
and the lights and the scale and the Europeanness of it. He and Julie, who
had both known hard times, felt that their lives were moving into a happier phase and that each was a part of this. Bill invited her to Hamburg for
Christmas. He would not be on holiday for the whole time—he was on
duty at the Bank—but they would have a chance to spend more time together than anytime previously.

For Julie, though, this presented a big problem. To understand what
she did next we have to take stock of her life so far. She had already suffered two devastating setbacks, one in the reaction of her parents when
she left the convent for the first time, and the other in the death of
Nicholas Royle, whom she had loved and intended to marry. She had had
another crushing disappointment a little over a year before, when her en-

gagement with Tom Aitkins was abruptly broken off. She had spent fifteen years in convents, and was frightened that it was far too late to begin living her own life. She was convinced that the crucial factor in the breakup of her engagement with Aitkins was her age; that, she felt, was why his mother had been able to make him end the relationship. Her own equivocations and the wasted years in the convent had cost her the remains of her youth, and her last chance to have children. She was hitting forty—which, in 1960, meant a statistically tiny chance of having children. And then she met Bill. He was, in most respects, perfect. But he was explicit about wanting a big family.

The invention or creation or simply the use of "Shivaun Cunningham" was, I think, indispensable to what she did next. To register the full import, you have to understand that Julia was the kind of person who felt nervousness verging on a panic attack when she parked on a single yellow line out of hours, or returned a library book a day late. Her anxiety about obeying rules and laws was flat-out neurotic. (And for anyone with an even slightly more relaxed, or indeed sane, point of view, maddening.) She paid bills on the day she got them, answered all letters of a business or financial nature immediately, worried about whether she was on the electoral register and where she had written down her National Health Service number, never got a parking ticket, hyperventilated if she was spoken to by a Customs official or a policeman, was nervous about asking the doctor for anything at all. Neurotics are often very tough—they have to be, to withstand the blast furnaces of their own neuroses. By the same token, tough people are often highly neurotic. Julia had both sides of that circle in full. She was also very comfortable occupying the moral high ground—as you might expect in a person who had spent fifteen years in religious orders. She liked being in the right. The letter reproving Bill for being dumped by his French girlfriend shows that; it is extraordinary to think of the gap between that high-minded, sermonizing, not-far-from-priggish tone and the lie Julie was about to tell.

But she was falling in love with Bill, or preparing to. And he wanted a big family. And she was going to be forty before she even went to Hamburg for Christmas. If he knew her age, he would not marry her. That's what she told herself, and she was right, I think. Bill did want children, and having waited already till his mid-thirties to marry, he could be prepared to wait a bit longer. If she told him her true age, she would lose her chance of marrying him; she would be the ex-nun who had left everything too late.

So she did something so simple, radical, and criminal that I, even with the documentary evidence in front of me, can hardly believe it. What Julia did was in its way brilliant: she sent off to the Irish Record Office and asked for a copy of the birth certificate of her sister Dilly, who was a full nine years younger than she. Then she used that birth certificate to apply for British citizenship, and lo and behold, Julia Immaculata Gunnigan became Bridget Teresa Gunnigan and, after her marriage, Bridget Teresa Lanchester. B. T. Lanchester, or sometimes, when she could get away with it, B. T. J. Lanchester. That was the name on all her official paperwork for the rest of her life. It is the name on my birth certificate—so the person named there as my mother is in reality my aunt Dilly. In short, Julia simply stole her sister's identity, and kept it for the rest of her life.

You may wonder why she went to such lengths, why she wasn't content to lie, or rather, to lie in person only, rather than lie in person and legally and in her official paperwork. The answer is that she knew she would be found out. Julia had already disappeared once, when she ran away from home and was out of contact with her family for years in her youth. She knew what it took, and how important official pieces of paper and official identities are. She also had experience of international travel and official formalities; India is a world center of bureaucracy and form-filling and paperwork. She knew there was no chance of indefinitely keeping the real date secret from her husband. She was right, too, since even the basic process of registering to get married in Hamburg involved giving details of her parentage and birth—so the purely spoken lie wouldn't have lasted through the engagement. She was right to go whole hog.

There were, I believe, three reasons why, once she had the idea of legally becoming somebody else, it was Dilly's identity that she stole. There were six other sisters to choose from, after all. The first reason was age: Dilly was not just younger but significantly younger, almost a whole decade. If she clipped off only a year or two it would still have left her in her upper thirties, on the high side for starting a family in 1960. By pretending to be Dilly she was pretending to be thirty-one, with every chance of having not just one child but several children, per Bill's expressed wishes.

The second reason was Dilly's real name. If Julia and Bill married, however much distance she managed to keep between herself and the family back in Ireland, there would inevitably be talk about her relatives. Until recently she had been living with Peggie, who had given her sympathy and succor and support in every practical way after she had left the convent in India. However she tried, Julia couldn't hide from the other Gunnigans forever—which meant that there would be talk, which meant that the other sisters were likely to be mentioned in Bill's hearing. But Dilly was always referred to as Dilly, then and to this day, and never by her given name of Bridget; and you would have to know vernacular Irish English quite well to know that Dilly was a diminutive of Bridget. Bill could hear Dilly mentioned without ever wondering why the Gunnigans had two daughters with the same Christian name.

And the final reason for choosing Dilly may have had to do with Julia's analysis of her sister's character. Dilly was already married and had started a family: she was based in Claremorris, near her birthplace in the unchic part of Mayo, and was fully involved in her life there. She almost certainly—Julia calculated—did not have a passport; she had no reason to have one. Furthermore, she was even less likely to apply for a British passport—there was essentially no prospect that she would ever do that. If Julia could obtain the birth certificate, she would be in the clear. She did, and she was.

Once the birth certificate arrived, Julia applied for a British passport under her sister's stolen identity of Bridget Teresa Gunnigan. It came through in December 1960, and from then on, that was who she legally was. Julia Immaculata Gunnigan disappears from the paper trail, never to be seen again. It was Bridget Teresa Gunnigan who went to stay with Bill in Hamburg over Christmas.

The visit went well. Afterward Julie would joke that Bill, who had

Christmas 1960. You sense that this is not people's first drink.

grown accustomed to servants in the East, realized how useful it would be to have a woman around the place. But there was obviously much more to it than that, and it was only a matter of a few months and one more visit before the inevitable happened. Bill proposed marriage, and Julie accepted, on May 27, 1961. Lannie, now retired and living at East Looe in Cornwall, sent a congratulatory telegram. The engagement ring drew favorable comments from Julie's students in London, as she wrote to Bill:

'Cor, that aint half a sparkler, Ma'am,' and 'Thinkin' of floggin' it, Ma'am, that'd get you some lolly,' and then 'Are we havin' you until the end of term?' The staff, when they saw it, said more to the same effect, and also remarked that a ring like it had never appeared in the school before. Liz Wagenmaker said that she thought the extra light in the staff room this morning was shining from my face.

They had to attend to the practical arrangements for the wedding, which involved Julie's sending Bill her details of birth and passport and so on.

7 June 1961

Dearest Bill,

Thank you very much for your letter received last night when I got back from school and the dentist. I don't know what to say about the cheque you sent me—for three hundred pounds—£300!! You are far too generous; it makes me quite ill when I think of all the money you have spent on me. Thank you very much—I can't thank you enough, you are far too good. I did a little bit of shopping last week and now I am planning some more as you can imagine. I am determined to get as good value in goods and enjoyment out of it as possible, but I'll tell you more about that later.

My baptismal name is BRIDGET TERESA (without the 'H') JULIA but on my *birth* certificate, as distinct from my baptismal certificate my name is given as BRIDGET TERESA (without the JULIA) and BRIDGET TERESA (in that order and that spelling) is the name on my British passport No. 581537 dated Foreign Office 2 December 1960. The story goes that when my birth was registered either my father or the local registrar were drunk (or both were) and they omitted my third name. I prefer to use the three, especially as I am called Julie, but when I asked them at Petty France (the Passport Office) they said they use the name on the Birth Certificate only. I am a British Subject as I applied for registration as one when I got the passport and I have a certificate from the Home Office to that effect. I will fish it out and send it to you, though I may not have time to do it this evening as I have to go to the dentist again today.

Thank you once again for all your generosity, darling. I hope you are not going short yourself on my account. I will write again soon. Much love and God bless you.

Julie xxx

It's artfully done. You wouldn't spot the lie in that letter unless you already knew it was there—though there is the tiniest clue, the merest tip of the hand, in the locution "the story goes that . . ."

The thing that shocks me about that letter is the date. She had taken out the false identity in December 1960. From that moment on, she must have known or suspected that something like this was coming. She made a plan, and it came to fruition seven months later. So all during the process of going to stay with Bill, falling in love, writing and traveling back and forth and all the other things they no doubt did, her scheme was working itself out. As their relationship moved into a new level of intimacy, she began a new level of planned and meticulous deceit. She of all people had the strongest imaginable views on the subject of lying and liars; yet here she was, building her entire future on a lie.

George William Lanchester, known as Bill, and Bridget Teresa Gunnigan, known as Julie, were married on August 25, 1961. The wedding party was given by "Daddy" Soul, he who had carried a revolver in Mukden in

the wild 1930s. The couple went on a long weekend to the beaches of Denmark; the real honeymoon was to be in Italy in the autumn, zooming around in Bill's Porsche. When that holiday came, though, there was to be a complicating factor, because the low-slung sports car and the twisty roads combined to worsen the acute morning sickness from which Julie was suffering, caused by me.

POSTCOLONIAL BOY

❖

· I ·

I AM THE HAPPY ENDING. That is a big part of what is strange for me about the story of my mother's early life. I am the symbol of her lucky escape, the thing that prevented her life from being a cautionary tale about an "ex-nun." I am the reason everything turned out all right. Except, of course, nobody's life feels like the happy ending to somebody else's. We have our own lives to lead, and our own messes and unhappinesses to make, and our own happinesses, too. The convention in comedy whereby a wedding signals a happy ending is no more than that, a convention; if you haven't realized that by the time you're an adult, you're in for some surprises. So I am not the happy ending to my mother's story. Nor was my mother's story ended when I was born. That's the first thing to say.

Another warning: As I turn from the part of the story I know through research and other people's recollections and what other people have told me (or didn't tell me) to the part I know firsthand, I have to record my sudden feeling of how complicated it is to speak about deeds and thoughts and feelings and motives. We talk so blithely when we talk about other people, of somebody doing X because of Y: she went to

university because she wanted to get a good job, she was attracted to him because of his looks, they moved to the city to look for work. When we think about our own motives, though, it becomes dramatically more difficult to say anything completely accurate about why we have done what we have. I would struggle to give a full account of why I am doing what I am doing at this very instant, sitting here at my desk writing this book. I know that I feel I have to do it, but beyond that I'm in a sense speculating—and that's speculating about myself, and about what I'm doing right now. Ask me why I did what I did a year ago and my answer would in all honesty be equally vague, though the false perception of hindsight might make me say something much more confident- and decisive-sounding. The only honest answer would be some blend close enough to a simple *I don't know.*

So how can I know why people do what they do, and why my mother

in particular did what she did? English common law embraces a maxi
once laid down by a judge about the question of motive: The state of a
man's mind is as much a fact as the state of his digestion. That is a principle that any legal system must embrace, in order to determine whether
my shove on your shoulder (the one that caused you to slip and crack
your head and suffer irreversible brain damage and die) was a slightly too
rough gesture or a successful attempt at homicide. The state of intent,
not the outcome, is usually the gauge of a crime. It's fair enough that
courts should take such a robust view of motive—but at the same time
this is a falsehood, a convenient fiction. The state of a man's mind, most
of the time, is not a fact. It is not knowable, not even to the man himself,
not in any of the most important ways. After having spoken so confi-
dently about other people's motives and intentions, and before going on
to talk about my own, I wanted to record this double caveat: that our
motives aren't knowable, and our selves are not fixed. And now, since you
can't actually write or think or tell stories about yourself without ignoring these truths, back I go to writing as if neither of those propositions
were the case.

B Y THE TIME I was three years old, I'd lived at ten different addresses in six different countries. The Bank was a good employer in some respects (pay, security) and a merciless one in others. When it came to posting a small family with a young child around different bits of the Far East, the company showed no pity. Most of the time I spent in Hamburg I spent inside my mother's womb, because we left when I was six weeks old. Our address in the city was—I can hear my mother saying the words—*"Sehrigstrasse achtunddreissig,"* Sehrigstrasse 38. The flat was a tram ride or lengthy walk from my father's work. Just downstairs was a bar, the Cosmo Club, which had proved especially handy during Bill's bachelor days, as it served good food, especially a Holstein schnitzel famous for being so big that nobody ever finished an order. My mother always told me that if I was every truly, desperately hungry and in Germany, the thing to order was a Holstein schnitzel.

My parents were happy in Hamburg. Bill would have liked to wait before Julie got pregnant, but she had a different agenda, to have a baby as quickly as possible; she was pregnant at the time of the wedding. This means that they kept the date of the wedding a secret, never spoken. I learned it by looking at their marriage certificate. In Hamburg my parents had only two sources of worry—a low, indeed worryingly low, number for people who depended on worry. One was the fact that Bill was likely to be posted back out to the Far East at fairly short notice. The Hamburg job was specifically for a single man. That was no big deal; Bill preferred the East, where he had been brought up, and his main reason for wanting to be in Europe had been to meet English girlfriends. Now he had an Irish wife, so that wasn't an issue. Still, the business of not knowing where you would be living in six months' time, which had been a source of excitement all his adult life—and was no doubt rooted in his itinerant childhood— was more complicated now that he had a wife and son "in tow." The other source of worry was my mother's acute morning sickness. She had never felt anything like the all-day, all-night, all-terrain nausea I was giving her. There was a wonder drug on the market to treat morning sickness, and she went to her G.P. to ask for it. He said that he didn't trust wonder drugs, and that instead of taking this thalidomide she would be better off drinking a half-liter of beer.

I was born in the Johannes Allee Klinik in Hamburg on February 25, 1962. The hospital avoided anesthesia during childbirth on principle. When my mother told me that, it was in the context of explaining how

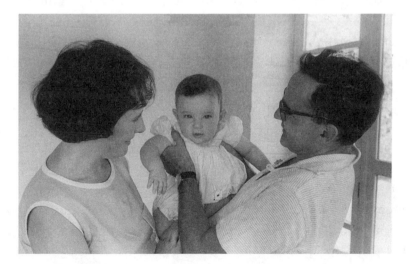

awful childbirth was, and how God had had to make sex something truly remarkable in order to make up for the terrible experience of bearing children. It can't have helped that the doctor and midwife spoke no English and my mother spoke almost no German; it was, as she wrote years later, "quite an experience." As I was lifted in front of my mother, she reached forward and kissed me. The Lutheran nuns who staffed the hospital tutted and snatched me away and told her that kissing a newborn baby was unhygienic.

Julie did not tell anybody then that I had been born. "She told us of your arrival in May," Peggie remembers. In other words, my mother postdated my birth to nine months after the wedding. "She didn't tell us your real birthday until years and years afterwards. When we got the telegram saying you had been born I went out and arranged for a huge bunch of flowers to be sent through Interflora. What must have been thought of the silly card I sent her. . . . I suppose she must have told Bill. But that was quite unnecessary. Vincent and I had lived together—it was literally easier for us to share accommodation for a few months before we got married, and we just couldn't see a reason why not. People talk about the fifties and how puritanical everybody was. Not true. Lots and lots of people did it, it was hardly worth talking about. We wouldn't have been the least bit surprised, if Julia had just told me. But she obviously thought she couldn't. She certainly couldn't have said it to my mother, or to other members of the family, but she could have said it to me."

Some of this reticence had to do with embarrassment: you might expect a woman who had spent fifteen years in convents to be a little shy about sex, and so Julie was. Having sex before marriage was, in her religion, a mortal sin—one that would cause her to be damned for eternity, unless and until she had it absolved. And it's true, too, that some of the family would have been deeply shocked to know that I had been conceived outside marriage. But those are not the only reasons for this silence about my exact birth date. This was also the beginning of the process by which Julie put distance between herself and the people who might be in a position to give away her secret, starting with Peggie. This was something that was going to cause a great deal of pain.

Bill's new posting was Hong Kong—deeply familiar to him, wholly exotic to Julie. He sold his proudest possession, a secondhand Porsche 911, which he had been driving for the past year. It was a relief to be selling it because he was moving, and not because he was now a father and family man; that would have been too much of an existential shock. At the very last moment of packing frenzy, Julie was jamming stuff into boxes as the moving men looked on, loaded them up, and took them away. I was in my cot in the bedroom, crying. The movers disapproved of the fact that my mother was dealing with them rather than with me. *"Rabenmutter,"* they said, or rather, muttered. "Raven mother"—a lavishly rich insult, and one that outraged and amused Julie so much that she never forgot it.

Our first address in Hong Kong, when we arrived in May 1962, was in a small block of flats called Fung Shui, a building where the Bank housed young families and where we were to live on three separate occasions over the next few years. I remember it from our subsequent times there, in the mid-1960s: a low, squat block of apartments with a wonderful view out over the harbor and across to Kowloon, on the all-too-infrequent

Fung Shui.

days when it wasn't misty. There were always families in Fung Shui, and therefore a rotating cast of children with whom to play, even though Bank postings and maneuverings were such that people seemed never to stay around for very long, not even from a child's perspective. There was a patch of grass—rough, broad-leaved tropical grass—that tended to wear thin under the abrading of tiny feet, and a kitchen garden, screened off from the road by bamboo and supervised by the *fah wong* (gardener), a fierce man who always worked in black pajamas, like a member of the Vietcong. I was frightened of him—a fear based on guilt, because I used to raid his garden to dig up and eat the carrots. I was obsessed with these carrots; I used to stake out the garden and wait for times when the *fah wong* was absent, then go on stealing expeditions. I learned by trial and error which carrot tops had substantial carrots underneath, and which were only tiddlers, best left to grow bigger. They were incredibly sweet—that was why I liked them. I would pull them up, wipe them with my hand and then on my shorts, and eat them. I knew that this was both naughty and reckless, but I had such a craving for the *fah wong*'s carrots that I didn't care. I was never caught, but the *fah wong* knew who it was, and gave me the death ray whenever we met, which was as seldom as I could manage.

That first stay in Fung Shui lasted for about eight months, and in the course of it we lived through the legendary Typhoon Wanda of 1962. Wanda was up there with the biggies, like the typhoon that Lannie remembered from the 1930s. That one had taken a ship with all its anchors set and its engines going full throttle and dragged it backward down the harbor at thirty knots. In Fung Shui, our flat had sixteen windows, and Wanda broke thirteen of them; she also sucked out one of the air conditioners. This was old typhoon lore: if you lost one window, the resulting change in air pressure would mean that you lost many more; if you lost an air conditioner, it was always sucked out of the room, never blown in.

The center of that storm passed directly over Fung Shui. I experienced this myself firsthand twice more, with Typhoon Rose in 1971 and Typhoon Hope in 1979. Typhoon Hope in particular terrified me, not least because my father, who enjoyed and wasn't scared of typhoons, opened the French windows and went into the garden to take the air (this at two

Photograph taken by Julia during Typhoon Hope.

a.m.). I begged him to come in, but he said that it was safe and that we would hear the winds returning before it hit us. I'm assured by experts that this is utterly untrue. He walked around for a quarter of an hour or so and then came back in, and the winds came back a couple of minutes after that. He told me that the second half of a typhoon, after the eye passes, is not as bad as the first—and this, too, isn't true, since the wind now faces a different direction and thus its effects can be as bad or worse. But his reassurance at the time helped me get back to sleep. For Wanda, he sat up enjoying it and mopping up, my mother sat up worrying, and I slept.

Our next posting was to Rangoon. It was a promotion for Bill, who looked forward to it for that reason, but it was also something of a hardship post. The military junta that now ruled the country was cracking down on all forms of civil and economic liberty and was trying to sequester foreign assets. Bill predicted trouble, and was not disappointed. We arrived in Burma in January 1963. On February 23 the junta announced that it was nationalizing the assets of foreign banks. We were put under house arrest; my father was allowed to leave home only to go to work and take part in winding up the Bank's business in Burma. My mother began to prepare for the return to Hong Kong. Our camera was confiscated—it is the only place we lived of which I don't have a single photograph. That's a pity, for several reasons, one of them being that the Bank house where we lived on University Avenue was near the home of the family of the late General Kyi, assassinated hero of the war and the struggle for independence. His daughter Aung San Suu Kyi, who would have been not yet eighteen while we were in Rangoon, is still living there to this day, under house arrest, kept alive by the international attention that brought her the Nobel Peace Prize.

Part of the culture of the time and place was that expatriates were expected to employ servants. It would have been bad form not to; it would have been denying a source of employment. In Rangoon, this reached an all-time high of extravagance: in addition to my amah—nanny—Ah Luk, who had begun working for us in Fung Shui, we had nine servants, none of whom worked directly for us but who were instead employed by the Bank. There were a cook, a butler, a bearer, a maid, a cleaner, a driver, a gardener, and I can't remember the others. I'm not sure what a bearer did, but it was a job in the old colonial East. As in a nineteenth-century Russian novel, basically the servants were in charge of the house. My mother's principal complaint about Rangoon was not about the house arrest per se but about the resulting boredom, and especially about the rigid etiquette among the household staff. To have a cup of tea involved asking the butler, who informed the cook, who boiled the water and got the tea from the cupboard, whose sole key was in the possession of the bearer. This was a tradition of inviolable antiquity. It meant that on three afternoons a week—the days any one of the men had off—Julie couldn't get a cup of tea, since one or another link in the chain of command was missing, and the division of labor was so rigid none of them was allowed to do any of the others' work. Julie longed for Sundays, when the bearer lent her the key and the other two men were away and she could have a cup of tea whenever she liked. This was the big story about our months under house arrest under the military junta in Burma: the drama and difficulty of getting a cup of tea.

We returned to Hong Kong. Several months later, in October 1963, we sailed to England for a holiday. While we were there, the news came through that my father would be posted back to Calcutta. This fact—which took a while to come through clearly, after the usual rumors, prevarications, and counterorders, all of which always reminded Bill of life in the army—gave him a heavy heart. He had not loved his previous time in Calcutta and he was worried about my health, but not as worried as I would be if I were moving there with a baby who was not yet two.

Julia had this photograph taken for a visa while in Rangoon.

("Children under four seem to do well here, despite all the illnesses they get"—that's from a letter Bill wrote at the time.) His trepidation, though, was nothing compared with the effect this news had on Julie, who was thrown into full panic. She was desperately worried that she would meet somebody who had known her as Sister Eucharia. She had been a well-known figure in the not enormous Catholic world of India; she couldn't get out of her mind the notion of some humiliating encounter that would expose her as who she had been.

Bill saw Julie's attitude to Calcutta at first as an aversion, a dislike, and then realized it was approaching a phobia. He began to see that his wife was different—more neurotic and more strong-willed—than he had thought. So he suggested a compromise. He would go to Calcutta and ready the house for Julie and me, and settle in at work, and then we would come out a month or two later. In the meantime my mother and I would stay with Lannie, who for the moment was living closer to her birthplace and her family, in Walkden, near Manchester. Julie had been friends with Lannie before she knew Bill, so that was not a problem. Bill was not especially happy with the arrangement, but he accepted it.

Bill was busy in Calcutta, and the time passed quickly. His main work there—the reason he had been sent out at short notice—was to resolve a number of fraudulent, inadequately secured, undocumented, and interlocking loans on the Bank's books. His letter to Julia about it interests me because it is one of the few glimpses I have of Bill at work.

> Mr E is not a crook but he is, for some reason unfortunately not known to us—he won't tell us—now desperate. We wanted to have an account-ant check his books, but he refused, despite our pointing out that we couldn't help him if he wasn't willing to come clean. It has all been very interesting and very like X—it almost seems there is a pattern to this type of man, and business. The same inability to get *any* coherent logical account—details which alter, halve, double, are denied, counter-denied, repeated, accusations being made against nearly everybody, 'I'm a reli-gious man and a good boy', 'It's not my fault', 'I will be honest with you . . .' 'You are accusing me of dishonesty', 'Just give me a little money

to keep going and I will have the whole thing straightened out in two months' etc, etc. It is fortunate that one needs to be so clever, and to have a fantastic memory, to be a good liar. There are few people who can talk and answer questions for two to four hours and lie successfully. It can be done of course if someone has prepared his story carefully and if there is not too much fact already known.

Jonathan Coe once wrote that "most of the things called 'ironic' in books are, in real life, painful." In that sense, there is a big irony here: Bill had no idea that it was precisely to cover up her own lie that Julie was reluctant to join him in Calcutta.

I was, apparently, happy in Walkden. In a photo of me at the seaside with my amah, Ah Luk, I certainly look happy enough. On the other hand, I hated Calcutta, and according to what I was later told, I cried more or less all day every day for the three months I was there.

On October 21, 1963, my parents and I took a boat from Calcutta to Singapore, and then flew to Brunei and my father's next posting, just off the coast of Borneo, on the island of Labuan.

· 3 ·

L ABUAN IS WHERE my own memories begin. Some of them are on
that margin between recollection and imagination where early
childhood memories live, and where it isn't always easy to distinguish between what I genuinely remember and what I'm constructing as
memory from stories and photographs and later memories projected backward. But there are some things I remember clearly and for sure. We had
a little patch of garden—not that it seemed little to me at the time—
with a kitchen garden planted in one corner, and a tree whose branches
hung down so low I could almost touch them. The house compound was
surrounded by jungle, which was overhanging and humid and damp and
in which, because of all the foliage, the light seemed to be colored green.
Visitors to the house would usually come by canoe, which was quicker
and in most weather more reliable than coming on the very bad road
from town; but when my father went to work, he always drove.

We seldom went into the jungle, but there was a path through it we
would sometimes take on weekends to head down to the beach. You
couldn't swim off the beach—I don't know why not: perhaps the currents were too dangerous—but you could walk on it, and if you went far

enough there was a burnt-out, rusted Allied landing craft left from World War II. The star attraction of the garden was a huge monitor lizard, four or five feet long, with a blue tongue; it would pad heavily across one corner of the garden most afternoons. The odd thing about the monitor was that it did not come every day, but when it did, it always did so between quarter to five and five and always followed the same route, a diagonal shortcut across one specific patch of lawn. (I say "lawn"—rough tropical grass, again, with sand underneath.) The lizard never gave any sign of noticing us, but I was warned to steer well clear of it, since the bite, although not actively poisonous, would involve contact with saliva so dirty it was the next-best thing.

Labuan was an interesting place to be, perhaps the most interesting posting my father ever had. Uniquely at that point in its history, it was a place of larger global strategic importance. Labuan lies just off Borneo, a huge island divided into two main parts. The bigger part, Kalimantan, belongs to Indonesia. The rest is a group of smaller states, two of them part of the Malay Federation, the third being Brunei. Sukarno, the president of Indonesia, had designs on the Malay part of the island. He had launched a series of incursions and provocations over the border, designed to start a war, which the huge Indonesian army would certainly win. Its opponent in this war was the British army, which, out of residual colonial feeling for the Malay states and a desire to protect the oil that had been discovered off Brunei—the same oil that was to make the country rich over the next decades—was sent out to stop the man unaffectionately known to British troops as "the mad doctor." A fifth of the British army fought in this war, which I think has the distinction of being the least well known of the British Empire's twentieth-century wars. It helped that it was never called a war, but was always referred to as "the Confrontation." The main British army headquarters for the Confrontation was on Labuan.

As a result, my father was immersed in a busy, lively, much more interesting version of a place that had previously been pretty much the ultimate colonial backwater. The island was full of soldiers and Royal Air Force people, and as a result social life was a lot more lifelike. (Part of the grimness of expatriate life in these places was captured by a piece of advice my mother once gave me: If you live in a place with a small social world, and you cook something that is a great success, and people ask you for the recipe, you must *never* give it to them. They will *always* make short-cuts and small alterations and turn it into something far inferior, which they will then [a] serve you when you go to their houses, and [b] make themselves sick of, so that when you next try to serve your superior original version they will inwardly groan, and feel sick and mutter, "Not again." Something a lot like this happens in the world of writing, when a successful book has so many imitators that it puts you off the original—but that's another story.)

Bill liked being the sole boss of the office: he felt that finally, after his thirteen basically boring years working his way up the Bank hierarchy, he was starting to get somewhere. It was nice to be reunited with his family, too, after the strange bachelor flashback of Calcutta. There's a bit of an irony here, that Bill should have spent all those years in Calcutta, one of the world's most overwhelming cities, and ended up knowing twenty or thirty people, and have come to a place with a permanent population of a few hundred, and then suddenly find himself hanging out with Gurkhas (some of his favorite people for the rest of his life), and making a close and lifelong friend of Rob Butler, a laconic Australian who looked after the Allied war graves. Once, while dropping in to visit Butler at the cemetery—which, though it may sound odd, was so beautifully kept and peaceful and gardenlike, in the midst of the jungle ecosystem, that we used to go there for walks—Bill spotted another of his new best friends, a young American, walking around the graves in deep conversation with a Malay man, and visibly embarrassed to be seen. Bill realized that the American was a spy, probably a CIA agent. It all added to life's rich tapestry.

Labuan's energetic social life meant much more entertaining, which Julie enjoyed. She tried not to show how nervous she felt as a hostess. These parties were a severe strain on Ah Lee, the cook. He was under normal circumstances very good at his work, but he had started smoking marijuana while in the Merchant Navy—in those days, my father told me later, the Merchant Navy and jazz musicians were the two sets of people who dabbled in dope-smoking. Ah Lee would resort to marijuana while under stress, with the result that immediately before a party, he would get so stoned he could no longer speak and could communicate only by leaning against a wall and pointing.

The strain and strangeness for Julie were even greater. A peasant farmer's daughter from Mayo turned nun turned schoolteacher turned housewife had no training in the business of giving cocktail parties—indeed, she had never drunk a cocktail in her life until Bill took her to dinner at Sheekey's in London in 1960. (She had a dry martini, my father's preferred drink—a rather heavy initiation, I can't help thinking. Dad drank it made with Gordon's gin and Noilly Prat vermouth, six to one, shaken not stirred, and with an olive. He said you could tell a well-made martini because you felt the effect in your shoulder blades.) The business of being a wife and hostess, which seems a strange thing to want to be for a woman who used to run a school, touched a deep sense in Julia of having escaped, gotten away, become someone else. As for what she did with the rest of her time, I have no idea. She had no job, and an amah—still Ah Luk—to tend to me. How she described this change to herself I don't know.

I would like to be able to say more about Ah Luk, but the truth is I "remember" her only from stories and anecdotes. I was apparently very fond of her, and she of me. She had a mouthful of gold teeth—photographs confirm this—and was gentle and kind, with a sly sense of humor. Often she and I would walk down the street, she pushing my push-chair, or hand in hand, while my parents followed. Ah Luk didn't speak much English, and she and I communicated in a kind of English-Cantonese pidgin. One upshot of this was that until I was about eight I could make myself understood in rudimentary Cantonese. I would translate for my mother at the markets, that sort of thing—and because Cantonese is a good language for swearing, and no doubt also because of Ah Luk's sense of humor, I spoke the Cantonese equivalent of barrow-boy Cockney. When I asked the price of something on my mother's behalf, I would say something like, "Oy, cock, how much is this fucking fish?" The stallhold-

ers would laugh and tell me the price. I would then tell my mother. My mother would then ask why they were laughing, and all they would ever say was, "He one very clever piecey small boy, missy." All that was thanks to Ah Luk.

The emotional ties between amahs and their charges aren't often discussed; I suppose the children forget as they grow up, and there are no written accounts, as far as I know, from the amahs' point of view. It's a pity. In colonial days—until the late fifties or early sixties—families who were returning to England for good could buy a special group ticket that featured one-way first-class travel for them, with a free third-class roundtrip ticket for the amah thrown in. It's a sad image, those amahs on their solitary journey home.

As for me, I was in love. The gardener's daughter, Ming Jah, was the object of my affection. In my memory she was infinitely older than I,

glamorously near teenage, though looking at a picture of her now, I see that she can have been only about six or seven. We spent every possible moment together—which I suspect means every moment she could bear until she got bored of having a devoted almost-three-year-old following her around. Ming Jah spoke no English, so we communicated in Malay. This eventually became a problem, and my parents stepped in to separate us, because after a few months my Malay had overtaken my English, and my mother's pedagogical worries kicked in. Before that I was as happy as an unsupervised almost-three-year-old can be. Ming Jah and I spent most of our time playing in the garden and underneath the house, which was, in an allusion to the local style, raised on stilts. It had a strange, humid, musty smell, one I have since occasionally caught when visiting a tropical greenhouse—a hot, wet, green smell. When it rained in Labuan, it did so in huge, overwhelming vertical cascades; there was no such thing as being out in the rain, it just wasn't possible. When the rain cleared, every-thing would be impassably muddy.

We were all, in our different ways, happy in Labaun. But we were there for only eighteen months—well, I say "only," but this was in fact the longest we as a family had been anywhere. There is a slightly poignant note from my father, requesting a brochure from a boarding school in England: the school, Gresham's, was the one I ended up attending, seven years later. Dad asks the school to send the prospectus in care of the Bank in Hong Kong; he says he can't give a return address because he doesn't know where he will be living.

We were back in Fung Shui not long after my third birthday. From this time on—spring 1965—we lived in Hong Kong until my father took early retirement in late 1979. If I were a character in a novel, a bildungsroman, it would be probably around now that the penny drops in the reader's mind that this is a story about a particular or peculiar kind of post-colonial childhood. I am a postcolonial boy. I say "peculiar kind" because I was postcolonial not in the sense that I had a copy of Fanon's Les damnés de la terre perpetually sticking out of my back pocket, or that I grew up a Bengali intellectual reading Dickens in Calcutta, or that I had to speak the language of the oppressor in preference to my own tongue; I was postcolonial in the sense that we kept getting kicked out of colonies that didn't want to be colonies anymore. Burma was in a convulsive moment of postcolonial revolutionary coup (one, incidentally, that has proved disastrous for all its citizens, making it one of the few places on earth that one can unequivocally say was better off under colonial rule). India was nationalizing banks and expelling foreign capital; Labuan was in the grip of a war with a would-be new imperialist, fought by the armed forces of the old empire; Hong Kong was in the last decades of the winding-down former empire, the clock ticking to 1997 and handover/reunification. The character based on me would be a comic figure, one who has only to step through Customs on arrival in a country for the local population to rise and revolt against the colonial masters. But it didn't feel like that at the time—though it did a little to Bill, I think, who grew up when the British Empire was still a reality and who lived to see it disappear. I don't think that he felt nostalgic for it, but perhaps there was a way in which the contraction of British power matched the contraction in possibility he came to feel in his own life: his sense of his place in the world shrank as Britain's place in the world also shrank. A process can be inevitable, and right, and necessary, without being any the less painful for all that.

Another point to make about the last days of empire, from the perspective of a postcolonial boy, is that it is not as if the colonial bubble were something one could physically feel as a protective membrane. There may have been a time when Britons abroad felt like masters of the universe, automatically more important than the natives wherever they might be—a little as some Americans do today perhaps, and as the citizens of any empire are likely to do in their prime imperial moment. By the 1960s, when I was growing up, this was over for the British. The residual effects had to do not with the psychological apparatus of empire, but with the fact that you could go to these exotic places and make your living and have your life, all in English, and then go away, and somehow the place would not have entered into you, nor you into the place. Easy come, easy go. This was very little different from the way in which the international upper middle class travel around the world for work today, educating their children in the language of their home country and living insulated from most of the realities of wherever they are, so that a job working for a bank or advertising agency or—whisper it—aid agency or whatever differs very little whether you're in São Paulo or St. Petersburg or Sydney or Bombay. The furniture and trappings and weather are a bit different, but in truth not so much so that the essential reality is much changed. This capitalist bubble seems to me to be at least as effectively insulating as the old colonial one, with which it overlapped and with which it has a great deal in common. My father grew up in the colonial bubble, which was punctured by war, and his sense of safety never returned. I suppose the bubble in which I grew up was a hybrid, postcolonial-to-capitalist bubble; the new bubble, a capitalist one, has a thicker membrane than any of its predecessors, I think, and is showing no signs of going away anytime soon.

I would be lying if I claimed to have noticed any of this at the time, or

at any time before I sat down to think about it as an adult. What I did notice, though, was that my childhood left me with a kind of reverse exoticism. When I came "home" to England, which hadn't been home for
either of my parents, I couldn't help noticing how alien everything
seemed. Everyone was so white, for one thing, and so restrained. It was
cold—though I quickly grew to like the cold and to prefer it to the permanent mugginess of Hong Kong. But much more than any of these
things, it was cultural. Today this is easier—children from Shanghai to
Shreveport know about Nike and Nintendo and can quote from favorite
episodes of *The Simpsons*. That wasn't true when I was growing up, and I remember spending a great deal of intellectual effort on trying to figure out
what people were talking about and/or pretending that I already knew.
What was the Tube, and in what respects did it differ from the Underground? Was it always underground or were there bits of it that weren't,
and were they the bits that were called the Tube, and what was *The Magic
Roundabout*? What was a jumper, and what was the difference between it and
a sweater or a pullover, and was there one name it was all right to use but
another that would be babyish or stupid? This didn't happen all day, every
day, but it happened a lot, and the feeling of not knowing what people

were talking about gradually wore down to a slight but chronic cultural dislocation. Someone once said that for V. S. Naipaul's characters the most difficult question was always "Where are you from?" I felt—feel—that. There was a constant sense that I was, to use the period phrase, "picking up fag ends"—overhearing scraps of other people's talk, or understanding scraps of it, and trying to put these together to make a coherent story. Trying to work out what they meant, with the emphasis on work. All children do this, to an extent, as they try to crack the codes of adult talk and adult lives. I'm not claiming to be unique, just that I did a lot of it. To sum up, I was an only child who had an unusually isolated childhood, a geographically fragmented early childhood, and who grew up with a powerful sense that everybody had secrets that could not be asked about directly, and that I needed to work out by myself. The thousands of hours I spent playing on my own, with a powerful motive for fantasy and imagination and working things out through hypothesis, and a linguistic dislocation so that English was my real home, much more than any specific place—these were a big part of what made me become a writer.

In about 1970 we moved to a three-story block of flats called Highclere, in Middle Gap Road, looking out over the back of the island and the harbor of Aberdeen toward the island of Lamma. It was, and is, a lovely

view. At first we were on the third floor; after a few years we moved down a floor, then finally we lived in a ground-floor flat, which was blessed with a tiny but very welcome garden. We had an Irish terrier, Barney, whom my parents ordered from Harrods. He was delivered in a crate to Kai Tak airport, and when we opened the crate he came bounding out wagging his tail, exactly unlike a young dog who's just spent twenty-four hours in a wooden box in the hold of a 707.

I suppose all children are self-absorbed; all lucky children, anyway. In my case this was compounded by the isolation we lived in, the post-colonial bubble we had carried around us to Burma and Labuan and Hong Kong. My parents were friendly, gregarious, chatty, and profoundly isolated people; they had social friends but not intimate ones, and our contacts with other families tended to be special-occasion affairs, Sunday lunches or days out on one or another borrowed boat. We had a boat of our own for a time, a tiny launch called *Carousel* with a rattling engine and a small, smelly downstairs cabin. She was great fun, until she sank in a typhoon in 1974. One of my favorite adventures in childhood was the time we stayed out overnight and I spent the night on the roof, watching shooting stars with my best school friend, Graham Semple. His father was in the army—I was at an army school, because of some theory of my mother's that ignored the fact that, since everyone moved on from the school to new parental postings after a year or two, it meant I had no permanent friends. Graham Semple's dad worked at the listening station that spied on Communist China—something I wasn't supposed to know, but did because the dads of most of my friends worked there. They were the only people who weren't transferred from Hong Kong at the end of every tour; and they were all recognizable from the fact that they spoke Mandarin, not much use in Cantonese-speaking Hong Kong, but essential for eavesdropping on the People's Liberation Army.

Lannie would come out and stay with us at Christmas or Easter. We would visit the graves at Stanley—officially, John Fraser's grave, but also, I now know, that of her lover Leslie Holmes. Two or three times on these visits she came down with malaria, a flareup of the illness she had picked up in Hong Kong back in the 1930s. The malaria meant a couple of days in bed, waiting for the fever to break. She used to like for me to be in the room, so I would sit in a chair by the bed, reading while she dozed and occasionally chatted; sometimes she would think I was my father, and would call me Billy. Sometimes she would slip back in time and talk about wanting to go out to Lantao when she felt better. Then—usually at night—the fever would reach a peak; she would be in a delirium, her face covered with globules of sweat; and the next day she would be weak and pale but fully herself again.

In childhood one doesn't usually experience one's own life as a narrative. Things happen one after another, but it's only in special circumstances that your own childhood is experienced as a story. Big shifts in how you live will do that, and so will changes in location, and bereavements. Once we had settled in Hong Kong, I didn't have any of these things. I was keen on reading, on Tottenham Hotspur (I never saw them play, even on TV, because we didn't get English football in Hong Kong; in fact, until I was about eight I thought Tottenham Hotspur was a man, not a team), on chess (but there was no one to play except my dad, who hated it because he said it was too much like being in the office), on Barney the dog. Once a week my mother, who couldn't swim and was therefore superkeen for me to learn, took me to a swimming lesson, crossing on the Star Ferry to Kowloon and the YMCA there, and I would have an ice cream soda afterward as a treat. (Ice cream soda seems to have passed from the world, which is a pity. 7UP with a scoop of vanilla ice cream in it. Try it on a child—I've not seen it fail yet.) On Wednesdays school ended at lunchtime and I would have a friend—usually Graham Semple—home to play. Some evenings my father would go down to Deepwater Bay Golf Club to hit balls at the driving range; I would go, too, mainly to watch him. The balls would soar off into the floodlights with the hills of the bay around them in a dark amphitheater. All the while I would secretly be craving the post-golf treat: the portion of french fries served with a glass of freshly squeezed lemon juice that you sweetened yourself with sugar and then topped up with soda water. I had a variety of techniques for distracting my father at the crucial moment so that he wouldn't notice just how much sugar I was putting in.

In general, all through my childhood, I was happy; but I was also, often, afraid. Conrad once described imagination as "the enemy of men, the father of all terrors"—which is an odd thing for a novelist to write, but which does tell the truth. I was very imaginative and very good at cooking up things to fear. On our weekend boat trips I never wanted to be too far away from Hong Kong Island, and indeed preferred being at Lamma, which was actually in sight of our home, to being at Clearwater Bay or any other of the prettier but farther-flung beaches and coves. I miserably nagged my parents to go somewhere I would feel comfortable—though the fear was all in the anticipation, and I would forget it when we got to wherever we were going and there was a chance to jump off the boat into the translucent water. This fear was partly that the boat would stop working and we'd not be able to get home; on the Star Ferry, I would worry that the engines might cut out and we would be swept out to sea, or that the pilot would forget where we were supposed to be going and head for open water by mistake.

Being away from home was another problem. My first day at nursery, when I was about four, I still remember for the pure intensity of my anxiety. This was a fear not about separation per se but about distance, about the sheer length of the trip home. It would have been all of a mile and a half, perhaps even less—but perspective, by definition, plays no part in these fears. The nursery was on the Peak, and I made a terrible spectacle of myself; I remember my mother visibly not knowing what to do as she tried to get away. She was bad at soothing my fears, while my father was able to calm them as much by his presence as anything else. But Julie didn't seem to know how to bring that part of herself to bear. My first attempt at staying at a friend's house for a sleepover, when I was about eight, was another bust. His home, too, was on the Peak, and again I was terrified that it would be physically impossible to get home; the house would be washed away, or the road would be washed away, or some such thing. (I had seen the effect of floods, and had once seen this very road washed away, so I knew that things did sometimes disappear down the

Bill's photograph of the landslide.

hill.) I made a big-enough fuss for my parents to have to come and collect me. A school outing overnight to Lantao for two days' camping was another predictable disaster; after the first night in a disused army barracks, I calmed down enough not to be sent home a day early, but only just.

The fear of awayness encompassed my parents' evenings out. I would be fine until our cook, Ah Ho, left to go to bed in his quarters, as he would do around nine or ten; then, if I woke, I would be in a state of intense anxiety until my parents got home. Once or twice I rang the host of the dinner party, who would always be exaggeratedly polite and treat me like a grown-up before going to get my mother or father; they, happily half drunk, would vow to be home any minute, or claim that they were just leaving; and I would go through to the spare bedroom and listen for the sound of the Morris 1100 struggling up the short steep beginning of Middle Gap Road. There was next to no traffic at that time of night, so I would hear every car with great clarity, but could never be sure whether it was the right one until I heard it brake to turn into our driveway. I was made to feel that I was being a tremendous fusser and crybaby, a view I accepted but didn't feel I could do much about. (As a parent myself, I now think that eight is rather young to leave a child on his own, without a babysitter. *Autres temps, autres moeurs.*) As I got older, I would imagine with increasing vividness what had happened to my parents: their car had crashed or gone over the edge of the road; they were dead; I was an orphan. It was a terrible thing to imagine, the worst in the world, of course it was . . . and yet it had a tingle of thrill to it as well. How distinguished, how different I would be if my parents were dead and I was left alone. I would have to be so very, very brave. . . . People would think, Isn't he brave? . . . As James Fenton wrote in the opening line of one of my favorite modern poems, "A Staffordshire Murderer": "Every fear is a desire. Every desire is a fear."

As for what underlay these fears, some of it was obviously genetic. People have different innate levels of anxiety and experience it with different levels of intensity. Mine is on the high side, and part of that is just the luck of the genetic draw. But part of it, also, I've come to believe, has to do with my parents' way of being. Specifically, with ways in which they were not there. My father was a lovely man, but he was scared of strong feelings and tried to avoid them; he felt—he knew—that they were dangerous. And my mother had secrets that, to her, felt explosively dangerous. She was scared of things inside herself. She knew things that no one else must be allowed to know. This was the source of my feeling that there were places inside her that were off-limits, that her psychic territory was marked with "Keep Out" signs—or more, perhaps, were a kind of interior Area 51, a place whose existence was officially denied. That left me with a feeling that there were things inside my parents that were not safe; that they were not a secure repository for their own feelings, let alone for mine. I could tell that something wasn't quite right. And that left me anxious.

These anxieties were not the whole story of every day. I had a happy childhood. Most days, though, there was an anxiety somewhere, to which I stood in some relation—it was growing worse or better, leaving me alone for a moment or not. It didn't prevent me from getting on with my childhood, and it didn't make me miserable—just, often, anxious.

This nervous child, who panicked at the idea of being away from home for a night, or on a boat trip out of sight of his family home, might not sound like the ideal candidate to be sent to a boarding school eight thousand miles from his parents. But as I've said, I was a happy little boy as well as a scared one, and—since every fear is a desire—part of me absolutely pined for the idea of being away, away, as far away as possible. By the age of nine or so I was very much aware that there was a much, much bigger world than that of Hong Kong. There were places, for instance, where I could have a bicycle. A bicycle! Hong Kong, which is essentially a single steep rock permanently choked with traffic, was not a place where a child could head off on a bicycle—though I did have one, a chopper on which I would forlornly go back and forth outside the garage, and would sometimes push to the top of Middle Gap Road (it was too steep to ride up) and cycle a half-mile or so to the place where the paved road ran out. Roaming wild and free it was not. If I went to boarding school, I would have a bicycle, and—perhaps the single thing I wanted more than anything else—friends who were there all the time, not just on half-day,

Wednesday afternoons, and people to play football with whenever I wanted. Everything would be bigger. I thought these things over and announced to my parents that I wanted to go to boarding school a year early, at ten. They were surprised, even a little shocked, but they had by then no real way of talking things over with me. When I said something that made them have strong feelings, they would not respond, but would go away and think about it and come back with an answer a day or two later. So the answer came back: Yes, you can go to boarding school a year early. I would start going when I was ten.

I know that for many people the school years are a primal scene, a defining set of experiences that shape the rest of their lives. That's always struck me as a bit pathetic. Perhaps the English are particularly bad about this; I notice that although there is a lot of American popular culture, especially movies and TV programs, about high school, adult Americans don't talk about their high school years much, whereas adult Britons not infrequently do. Anyway—my school years weren't central to my life, and I'm not going to write about them as if they were. I was sent to Gresham's in North Norfolk, an academically good-enough school with a

My first holiday home from school, Christmas 1972.

strong outdoorsy, gamesy bias. I don't know whether my parents knew about that emphasis; indeed, I rather think they didn't—they told me that the school was known for teaching mathematics and science, which is what at the age of ten I thought I most wanted to study. Yet the great virtue of the place was that it was so structured, so active, and so friendly—not without its ups and downs, of course, but there were people I could call friends around, every day, all day. That was what I had most wanted, and as a result I was happy at school. There was compulsory sport four afternoons a week, semicompulsory army corps one day a week, semicompulsory because the alternative was "granny-bashing," or going to visit people at the local old-age home. I preferred corps, which involved a lot of marching, going on field expeditions, et cetera, and is the reason I have the relatively modest practical skills I have (tying knots, first aid, that sort of thing).

As for the awayness that had bothered me so much when I was younger, I didn't really feel it. I did have a couple of episodes of homesickness, which was an acknowledged risk; it was spoken of as a specific illness, like measles. The odd thing is, it felt a bit like that, too. You missed home like a physical sensation—it was a kind of ache. It could come and go at unexpected times, and sometimes did not go at all, and the children who had that form of homesickness couldn't cope with boarding school and would usually leave. That would sometimes happen with tough and abrasive boys, who turned out to be deliquescent with grief at missing their mothers. Boys who would tease, mock, and denigrate one another mercilessly on every other subject and at all times never ridiculed the homesick. I had it badly my second term—my first at the eight-thousand-mile distance from my parents, since my mother had been in Norfolk for the first term. It lasted for about two weeks, then went away and never came back.

I suppose my Far Eastern childhood was, by contemporary British standards, about twenty years out of date. Gresham's, isolated in Norfolk, was about ten years out of date, so it was a good way of gradually catching up. All through the years I was at boarding school, the reverse exoticism I've mentioned was a big factor. To an only child brought up in the tropics, nothing could have been more exotic, alien, bizarre, otherworldly than sleeping in a freezing-cold dormitory with twenty other boys. And in the eight years I was at boarding school I don't think I was lonely, not once. It helped that while it was a physically strenuous and in many respects spartan school—where punishments might involve detention on Monday at six a.m., or a three-and-a-half-mile (three bridges) run, or doing "sides" (punitive essays) on "RLP" (red-lined paper), or collecting five perfect signatures from five different boardinghouses at eight in the morning—it was also relaxed and unpressured.

For all these reasons, principal among them the sense of structure that boarding school gave, my fears were largely absent through these years. Looking back, I think I was remarkably cool about the fact my parents were all those thousands of miles away. There was one source of friction with home, though. Letters were a bone of contention, a sore point, an "issue." Boarders were supposed to write home once a week. My parents let me know they looked forward to my letters—depended on them, even. Once or twice, when I failed to write, they shopped me to my housemaster and I got in bad trouble (aged about eleven) and semi-bad trouble (aged about fifteen). To me, this was hypocrisy. Since they could, at all that distance, with letters taking a week to arrive, have no idea how

Easter 1976, taken by me with a self-timer.

I actually was at any given moment, why make a fuss about it? If they minded that much about my state at any given moment, they shouldn't have sent me to boarding school—that was my view. My mother tried to emotionally blackmail me by telling me about my father's failure to write to his parents during their incarceration in Stanley. I felt sorry for my dad, but didn't feel the cases were at all similar. I wrote when I felt moved to do so, and when I didn't, I didn't. They had put me out of sight, so I put them out of mind.

I have claimed that I was calm about being so far from home. At least, I was calm about being there. Getting there, actually having to travel those eight thousand miles, was different. I dreaded, deeply and viscerally dreaded, the flights to and from Hong Kong, a trip I made two times a year—out and back for Christmas, out and back for Easter. (In summer my parents came to England for their annual leave.) The flights were horrific. In those days—1972 to 1980—terrorism was a risk to airlines flying through or over the Middle East, so passengers would often not be allowed to disembark from the plane. It would fly to Rome (or Zurich), Dubai (or Abu Dhabi), Delhi (usually) or Bombay, Singapore (or Kuala Lumpur), and then to Hong Kong. The 747s in those days flew a shorter haul than they do now, and the Vietnam War meant the planes were not allowed to fly on more direct routes over China and Southeast Asia. So the total flight time would be twenty-one or twenty-two hours. That's a lot for anyone; for a ten-year-old traveling on his own, it feels like a lifetime. I spent the flights not so much in a paroxysm of fear as in a suspended state of near-panic, waiting for things to go wrong, and jumping half out of my seat at any unexpected move, noise, bump, change of altitude, or engine noise, or just if the sky looked funny. Because part of the flight involved crossing over the Himalayas, and because weather-avoidance systems were less developed in those days, there would often be a patch of frightening, banging turbulence. And all the while spent waiting, waiting, holding my breath for the minutes to pass. I coped well enough at the time, apart from the paralyzing sense of dread; and in a way the fear served me well, since it displaced the emotions I felt about being so far away from home onto the business of traveling back and forth, rather than onto the fact of distance itself. But it left me with a fear of flying that is still vividly with me to this day.

My last term at Gresham's was the winter term of 1980. I was staying on a term to take my Oxbridge entrance exams, which I passed to win a place reading English at St. John's College, Oxford. That made my parents very happy. I was head boy, captain of the second fifteen at rugby, second eleven at hockey, and played for the first eleven at cricket; I had a Duke of Edinburgh silver award, a gold badge for swimming and a bronze medallion for lifesaving, a St. John's ambulance first-aid certificate, three A-Levels, two S-Levels, and eleven O-Levels. (These were, respectively, the compulsory exams taken at sixteen, the advanced and more specialized exams taken at eighteen by students who wanted to go to university, and the optional extra exams taken at eighteen by those who wanted to go to Oxbridge or otherwise show off.) I had had several crushes and near-misses with girls, but hadn't yet had a proper girlfriend. I had played the doctor in *Macbeth,* the common man in *A Man for All Seasons,* and Jack in *The Importance of Being Earnest,* all very badly. I had edited the school magazine. And I was completely, definitively illiterate about my own emotions. I was about as far out of touch with my emotions as it is humanly possible to be. I was an expert on not feeling things. Nothing at all unusual in that—a great deal of the way boys are, or were, brought up is an education in suppressing their feelings. The process begins by focusing on the manifestations of emotion and then turns inward, so that in the most successful cases it produces men who not only don't express their feelings, but don't feel them. This might sound like fairly radical psychological surgery to perform on yourself, but if you think about it, not feeling is a good solution to the problem of not being allowed to express feelings.

That, I think, is why the flights to and from Hong Kong were such a big deal—they were exercises in not feeling. The storm of emotions I must have felt at leaving home and going away—the mixture of fear and rage and sadness, of longing and distance and grief—was, for twenty-one hours at a time, simply squished down. The flights felt so nightmarish because they were sustained exercises in squashing my emotions and locking them up; I was hiding myself in a trunk, I was dismantling myself and hiding myself under the floorboards. For years I had a nightmare about having committed a murder that involved chopping up a body and hiding it. My main feeling was fear of being caught. Then one day I realized that the dream was a kind of pun: dismember, re-member. The body was me, and I had cut myself up.

So that was me at eighteen. The good news was that I was lively and curious—curious about everything, burning to know everything, hungry for knowledge and hungry to imagine and keen to the point of desperation for my life, my real life, to begin. The bad news is that I was about as cut off as possible from my own feelings as someone can be and still be sane. A letter of my mother's from the time refers to me being "more human" than before. (Not a letter to me, obviously.) That is cruel but fair; the divorce between thought and feeling was so complete that I barely counted as human.

In all probability I would not have been much inclined to feel things anyway; by temperament as well as by training, I squash things down rather than blurt them out. My father structured quite a lot of his emotional life around the avoidance of painful feelings; my mother kept many things about her life locked up and out of sight. All these things helped make me this way. And perhaps I sensed that the secrets involved were, to the people who carried them, dangerous. And perhaps there was a failure of imagination involved, too. For whatever reason, a cocktail of unconscious wishes and needs set up a limit to my curiosity about my parents, my mother in particular. I just didn't want to go there. Genetics, family dynamics, education, and my own choices had conspired to produce a young man so strongly compartmentalized that I was not conscious of having any feelings at all.

WHO KILLED SHIVAUN CUNNINGHAM?

· I ·

OF ALL THE THINGS I feel I understand better by researching my mother's life story, and thinking about it, and empathizing with it—the triple detective work I wrote of earlier—the one that has most helped me to understand my own childhood is the effect on my mother of emerging from a convent after all those years. Accounts by women who did it are unanimous that the feelings of bewilderment and numbness take many years to wear off. The two perhaps best-known accounts, by Monica Baldwin and Karen Armstrong, were written years after they left enclosed orders, and report a general sense of astonishment and numbness on emerging into the world. *Beginning the World,* Armstrong's book about life after the convent, was artificially breezy and made too light of how wrenchingly strange the experience of getting used to life in the world was. She retold her story in *The Spiral Staircase,* which is especially moving for me because it is a book my mother might have written if she had been able to express herself fully and honestly. Two of the principal emotions it reports are disorientation and sadness. My mother, who was in the convent twice as long as Armstrong, was, I think, lost and grieving and confused for many years.

Julie's life on leaving the order was such a blur of events that it may have taken her a great deal of time even to realize what she had done. I suspect that it probably took her about a decade to reconcile herself to the experience of leaving the convent. That's what other former nuns say they went through, just in terms of leaving the convent, in and of itself. Then we have to consider the specifics of what Julie experienced: not simply the leaving itself, but the flight, the drama of the clothes, the flat, finding a job, the effort of inventing a new self to take into a secular world, the huge task of learning how to act and talk and walk and dress and be, the hard-to-admit sense of her biological clock running out, the desperate urgency of earning a living, the anxiety over what to tell people about herself, the permanent need to fight off a sense of shame and failure, the experience of getting to know a man and the crushing humiliation of being rejected by him, the unformed and unregulated nature of life in the world, the feeling that she was always on the verge of drowning, the constant anxiety and sense of pressure and rush and of no backup or safety net, above all the sheer wrenching strangeness of this new life. And then meeting Bill, and coming to like him, and falling in love and conceiving a baby and getting married and being a wife and having a baby and going to live in Hamburg and Hong Kong and Rangoon and everywhere else, all now as a wife and mother and person completely different from the person she had been for most of her life. This was a huge psychic load to bear. I think that until, during, and after her marriage, Julie's main feelings were an overwhelming sense of numbness and bewilderment. I think it took years to wear off. I would not swear that it ever fully went away.

As for how this manifested itself, the first and perhaps simplest way can be addressed through a question that, when I was growing up, never crossed my mind: What did my mother do all day? It never occurred to me to think about this as a child—she was just being Mum, that was self-evidently a full-time job. Besides, once I was at boarding school, I was in an environment where every moment was structured, from first bell at seven-fifteen in the morning to lights-out. Time was the biggest luxury imaginable. Just as I used to look at chocolate and sweets in shops and be utterly mystified that adults, who could afford them and had no one to tell them not to eat them, were not pigging out on them all day, I couldn't understand why anyone who had any choice would want to do anything, when doing nothing was so much rarer and more precious. Why would Mum do anything, when doing nothing was a serious alternative?

Now, though, looking back, I wonder. Julie had been an important person in her world. She had been the principal of a well-known school, and had had power and responsibility and recognition, and had been, every day of her working life, run ragged with busyness and burdens. She had worked flat-out for years; her days were not her own, either in practice or in theory. The convent was a closed world but in many respects not a sheltered one, and the life of the community made extra demands on top of those of running a school, which was a full-time job in itself. She had gotten her degree and her teaching qualification, while working full-time. Then escape, and London, and the very different English schools, and living in a flat and beginning to come to terms with life in the world, and then men, and Bill, and Hamburg, and me, and then—well, perhaps it makes perfect sense that Julie would want to slow down and look around. She had full-time help with the house, with the cooking, and with me, when I was there. It isn't clear to me what she did with her days, other than that she always managed to seem, and to speak of herself as if she was, busy. This was partly social—having people over for tea, going to see people for tea, planning dinners and cocktail parties. She read a bit; she took an interest in cooking, and was a great one for cutting out recipes. (I still have the scrapbooks.) But that was about it. It seems an extraordinary contrast with her old life. She at one point spoke to Peggy about her intention to find a teaching job in Hong Kong. Nothing came of it, and Peggie always wondered why. Julie would soon have realized that she couldn't get a job, because she could not use her certificates and references. This in itself must have been a huge psychic strain.

Many former nuns speak of an overwhelming sense of sadness at leaving the convent. I think Julie had that. And there was another, more concrete source of pain and loss. For the years of my early childhood, Julie's life was dominated by the attempt to have another baby. If she had done that, she would, as if by magic, have managed to square the circle between the version of her life she had given Bill and the truth. It would have meant that although she had lied to him about her age, she would also have balanced the consequences of that lie by giving him his heart's wish, another child. He deeply did not want me to be an only child. They hadn't had anything like as much time together before children as he would have wished, but the silver lining as far as he was concerned was that the mission to populate the world with little Lanchesters had begun. Onward!

So they tried, again and again. They succeeded, too. Julie was pregnant four more times after I was born. Every one of the pregnancies ended in a miscarriage. This was the great sadness of my parents' life together, and it was something about which I had absolutely no idea until one of my Irish relatives told me about it in the mid-1980s. I believed that, because I had no reason not to; but it still seemed to me hardly credible that all this could have been happening without my knowing about it, at the time or afterward. Then, late in the process of writing this book, I found a handwritten note of my mother's, two pages of letter paper under the heading "Random Notes (Before I Forget)." It confirms, in the saddest and flattest way, that Julie did indeed miscarry several times. The first miscarriage was in May 1963, a month after our return to Hong Kong from Burma. The second was in October 1963, on the ship to England. The third was in March 1965 in Labuan. The note Julie left mentions only three miscarriages; there was one more, and it provided the only hint of the subject I had, when I was about seven or eight.

One day at Highclere, walking down the steep-stepped shortcut through the vegetable garden to the bus stop, my mother, without turning around to look at me, said, "How would you feel about having a little brother or sister?"

The truthful answer was that I had never given the subject a second's thought, and had no intention of starting now. I could tell that wasn't what I was supposed to say, though, and so I said: "Great!"

"Well," my mother said, stopping on the shallow, precipitous steps and turning to me, "you may be going to. But you mustn't tell Dad."

"Okay," I said. I don't think I gave the subject any more thought, and it seemed to go away on its own without my having to raise it again. I guessed that my mother had been misinformed. She never brought it up again. That must have been the last of the four miscarriages. The fact that my mother was so bubbling over with happiness and excitement that she could not hold back from telling me, even after the losses she had already suffered, is still freshly sad.

So this river of hope and pain was running through my parents' lives and occupying far more of their thoughts and feelings than I could ever have guessed. Julie regarded my birth as a kind of miracle—more than once she told me that my name was derived from the word meaning "gift" in Hebrew, and that that was what I was, a gift. She would have regarded a second baby as even more of a gift, as she headed into her middle forties at a time when that was long past the norm for having a child. But the second gift never came, and Julie began to feel that if she was not exactly being punished by God, then He was withholding from her something that she wanted. Her belief in God was intact, and even survived the experience of going to see a priest in Hong Kong to discuss my religious status—whether there was some way in which I could be brought up secretly Catholic. He responded by making a sexual advance to her. Her shock and outrage over that was such that she didn't attend Mass for about a decade—and she never told my father what had happened, because she had gone behind his back in the first place, and because he "would have been too upset." You have to wonder what the priest was thinking; perhaps he realized that since she was acting in secrecy she would feel that she couldn't tell anyone. If that was his calculation, he was, depressingly, correct.

The fact that she went to see a priest at all is an indication that her religious feelings had not waned since she left the convent. (If you wonder how I know all this, given how little I know about so many areas of my mother's life, it is because she told me. Religion was one of the subjects on which we spoke freely later in her life.) Her argument was not with God but with the hierarchical, authoritarian, and sexist nature of the Catholic Church, especially in its pre–Vatican II form. She did not begin going to Mass again until the mid-1970s, and then not in Hong Kong but only when she was in England in the summer. It was after my father's retirement in 1979, when my parents settled near Norwich, that she began attending Mass on a weekly basis. I don't think her views changed much over this period; I think she just missed receiving communion. The rituals had changed sufficiently for her not to be overwhelmed by memories of how the Church used to be—she never expressed any nostalgia for the Latin Mass, or any of the pre–Vatican II ritual trappings. She never made any attempt to enter into the life of the Church as a community.

Julie still believed in God. He had given—her escape from the convent, Bill, me—and now He was taking away. But why was He taking away? Perhaps the darkest thing about these years, darker even than the miscarriages my mother suffered, was the cost of her lie, and the way its consequences seemed to grow and ramify. I don't think she had thought this aspect of her choice through; I believe it seemed to her more like a moment of decisive action, which would free her from her old life and let her begin a new one unencumbered. It was a lie, and lies were wrong; but she deserved a chance at being happy, she loved Bill and was loved by him, and was sure that they could make each other happy. She had been trained in a theological tradition that taught that in certain circumstances the end could justify the means. She had been cheated of one lover, one husband-to-be, by death, and rejected by another man because of her age. All she had to do to marry this man was tell a lie; so she did. It was like a test of her courage and her will to live her own life, just as leaving the convent had been. I think that was the spirit in which she began her new identity.

What gradually happened, though, was that this decision, which seemed clear-cut, finite, and limited in scope—a turning of the key, the cutting of a knot—had psychological consequences. "Take what you want and pay for it" is a good maxim, and it was what Julie thought she was doing. But the pain did not happen just once; she kept paying; the impact of her choice on her life kept mounting, and ramifying, and corroding her relationships and her sense of self. It poisoned what should have been her happiness.

The greatest damage done by my mother's secret was to herself. First, she couldn't tell the story to anyone else. That cut her off from people. She was never a trusting person; by giving her a sense that there was something she could never talk about, this also gave her a concrete reason not to trust anyone. That, humanly, was about the last thing Julie needed. But the secret did something else. It was impossible for her to talk to anyone else; and I believe that it became impossible for her to talk to herself about her own life. The story she had told about herself for her first forty years was that of a person who had tried to be good—that was central to her sense of herself. By lying to the person she loved most, she damaged that sense of self, in ways that made it hard for her to make coherent sense of herself. She found it difficult to integrate her experiences into a story; she found it difficult to integrate her experiences, period.

Then there was the effect on her relationship with Bill. She loved him, loved him more and more as time went on, not least for his goodness and innocence. A man with a thicker carapace, a more worldly and cynical man, a man not above telling the odd lie himself, would have been much easier to lie to. As the miscarriages followed one on the other, this feeling grew ever more certain in Julie: Bill must never know. So there was a secret sadness—her love for him was undermined by the knowledge that she was tricking him, hurting him, and without his even beginning to suspect. She had been brought up in circumstances where it was not unusual to have to lie to those around you—to have some secrets, just to get a bit of psychological space for yourself, a bit of mental territory with a "Keep Out" sign. The convent was in some ways a training in lying, too, since life in an institution more or less forced you to have secrets and privacies of your own—and when Julie decided to leave the Church, this feeling intensified, and she began systematically deceiving the institutional body around her. So her training in lying was in impersonal deception, deception of a force larger and more powerful than the individual. She knew she could live with having committed that kind of lie, a lie to the family, to the Church. She began her life with Bill by thinking it would be like that, but then gradually came to realize that this new kind of lie was very different: she was lying directly, radically, to the person she loved most. He could never know the part of her she held back. The other kind of lie had a guilty pleasure to it, but this was bitter and hurtful and all too heartfelt.

The secret had a particularly crushing effect on her relationship with Peggie. Without the example provided by her sister, and without the practical support she gave, Julie could not have left the convent in the way she did. (One cannot prove a counterfactual, but my hunch is that she would eventually have left, somehow, sometime; I don't think she could have borne her sense of miserable trappedness indefinitely. But that is just a hunch.) Once Julie was married, she pushed Peggie away. She was living on the other side of the world, of course, which made it easier, and most of the pushing away was done via little sisterly signals and withholdings. But it certainly happened, and Peggie, who could have no way of guessing the real reason, was hurt by it. In her letters, Julie would sometimes talk about wanting to bring me up as a "proper English gentleman," a claim that, apart from being straightforwardly not true—since it wasn't what she wanted—made no sense at all in the context of who she was and who my father was. But it made complete sense when translated as the expression of a wish to keep her family at a distance. Later, when I was old enough, she would tell me that some of her family could be troublemakers, and I should be careful about talking to them and about what they said to me.

This was grossly, bitterly unfair. Julie was in effect blaming her family for her own lie. Contact with them was risky because somebody might blurt out her secret. All it would take was a mention of the age of one of her siblings, or Dilly's real name, or a date that did not add up. It could happen very easily. So she made it seem as if the family were the risk, as if there were something risky and toxic about them. I believe some of her family saw as snobbery her wish to get away from Ireland, to remake herself as Mrs. Julie Lanchester, wife of a sort-of English banker, mother of a sort-of English son. I don't think it was snobbery; I think it was a fear of exposure.

The way Julie put distance between herself and her family had more to do with omission than commission. It was less specific gestures and moments, and more a process of silences and absences—visits not made, birthdays not remembered, letters not written. (I would add phone calls to the list of things not done, but I can't blame my mother for that, because calling Mayo from Hong Kong was a hugely complicated and expensive process, involving speaking to the local exchange operator in Ireland in order to book time for the call. When direct dialing came, it was difficult to believe that all the drama and difficulty and local color had evaporated.) But there were some specific instances in which my mother was caught out in the act of distancing herself. When Molly Gunnigan, her mother, moved in with Dilly, the family agreed that they would send a little money each month by way of helping Dilly pay Molly's living costs. Dilly and her husband, Peter, a mechanic, lived in a small house with eight children and did not have much money. So Peggie suggested that the seven other siblings would each send a small check, say, two pounds a week. But Julie could not send a check, because her checkbook was the property of someone named B. T. J. Lanchester—and of all the people in the world, the person to whom she could least be revealed as B.T. was the real Bridget Teresa, her sister Dilly. So Julie sent cash instead. (She could have sent a money order, but that was a major chore in Hong Kong.) The cash was stolen in the mail, and Dilly's irritation at that—at Julie's not bothering to send the money, or not bothering to send it safely, when she was by far the most well-off person in the family—moved her to write an angry letter. Julie was furious when she read it, and she never sent money again. Relations between the sisters never recovered. And all because she couldn't use her own checkbook.

As a result of this, Julie had almost no real contact with her family for many years. I think she came to believe this new version of her family; she superimposed her new sense of needing to keep distance from them on her memory of her childhood grievances, and decided that she could not trust them and that they did not wish her entirely well. Just as she might have been growing out of her old grievances, she grew a new and basically fictitious set. When her caution about her family began to wear off, in the middle 1970s, she started to see more of her sisters, while keeping Bill and me at a distance from them. The usual pattern was that she would go to

Ireland and visit one or another of her sisters for a week or two in the summer; after my father retired in 1979 she would go more often and for longer. Her youngest sister, Jane, her goddaughter, had been very close to her; but she never saw Jane between 1949 and Jane's last illness forty years later.

Jane was the last Gunnigan sister to leave the convent, and I think she represented for Julie her own sense of failure as a nun—in fact, in relation to her youngest sister, Julie acted as if there were something wrong with her because she had left the convent. Jane went on to work in earthquake relief in Peru, then in a project looking after orphaned children in the Bronx, and then in an antipoverty project back in Ireland, but Julie stayed out of touch with her all those years. Indeed, I met Jane before Julie saw her again, on my first, mind-bending and eye-opening visit to my Irish relatives in 1981. She was an incandescent spirit, kind and warm and funny and good, living in a book-crammed chaotic bungalow near Waterford with Pat Brady, the former priest who had been her partner ever since Peru. She was upset that Julie had been out of touch for so long. And the real reason for the gap and silence of all those years was, yet again, Julie's lie about her age. Sometimes people speak of "a gift that keeps on giving." The lie was a taker that kept on taking. In Jane's case, it took away the sisters' relationship. The cancer of the bone marrow that killed Jane had been misdiagnosed as osteoporosis; nuns are prone to osteoporosis since they tend to undergo menopause early. The doctors paid too much attention to Jane's life history and not enough to the symptoms. When my mother finally went to see her as she was dying, Jane held her hand and told her, "You were always the beautiful one." It was a sad, terrible moment of reconciliation for the two sisters. Julie felt that she had gone to see Jane just in time. The deeper truth, though, was that she was irrevocably late.

Of all the selves she could have been and chose not to be, perhaps the central one was Shivaun Cunningham. The two things she had never had, when she'd thought about her ambitions to write, were time and freedom; these were now things she had in abundance, in excess. Most human beings live inside a role. Julie had been a daughter, a nurse, a nun,

a teacher, at a time and a place when these identities were powerfully encompassing, and left little room for a residue of self. Now she was a wife
and a mother, with full-time employees to do much of the work atten-
dant on both roles. Bill was gone from home by eight in the morning,
back at seven at night, and he worked on Saturday mornings, too. The
amount of time for Julie herself was vastly greater than she had ever had
in her life. There was nothing to stand in the way of her desire to write.
She had once felt sure she had the talent and the stories to tell, and a
writer was what she wanted most in all the world to be. And yet after that
promising start in London she never picked up a pen. She was finished
with roles, and was ready for the thing beyond a role, which was writing—
since to write is, for a serious writer, to move beyond the role and the self
into an encounter with something much more bare and exposing, un-
structured and unsupported.

That, perhaps, was the nub of why she could not do it—or one of the
nubs. Her secret gave her a profound fear of exposure, a sense that if she
opened herself up she would be shamed, destroyed, stripped bare. You
can see the way Julie's secret was antithetical to her writing even in one
of the stories she wrote and read on the BBC, "My Hair and Me."
That story is, I believe, entirely autobiographical, with a couple of small
but highly charged exceptions, both of which concern the narrator's age.
She speaks of her "older sisters," as though she were not herself the oldest, and of spending seven years in the convent, seven fewer than she
actually spent. The narrator also doesn't have the background of Julie's
earlier year with the Good Shepherds, or the years she spent nursing in a
sanatorium outside Dublin—so "My Hair and Me" makes the best part of
a decade magically disappear from Julie's life. Doing the math on the narrator's age, it comes out as 19+1+7+2+2=31. Which is how old Dilly was,
and how old Julie was claiming to be once she stole her identity. The story
was written in 1960, months after she met Bill, so it seems highly likely
that by then Julie was already contemplating permanent, structural
falsehood about her age, and perhaps even the identity theft that accom-
panied it. Any family member who heard her story, anyone who knew
her, would know that she was not being honest about her age. Most

people would think little of it, and say less. But for Julie, writing brought with it a terrible enhanced sense of risk. The fear of exposure grew. And eventually the fear of exposure kept her from writing. B. T. J. Lanchester, a semifictional self, smothered Shivaun Cunningham, another semi-fictional self, in her cradle.

The other reason for killing off Shivaun Cunningham had, I think, to do with me. It might be the easy thing to see this as a classic feminist story, the pram in the hall as the enemy of promise, the somber enemy of great art (to borrow Cyril Connolly's phrase). In this version, the years of looking after me are what prevented Julie from carrying on with her writing. But I don't think that's true, not least for the simple reason that Julie now had more time to herself than she had ever had. It's not the case that the burden on her increased after I was born; once we had moved to Hong Kong, with me six weeks old, she had full-time child care, she had financial support and, in the key phrase of Virginia Woolf, a room of her own. She had means and opportunity. The thing she no longer had was motive.

Julie had wanted to be a writer because she wanted to escape; she wanted to get away from home, from her family, from Ireland, from her own past; she wanted to be free. She wanted to be new, she wanted to be someone else. But with marriage and a baby, she had done all those things, and in a way that was, to her and in the context of her family, even more triumphant. She had gotten away, gotten married, gotten (in relative terms) rich, cheated time and the wasted convent years by having a baby; she wasn't Julia Gunnigan or Sister Eucharia, but Mrs. Julie Lanchester. My birth didn't stop Julie from writing because I was the opposite of writing, inimical to her ambitions, a succubus, a classic somber enemy of great art. My birth stopped her from writing because it fulfilled many of the wishes that writing had represented. She didn't need to make a getaway anymore, because she already had, and Bill and I were the living proof. Indeed, we weren't just the proof of it, we were it. So the answer to the question of who killed Shivaun Cunningham is the Lanchesters: Bill, John, but most of all B.T.J.

As for me, the main cost of my mother's secret was not so much in a feeling that she had a secret—I never guessed that, not consciously—but in a feeling that there were ways in which she wasn't fully present. There were closed compartments in her, places where you weren't permitted to go, and where perhaps she didn't go herself. I find it very difficult to put this feeling precisely into words, other than to indicate a general sense that there were things out of sight. If you told her something she didn't want to hear, and particularly if you expressed a feeling she didn't want to acknowledge, she would somehow disappear. If possible, she would do so physically—I remember when I asked her where I had come out of when I was born, she moved from room to room in the house with me dogging along after her, until it became clear that I wasn't about to stop asking, at which point she literally ran away. I think I was about six or seven at the time. I think I may have asked again the next time I saw her—I'm not really sure, but one way or another, I got the message that this question wasn't going to be answered and had therefore better not be asked. Later, when I was leaving to go back to school at the end of holiday trips to Hong Kong, she would usually vanish from the airport—I would look over and she would be gone. "Where's Mum?" I would ask my father, and he would say, "I think she's a bit upset," that being a perfectly adequate explanation for why she had gone off to hide. But that kind of literal running off and hiding was much rarer than its psychological equivalent, which was somehow to vanish internally so that you, or the thing you had said, or the issue you had raised, in some mysterious way no longer existed. The actual subject of discussion did not have to be, and in fact usually wasn't, one of acknowledged importance. If I was going to be out in the evening, say, and needed to inform her of it in advance, well, that was a huge act of courage and defiance, a flung gauntlet, a reckless charge over the top. I would have to summon all my nerve to say, mock-casually, "Oh, by the way, Mum, I'm going to be out this evening, don't bother cooking dinner for me."

She would make no acknowledgment whatsoever—not a blink, not a flicker. That was how I would know she had heard, because if she hadn't heard, she would ask me to repeat what I had said. My words were so out-rageous, so wounding, so emotionally violent, that they could not be acknowledged. It would be like permitting someone to offer you a flagrant insult. She would be imperturbable, masklike, a sailing ship not deviating from its course. The reason for that was the subject under discussion— that is, that I was rejecting her. And that could not be admitted or discussed, so better simply to pretend that the possibility of it *could not exist.*

That was how she seemed to me. As for how she seemed to herself, how she felt, what seemed like absences and silences inside her manifested themselves as depression. This cloud hung around her for years. It did not begin at the start of her marriage, but by the late 1960s and early 1970s, depression had established a pattern of coming and going, one made more painful and costly by Julie's difficulty in talking about how she felt. Here, yet again, the subject was made radioactive by its proximity to the big secret: Julie felt she couldn't discuss her depression without talking about reasons why she might feel guilty, remorseful, sad, and hollow. She couldn't discuss it at all, not even with herself. It was only in the 1980s that she began to talk about the depression she had undergone, some time after the worst of it had passed. The first time she mentioned it, we were watching the news together and a picture of Menachem Begin came on, unshaven and looking crushed, in the grip of the depression that seized him after the cost in Israeli lives of his invasion of Lebanon became clear. I said something about feeling sorry for the victims of the war rather than for him, and Julie said, in her maximum-force mode, "I've been depressed myself, and feel desperately sorry for anyone who's experienced it."

I suspect that the root cause of the depression had to do with injury she had inflicted on her sense of herself by lying. She thought of herself as good; that sense of her own goodness was central to who she was. Of her own free will, she had violated, permanently, that sense of who she was. She had destroyed the story she told herself about herself. And that led to a malignant sadness that lasted for years.

As for how that depression seemed to others, it manifested itself mainly in an enhanced, weapons-grade ability to project her moods. Depressed people can be like black holes, sucking up the oxygen around them. They are, more or less by definition, unreachable. There were long stretches of time when this was the case with Julie. She seemed angry and withdrawn, and it was not clear what she was angry about. I got used to this, insofar as a child can, when I was small—one reason why, when the time came to go to school a couple of continents away, it was less of a wrench than it might have been. I had grown used to my mother's not being there.

As for how she thought of herself and of her illness, I don't know. But I do know that one of the main reasons I am a writer is that she couldn't be one. And the reason she couldn't be one is that she couldn't tell the truth.

FAMILY
ROMANCE

❉

· I ·

BECAUSE WE LIVED in the same small block of flats for so many years, and because my father kept working at the same job, I saw his life as entirely static. It never occurred to me that his working life involved a trajectory of hopes and feelings and experiences.

For a couple of years after our return to Hong Kong, back from Labuan in 1966, Bill was working, first as deputy and then as manager, at the North Point branch of the Bank. In career terms, he felt that his best years were in front of him: he was serving a long apprenticeship as a relative junior, but that wasn't unusual in the Bank in its colonial days. He would still have expected to rise, and for big opportunities to open up. That might seem a naive hope for someone who had spent seventeen years working for the same company; but the pace of banking life, like that of other work, was slower in those days. His chance might yet come.

When it did, in the late 1960s, it was in the form of a transfer to the head office, at 1 Queen's Road Central. Today, that address is occupied by a famous building designed by Norman Foster—at the time it was constructed, the most expensive privately owned building in the world, and a highly ugly and impractical one, too. When my father worked there, though, the bank was a chunky stone structure with a lovely central hall illustrated with a mural of striving workers; it was so low, relative to the Hong Kong of my childhood, it was impossible to believe that when my grandparents were first in the colony it was the tallest building there. This was where Bill was to spend the rest of his working life. It's where I best remember him as a working man, when I used to drop in on him, semi-unannounced. I would either ring his secretary from the banking floor, or simply sneak into the staff elevator and go up to his section before asking to be taken in by the "boy"—a Cantonese man in his thirties who was the administrative manager of this section. Dad was always pleased to see me, and I him, and there was something very reassuring about my father in his office, at the center of all this bustle, a picture of me and my mother

on his desk. Lunch, in theory a quiet time, was often the worst moment to drop in, because he would often be having a snooze.

Although I didn't know it then, Bill was a disappointed man. He had climbed to the stair below the top one, in terms of the Bank hierarchy. He was now a senior member of the overseas staff, well paid and as secure as any worker in the world, the beneficiary of a pension plan that, as it happened, he was to help design. (He didn't benefit from it much, but my mother did.) The next level up was that of the head honchos, the people who decided things and set the course, as opposed to running things and keeping them on course. Bill never got to that level. He had a platform with a perfect view of the personalities and politics at the highest tiers of the bank, and he worked with three men who were eventually to run the organization, and oversee the process that took it from being a minor colonial bank to one of the biggest financial institutions in the world. Two of the chairmen he had known were, he said, diametrically opposite in their behavior to colleagues. One would scream and shout and berate colleagues, but he never sacked anybody. The other was mild-mannered and calm and never raised his voice, but was utterly ruthless and would sack and demote people without hesitation. I've kept that in mind ever since Dad told me, and it's been borne out: in every organization I've seen at close range, the bosses tend to be either screamers or stabbers. They have either a bark or a bite, almost never both.

The next promotion never came. Bill was the deputy head of the personnel department—in other words, he did all the work. (An observation of my own from institutional life is that deputies do either all the real work or none of it.) There were a few attempts by other, senior figures to poach him—once, by a friend who was setting up a merchant bank to wheel and deal, in what was to be the far more buccaneering style of banking prevalent since the 1980s. But Bill's superior fought off the move, mainly, it seems, because he needed Bill to do all the work and run the department. Bill saw this as a disappointment, and so it was, since what matters in life isn't so much what happens to us as what we think happens to us. I do wonder, though. The cure for being a banker wasn't to be a more interesting kind of banker; it was, probably, not to be a banker at all. But it's hard to accept, once you have been doing a thing for twenty years, that you have been doing the wrong thing. Julie and I were an important alibi for Bill in this respect. I think he would have stayed in the same job whatever happened; I think his childhood had left him with a desperate need for security and structure, which the Bank provided. Yet he told himself that he had a wife and a son to support and school fees to pay and a standard of living to maintain, and so he had no choice but to keep on doing what he was doing.

Duty was important for Bill. He was a good man; in his unostentatious and shy way, one of the best men I have known. He grew up in a culture in which duty and reticence and honor and privacy and lack of ostentation were regarded as forms of goodness and public-spiritedness. Plenty of people still believe in all these things, but they have vanished from our public culture, or at least from our publicized culture, and no one celebrates them anymore, or even admits that they were once seen, and not so long ago, as virtues. One aspect of his sense of duty was the good deeds he did, and another was that he never spoke about them. I knew that he was appointed to sit on the Hong Kong rent tribunal, overseeing arguments between landlords and tenants—a highly sensitive position in that place and time, and a great tribute to his reputation for fair-mindedness. It was also a tribute to the fact he had taken the trouble to go to night classes and learn functional Cantonese, something very few expatriates bothered to do, not least because it was so difficult. But there were other things I did not know. In our later years in Hong Kong, from the early seventies on, we came to know a group of Catholic nuns; they did a variety of demanding jobs, mostly linked to poverty relief; one was a surgeon, another the private secretary to the bishop of Hong Kong, Cardinal Wu, others were involved in medical aid work in Guangzhou. They had the unusual virtue, in Hong Kong, of being equal-opportunity skeptics, as unillusioned about the Communist Chinese as about Britain and the self-serving billionaires and big shots of the Hong Kong business community. I had always assumed that we met them through "the Murphia," my mother's Irish friends. It was only recently, on a trip to Hong Kong, that I learned that that wasn't true: we knew them because my father served unpaid as the treasurer of a hospital where some of the nuns worked. I had had no idea; he never mentioned it to me, not once. That is how you are supposed to do charity, with the left hand not knowing what the right is doing, and it was the best side of my father's reticence. On the same trip to Hong Kong in 1997, I found out something else I had not known: that my father had paid the fees of Ah Man, our cook Ah Ho's son, who was my near-contemporary and friend, to study electrical engineering at university. I was by now in a position to know that although we were well-off, we weren't that well-off, and that my father had had his worries about life after retirement. So this was no small gesture, and as it happens, it changed Ah Man's life. He founded a business making boilers and is now a multimillionaire. His parents, once our cook and maid, now live in a spectacular duplex by a marina at Sai Kung in the New Territories. It would have made my father so happy to know that, and it made me glad that such a private man, who had in most respects left so little mark on the world, has at least one place other than in my heart where his memory is revered.

My awareness of Bill's unhappiness at work was not a vivid thing. He did not complain at length, only in muted asides. He felt that he was brighter and more able than the people he worked for. This is something I learned more about from my mother than from him. As for his work, he hardly ever spoke about it. Only once did he show me papers he had brought home from the office, relating to a choice among three candidates applying for a senior-level job. He spread out the papers, explaining who the men were, then said that although one of them was obviously the best and brightest, he wouldn't get the job because he was spiky and cocky and probably wouldn't fit in. That, he explained, was how things often worked. People wanted to have a quiet time and didn't like to be disrupted, even if it was by someone who in other ways was the best man for the job. That seemed distressingly timid to me then, though since then I've seen that about ninety percent of the time, what my father said happens, happens.

I didn't learn much about Bill's work from him directly. I didn't learn much about his life, either. The defining event of all these years came in

1974, when my father had a serious heart attack while in the office. Until this point, in twenty-five years of employment, he had not missed a single day's work through illness, something of which he was very proud, especially because he had so often been sickly in his childhood. He was forty-seven years old and a smoker, getting through a pack of Benson & Hedges Gold a day, but apart from his being overweight—not obese, but overweight—and sedentary, there were no warnings. There may have been a connection, it occurs to me now, with the tuberculosis of his youth. Years after his heart attack he told me two things about it. First, he said, what was disconcerting was that the initial symptoms were so like those of indigestion that he never quite got free of the worry that what felt like indigestion was actually something potentially fatal. At the time I did not understand what a glimpse this was into a world of constant, tormenting anxiety. And second, he told me, at the moment of the heart attack he felt himself falling over, losing his footing as he collapsed, so that now whenever he began to lose his balance, say on a carpet slipping over the smooth floor underneath, he had a flashback to the moment of losing consciousness during the heart attack. Again, I didn't understand how terrible the ensuing anxiety and sense of apprehension must have been. The main thing I saw was the physical caution that never left my father afterward, and the regular angina attacks he would suffer when out walking, which would make him pause and catch his breath with his fists resting on his hips—a syndrome I now know is called "window shopper's angina." He kept his nitroglycerin pills on him at all times, and eventually we kept an oxygen cylinder in the closet. He gave up smoking, began to take regular exercise in the form of walking, and never ate so much as a mouthful of butter or bacon again.

This doesn't mean we ever properly discussed it, though. I was told, at school, that my father was not well, and I remember the house matron smiling at me in an unusually and unnaturally "nice" way—but as far as I knew, he was having an operation on his feet. Is it possible my mother wrote to me about his heart and I misread the word as "feet"? Looking over my parents' correspondence, I see that the heart attack is mentioned directly in letters to friends and to Lannie, but not to me. In any case, just as my parents didn't have a clue about my preoccupations at school, I didn't have a clue about things at home, and it was only very gradually that it became clear to me what had happened. My father spoke about it over the next years in asides, and from these I pieced the story together. The only time he directly mentioned it was in the summer of 1979, when he told me that he would be going to a London specialist to assess whether he ought to have a bypass operation. I was planning to go on a school-organized expedition that summer, to learn hang-gliding, but canceled it because I wanted to be around if he had the operation. In the event, he was told that he didn't need it; his changed diet and the exercise he had taken had done him so much good that the bypass was unnecessary. This turned out not to be true, but he was deeply relieved.

They were trying to protect me, I think. My parents did not want to frighten me by going into too much detail about my father's health and about the risks involved if he had another heart attack—and in one sense they succeeded, because I had no conscious fear that he might die. At the same time, I internalized a great deal of his worry, and I began to think, not consciously but vividly, of death as something that might descend out of a clear sky at any moment. This unconscious belief or conviction was to cause trouble in the future.

Bill had had difficulties with phobias and anxieties in the past. Wide-open spaces triggered moments of irrational fear, as did moving from dark places into sunlight; he once told me he thought the feeling might be linked to traumatic hidden memories about being born. He dreaded social situations that he couldn't get out of, and had a particular fear of restaurants; he would have to walk back and forth outside, summoning the nerve to go in. These anxieties were intensified by the heart attack, since he now had reason to worry that he might overtax his heart by panicking and then suffer another infarct. In other words, the anxiety gave him a powerful legitimate reason to feel more anxiety—a classic anxious spiral.

I don't want to make Bill's life sound grim. He was a popular colleague, and people were quick to like him; he was unpompous in a time and a place when that wasn't a common trait in men. (How many middle-aged men, in truth, are unpompous? A minority, certainly. One in five?) He was gentle, funny, intelligent, kind, and also had the deeply rare quality of actually listening to what people said. Women liked him. He had very few close friends and, I sometimes think, no intimate ones. He almost never spoke of his deepest feelings; I may be the only person apart from Julie to whom he did. But that made him seem not a closed or secretive man, merely a private one.

The material comfort he provided for his family was a source of pride to him. We were comfortable, and Julie very much enjoyed that; Bill himself liked that sense of security. In retirement, when money was tighter, he told me, "I like the feeling that if I wanted to go down to London and stay at the Ritz for a night or two, you know, I could." Not that he ever did, but I know what he meant: he liked the wiggle room, the psychic sense of space, that earning a good living brought. As I have already pointed out, this sense of potential freedom came at the cost of spending his days in wage slavery, and of effectively mortgaging his life away—but nevertheless, at least in some sense he felt free. He was proud of the good education I was getting, and very proud when I got into Oxford, and then even more proud when I got a first in my moderations, the exams at the end of my first year. Later, when I won a couple of university prizes, he was prouder still. He saw this, with reason, as a set of opportunities he had created. When my mother told me about his pride in these things, she would always use the same phrase: "He opened the window and flung his chest out."

By 1979, I was coming up to my last year in boarding school, and therefore the last year of school fees; in those days, university education was paid for by the state. (Obviously, given that he never discussed money, the fact that he kept working partly to pay my school fees was never mentioned. It's a connection I worked out in retrospect.) Bill had spent thirty years working for the Hongkong and Shanghai Bank. His health was what it was, a source of great anxiety, but it could be managed, with mild exercise and a lot of medication, much of it with unpleasant side effects—specifically, the eczema he suffered thanks to the combination of beta-blockers and blood pressure medication. But he now had a place he could retire to.

This was Alderfen, the house he and my mother bought in Norfolk in 1972. There was no ancestral connection of any sort with the area, but my aunt Peggie lived nearby in Norwich with her husband, Vincent, and daughter, Siobhán. Their presence was one reason I had been sent to school in Norfolk. In many ways Alderfen was an unfortunate choice. Village life proved to be unfriendly even by the standards of English village life—read: very unfriendly indeed. The site was windy and bleak; the house itself was an unlovely "chalet bungalow" of recent construction, a bungalow with a room upstairs that had a balcony. Because I was at a boarding school, in the summer holidays my friends were scattered all over and I didn't see them much; for my parents, there was no ready-made social life—Peggie and Vincent moved back to Ireland in 1973—and next to no culture in Norfolk. But Bill nevertheless loved the idea of owning his property, with no street address beyond that one word "Alderfen." The nineteen acres of land were mostly unusable, indeed unwalkable, marsh, but beautiful nonetheless. Bill now owned a piece of somewhere, and for someone who felt that he didn't belong anywhere and who had lived all his life in property belonging to other people, that was a novel and consoling feeling.

Thanks to those three decades with the same employer, Bill now had the option of taking early retirement. This might seem a no-brainer: to have reached fifty-three, and now to be rid of a job you are bored by, on a comfortable pension, free to do anything you want with the rest of your life. What's not to like? It was difficult for Bill, however, because it involved accepting that he wasn't going to get any further at the Bank and therefore that his central work ambition had failed. Retiring involved facing and accepting the fact that he was disappointed. He decided to do it anyway, and 1979 was our last year in Hong Kong; rather than take a summer holiday in England, he worked through and left the territory forever in September. For me, that summer was one of the best times I had in Hong Kong. Once an atomized place with a random collection of people coming and going, Hong Kong was now a place where I had some friends from holiday to holiday—specifically girlfriends, with the emphasis on "friends," but still. There were parties, there was hanging out, there were bars and clubs where the idea of somebody's asking for proof of your age never crossed anyone's mind. It was, I suddenly realized, a good city in which to be a teenager. Then I went back to school to start my A-level year, and Bill and Julie took the long, slow trip home that they had been discussing ever since he had decided to stop working: Thailand, Cyprus, and then Sweden, to buy a new Saab and drive it home across northern Europe. At school I received a sequence of postcards. Bill and Julie arrived at Alderfen sometime in early November, and the open-ended years of retirement began.

Bill went from a highly structured work environment with long hours and a built-in social life in a city where he had lived most of his life to a Norfolk village. I recently went back to the village, and the question that hit me with great force was: What were they thinking? To go from a life spent in the tropics, most of it in one of the world's great metropolises, to a sleepy, isolated, insular, literally and metaphorically cold piece of nowhere—what were they thinking? True, Lannie had, a year or so before, moved from her beloved adopted home in Cornwall to a small flat in Trowse, a suburb of Norwich—and that was also part of this arbitrary relocation to Norfolk. (Lannie's great friends at her new flat were the airline stewardesses who lived in the identical flat next door and flew out of Norwich airport. This was back in the days when being an air hostess was inconceivably glamorous. They were incredibly sweet to her and occasionally used to have envy-inducing parties, which I could hear through the thin walls.)

The fact that Bill saw much more of Lannie was the big positive about retiring to Norfolk. He now saw more of her than he had since he was evacuated from Hong Kong in July 1940. But Lannie had had a heart attack in 1979 and her health was not good. In February 1980, I was acting, very badly, as Jack in the school production of *The Importance of Being Earnest*. My parents came to see it. This in itself was a big deal for me, because it was the first school play they had been to see and the first time either of them had seen me act. Afterward they came to talk to me in the cloak-room. My father told me that he'd been with Lannie that afternoon; she had called them and asked them to come over because she wasn't feeling well.

"We were sitting on the sofa," Dad said. "Then Lannie gave a kind of start and she died. I'm sorry."

I don't remember feeling anything. In my clueless eighteen-year-old way, I wasn't even particularly surprised. Lannie was old, and old people did die. The funeral was a few days later. Lannie was buried in the cemetery in Norwich. I had the afternoon off school. We never discussed our feelings about her death. Now, looking back, I think it hit my father very hard.

This grief compounded Bill's other difficulties. The main one was that he was entirely unprepared for retirement. As a lively-minded man with many interests, no doubt he thought he would be free of the intellectual underemployment that can blight life after work; he had lived mostly in his head for many years, and probably assumed retirement would be more of the same. He began a two-year course in electronics at Norwich Technical College, pursuing an interest he had had for years and, characteristically, wanting to learn things from first principles. (The other mature student doing the course was twenty-four.) When he bought a BBC-made computer, one of the first affordable consumer models in the UK, he wanted to know how to program it and how it worked, software and hardware, from the bare machine code up. I said, "But what can it do? Aren't you more interested in the things it can do? Who cares how it works?" He shrugged. "Difference of approach," he said.

Bill looked after the garden and set up a mesh net to keep coypu out of the vegetables. Coypu, or nutria, was an introduced species that had escaped into the wild, after the bankruptcy of a fur farm in the 1930s, and the animals were now destroying Norfolk's dikes by burrowing into them. The coypu is a two-foot-long rodent with unforgettable orangey-red front teeth; at night our local ones made eerie human-sounding screaming noises. (They've been eradicated now, after a government program in the late 1980s.) Bill joined the local branch of Mensa and

Dad and me on the walls of York, 1982.

discovered that a typical evening's meeting involved sitting in the pub discussing whether or not to go for a pizza and then going to see *Eraserhead* instead. He turned down a retainer from the Bank because he wanted to be free to apply for other work; he did go for one job, as bursar of a Cambridge college, but he didn't get it. He studied the stock market and made investments not just for the fun of it but for the income to supplement his pension as well. He was bored out of his mind.

And then he died. Does that seem too sudden? It did to me. He was fifty-seven and I was twenty-one, in my third year at university. The summer holiday before his death, in 1983, I had taken him out in the canoe that was my great source of happiness at Alderfen—a neighbor and I would spend hours and hours on the small dikes, the river, and the local Broad, the most excitingly wild and natural place I, a city boy, had known. On some days I would see a kingfisher that lived near where we kept the canoe: the electric blue flash of its wings, so startlingly vivid amid all the greens and grays, would, whenever I saw it, be the high spot of my day. I hadn't known before that a natural phenomenon could be the high spot of a day. At the end of our narrow, overhung, nearly secret dike mooring, you could turn right and head to the Broad, or left and explore the cramped, shallow, shifting waterways impassable by any normal boat. We never saw a soul there, except on the one day we rescued a man who had gotten lost; we were in the garage playing darts when we heard him shouting for help—a trick of marsh acoustics, since, when we eventually got to him, he was well over a mile away.

My father didn't often come out in the canoe. I think he was worried that the exertion of paddling would overtax his heart. That day, though, was clear and warm, and I managed to persuade him. Instead of heading for the Broad, we went along the narrow dike that ran by the edge of our property—the only way of getting there, since the marsh was too boggy and treacherous to walk on. It could have been about four hundred yards from our house, no more. To my astonishment, the low, overshadowed dike had been transformed into a broad water avenue, and it took only a moment to see why: maybe a dozen trees on our side of the bank had been cut down. I was surprised and curious; my father was aghast. We canceled the excursion and quickly went home. A few days later I was back at university. Very soon after that I heard that my parents had put our house on the market and were planning to move.

What had happened was that a few locals had cut the trees down to provide access to the Broad for a mooring past our property. They knew the trees belonged to us, and had cut them down without asking, for the simple reason that if they had asked, Bill might have said no. Quite a few people knew what was happening, but they chose not to tell Bill. After all, he had had the house for only eleven years and had been living there full-time for only three and a bit.

The resulting feeling of betrayal was, for Bill, very sharp. People with whom he was on nodding and chatting terms had, he felt, done something behind his back. He had a deep sense of insecurity about the locals' untrustworthiness; he felt a lack of goodwill. So he got an apology from the parish council and sold the house and moved to Norwich, which is where my parents were living by the time of my next holiday from university, over Christmas and New Year's.

I went home the second week in December. My mother had gone to Ireland for a week, so my father and I had a few days alone together. I had gone home in some triumph, having just won a university prize exam, and Dad was very proud and happy—remember, his own finals result had been, by his own account, the worst day of his life. He was very glad to be in the city. "It was only when we got here that I realized that I was just so fucking bored," he said. "You can go out for a drink, you can go for a coffee, you can go see a film. In the countryside there's just nothing to do." We went to see Peter Weir's *The Year of Living Dangerously*, and he said it was uncanny how the movie caught what Indonesia had been like in the fifties and sixties. We had dinner together on a Wednesday night. On Thursday, my mother came back from Ireland and my girlfriend came to stay for a few days. On Friday, my parents went out for a drink after dinner and came back at about nine. My girlfriend and I were watching Polanski's *Repulsion* on TV when my father went out of the room. He was gone for about half an hour. My mother went to see what he was doing. She screamed my name. I ran upstairs and saw her standing over my father. "I think he's died," she said. My first feeling was a great surge of tenderness for her: I felt so sad for her. Not him, not me—her. I knelt beside her. She was right; my father was not cold, but not live-warm. He had had a massive heart attack.

We buried his ashes a few days later. The turnout was sparse, since Bill had so few connections with Norwich. In Hong Kong we could have filled the cathedral. I can remember those days with a terrible clarity. As far as I could tell, I felt nothing, nothing at all. This wasn't denial so much as simple inability to locate my feelings. I just didn't know where they were. And there was so much to do, too. There were phone calls to make, let-

ters to write, probate to arrange, my mother to look after. I wasn't prepared for anything about death, and one of the things I wasn't prepared
for was the sheer workload.

This was the first time I was ever impressed by my mother's religious
faith. Her reaction the night my father died was one of pure shock: "What
am I going to do? What will become of me?" she kept saying. But by the
next day she was deeply, passionately grieving. She told me that she had
always thought it would be she who died first. (I never asked why she
might have thought that; I saw it as self-dramatization. It never occurred
to me that there might be a reason.) She was able to feel the loss in a way
I simply couldn't, and at the same time I felt this was in some way connected to her ability to see something beyond the loss, a context or meaning provided by her faith. Somehow, because she could see beyond it, she
could also see it. As for me, partly because the loss of my father seemed
so random, so arbitrary and meaningless other than as pure loss, I couldn't
even acknowledge it, much less cope with any of the feelings it brought
up. Because I had no way of describing to myself what had happened, on
some level it was as if nothing had happened. It was as if I knew I had a
pair of keys somewhere, and knew that they would be in some way useful, but I couldn't find them. No: it was as if somebody had told me that
there were things called "keys" and that these things called "keys" were
essential, and that I would surely be able to find them if I looked, but I had
no idea where they were or what they looked like or even, really, what
they were for—just that somewhere, somehow, there were these things I
probably needed.

A year after my father died, the day before I was due to go back to
spend Christmas with my mother, she stepped in front of a car while out
shopping and was run over. Her injuries were not serious and she was in
hospital only overnight, but after about a week she was still feeling ill, so
she asked me to call a priest to give her last rites. Over the phone, the
priest explained that this wasn't something that was done only and always for the dying; it could be done for ill people to help them feel better, and the official Church name for the ritual was now the Sacrament
of the Sick. He came before lunch the next day, a scruffy middle-aged

man with stringy thinning hair who wore a dog collar and a definitively tatty anorak under which he was carrying communion wafers and wine in a small canister like a thermos. Something about his sense of rush and the way he carried the sacraments, and the smell of wine on his breath at ten in the morning from the Mass he had already said, and his uncharming, unsocial, hurried manner—something about the practicality and scruffiness of him—made me suddenly realize that he completely believed that what he was doing was an act of magic. He had come to our house to contact supernatural forces as part of his working day. The absence of any trappings and formality and stage setting made it all the more apparent that what was happening here was a piece of magic. I remembered the Church of England priest who had come the year before—"Are you Jewish?"—and I understood for the first time the difference between the Church as an institution that tried to be nice to people, and the Church as a body to which people belonged because they had a living, vivid, strongly felt and daily belief in the supernatural.

At this point, my mother was still in a cavern of grief. She stayed there for years. She disappeared into it; it swallowed her almost whole. She was still inside it when her own mother, Molly, died in 1988. Julie went to the funeral, but said little about it afterward. More or less the only consolation of these years was her lack of financial worries, thanks to the pension plan that Bill had designed. He had successfully argued that the Bank pension should pay unusually high benefits to widows.

One of the ways in which Britain has changed for the better in the last twenty years is that it is no longer socially unacceptable to be a widow in quite the manner it once was—as if losing your husband were bad form, or as if you had contracted a disfiguring disease, not lethal but embarrassing and best left unacknowledged. Some of the married couples who had been my parents' friends stopped sending invitations to my mother. I don't believe this was ever out of conscious cruelty; it was more out of inattention and the fact that they just didn't think of her, a single widowed woman, when they were devising social engagements in their couply lives. Other friends tried to keep seeing my mother, but made the, to her, unforgivable error of pitying her—something to which she was highly sensitized, and to which she reacted by cutting off all contact. If she even suspected that someone might pity her, she would not talk to that person ever again. It was as simple and final as that. She cut off contact with Bill's aunt Louie after a visit during which Louie said—after eating some boiled ham my mother had cooked—"Well, I suppose it was eating heavy food like that which killed him." That was characteristically thoughtless of Louie; it was equally characteristic of Julie that she never spoke to her again. When she did begin to pick up the threads of her life, she did so partly by collecting friends whom she could help, or whom she felt better-off than, or who were nice to her but not patronizingly so. A married couple, the owners of a local Greek café, became two of her closest friends; another friend was the woman who looked after the practical affairs of the cloistered order of Carmelite nuns at Quidenham convent; yet another was a widowed doctor in our old village, who was too brisk and brusque to pity anyone. But that was sometime in the future. For the moment she mainly just grieved.

· 2 ·

I STAYED AT HOME for six weeks and then went back to school to get on with my final year. I was in a state. My brain was racing—it felt like a machine for generating ideas and insights—but I could hardly sit still long enough to read a single page. In some ways it was the perfect frame of mind for taking exams, given that I had enough raw material in terms of basic reading. As for my feelings, they were lost to me. I knew that something wasn't right, but had no idea what, or how to put it right. I was essentially, I think, still in shock. Mostly I kept feeling a pressing, urgent, desperate need to run away—it wasn't clear where or to whom, but just to run away. I had vivid fantasies about heading down to the train station and disappearing.

So the exams came and went, and I had no idea whether I had done brilliantly or terribly. With each one, I spent the first hour of the three-hour paper more or less willing myself, against some unnamable psychic resistance, to begin writing. (I also vowed never to experience that feeling again, and to find a line of work where I wouldn't encounter it; and I've ended up in a line of work where I grapple with it every day. As tabloid editors like to say, "'No' is just an emotional way of saying 'yes.'")

After exams, I stayed in Oxford for a few weeks, until the results came out, and it emerged that I had been awarded a first. I had imagined that moment as a surge of redemptive triumph, as something that would make everything all right and heal the sense of waste and loss I had had since my father died. In the days after his death, the sentence "There must be no waste" would run through my mind over and over. No waste, no waste, there must be no waste. I had, on some not-conscious level, thought that if I got a first—it turned out, a week later, to be a congratulatory first, that is, one of the top four in my year—it would be the case that there had been no waste. And therefore everything would be all right. But that was nonsense, because what I had meant, without realizing it, was that there must be no loss—and the whole point of loss is that it is loss. Loss is the thing you can't get back, the time you can't reverse, the people you love whom you lose.

I should say here that I don't really believe in decisions. That's to say, I think people almost never make decisions, in the sense that a decision involves standing at a fork in the road, thinking which path would be best to take, and then taking it. Usually what happens is, you bumble along, until something happens that makes you look back and realize, Hang on, that was a fork in the road, and I went off in this direction instead of the other one. Normally we don't make decisions, we just do what feels necessary, inevitable. When you split up with someone, you don't sit down and think it through and decide; it's that circumstances mount up and you realize that you can't stay, that it's over, that you already have split up, and that you can't stay put for a second longer without suffocating. By my lights, that's not really a decision—it's just what has to happen next.

So after exams, I didn't decide to stay on at university, I just stayed on at university. Most of my contemporaries went off to do other things, things that, I soon realized, were more interesting, better paid, and much, much more connected to the wider world than being a graduate student. By staying put to do the next thing academically, I was, I thought, staying in the broad mainstream of life, the way I always had by taking the next academic challenge, back since I was about ten. But instead, I slowly realized, I had headed off up a weird tributary, uninhabited and over-grown and isolated.

This isolation wasn't literal: I was living with a group of friends in a shared house in Old Marston, a village just outside the Oxford city perimeter, with a couple of hundred inhabitants and several pubs—the latter because we were in South Oxfordshire, where pub closing time was eleven p.m., whereas a mere hundred yards or so away, in Oxford city, closing time was ten-thirty. My friends were trying to set up an experimental theater company. They were lively and busy and idealistic and they worked hard; I wasn't lonely. But I was lost. The structure of essays and exams had gone: now I had all day, every day, to try to fill with the mysterious activity called writing a thesis, a 50,000-word formal essay titled—I no longer remember how I cooked this up, or what I was thinking—"Rhetoric and Diction in Three English Poets of the 1590s." I had no idea why I was doing this, and no real interest in it, and I was gradu-ally understanding that I didn't want to be an academic. In fact, graduate work, which I had assumed was a logical continuation of undergrad-uate work, was something close to its opposite. Instead of being struc-tured, with regular short pieces being produced, and evaluated, against tight deadlines, it was formless; I saw my supervisor only once every few months, and had no other contact or support of any kind from the uni-versity. I would sit in the pub or college bar with other graduate students, as we all did a fair bit, and agree that it was like having disappeared off a cliff at the edge of the world in some primitive cosmogony.

What I did all day as a graduate student, in practice, was spend an in-credible amount of time and energy trying not to do any work. I would get up late—eleven or so—have coffee and take the bus into town. I would stumble into the Bodleian Library around noon, and perhaps go to the catalogues to order a book or two for the afternoon. I would hand in the book request slip and—because by now I would invariably have bumped into a couple of people I knew—would then head off for lunch at a café or college. After a good long chat and maybe a wander around Blackwell's to see if there was anything new, I might briefly return to the library to check whether my books had come and perhaps flick through the things I'd ordered, only to spot another friend and go for a coffee. Then a wander back to college to check my pigeonhole for mail, and then— oops!—it would be time to head back to a pub or bar for a drink before taking the bus home. I'd have supper with my friends and stay up reading until two or three in the morning.

A rich, full life it wasn't. You can live like this only if you are pretty seriously unhappy, and I was. Of course, there was no way I was going to get away with it. I began to suffer from panic attacks.

There is a mechanical account of panic. It can be seen simply in terms of physiology. What happens is this: It starts with the trigger, your personal trigger—spiders or snakes, or open spaces or closed ones, or the fear of fear, or for no reason that you can detect. You notice the signs of anxiety in yourself—increased temperature and heart rate, butterflies, a sense that the veil of reality is too thin, that you can tear it with your own thoughts. Most of all you become aware of your own rapid, shallow breathing. You overbreathe. Your body takes in too much oxygen and does not retain enough carbon dioxide; you have begun to hyperventilate. But breathing too much oxygen, paradoxically, feels like not breathing enough. You feel as if you can't draw a proper breath. (The trick of breathing into a paper bag works because it increases the level of carbon dioxide in your blood, which makes the respiratory system slow down.) You realize what is happening and that there is no way out. The cycle speeds up; the anxiety and the symptoms of carbon dioxide shortage both soar; and then you are lost to panic. Once you have taught yourself to do this, it is all too easy to do it again and again and again, and then to learn to fear it, and to fear situations where you may feel it, and then you have a new acquaintance in your life, called panic, who isn't going to leave you anytime soon.

That's the mechanical account, that's how the physiology of panic works. But it's not the whole story. A big part of panic has to do with being ambushed by feelings you have not acknowledged. You ignore something in the hope that it will go away—and let's face it, this would be a perfect strategy if it worked. The trouble is that it doesn't work. If the feelings are sufficiently important, then they—the bastards!—won't let you ignore them. Ambush is a good metaphor for what they do. They hide out of plain sight, giving their presence away only by the equivalent of a stifled cough or rustling bush: the night sweat, the forgotten appointment or unexplained surge of anger, the compulsion to open the second and then the third bottle, the inability to sit still. And then the sky falls on your head. Your unconscious, the thing you are trying not to think about, whose existence you are working not to acknowledge, suddenly turns into a nine-hundred-pound gorilla and says, "Oi! Try and ignore this!" The resulting panic blanks out everything else—blocks out all other thoughts and feelings, erases all consciousness of everything but itself. You become your own panic room. You enter a compartment of the mind that consists of pure fear, nothing else.

When you get out of that room—and it is part of the horror of panic that, at the time, you feel that you never will—you know that something isn't right with your psyche. You know that in the deepest fiber of your being, because your mind has just attacked itself. ("Mind attack," formed on analogy with "heart attack," might be a better term than "panic attack.") But you don't necessarily know what the problem, or set of problems, is—you just know that they are there. In that sense the alert-raising powers of a panic attack are all too effective. It's like an incomparably powerful alarm, but one you set off not only when there is a fire or a burglar, but also when there is a strong gust of wind, or a TV set left plugged in, or a fly in the hallway, or a curtain not pulled back, or a leaking tap, or anything. In other words, a panic attack tells you that something is wrong but doesn't tell you what it is.

My first real encounter with panic happened one day when I was walking to the upper reading room at the Bodleian and found myself abruptly short of breath. My heart was racing, my hands were sweating; there wasn't enough air. I had to get to somewhere safe—somewhere out of the building—which felt miles, hundreds of miles, away. Away, away! And down the stairs I ran; and as I did so, the panic eased. That was a crucial, fatal lesson. If you run away, it helps. For the moment, anyway. But if you run away you are more or less guaranteeing a recurrence of the phobia, which thrives more than anything on avoidance. Avoidance is a phobia's favorite thing; every time you avoid something that gives you even the initial flicker of fear—let alone any of its more flagrant manifestations—you are making it absolutely certain that the fear will (a) come back, and (b) be worse. So why avoid things, if it's so damaging? That's easy to answer. You avoid things because you're so frightened you feel as if you have no choice, even when you know you're just making things worse. Thanks to the diagrammatic, irresistible logic of avoidance, I never again walked up those stairs without fear.

In hindsight, I can see that that panic was linked with another thought I had had in the reading room. I was looking around it one day—I vividly remember that I was reading a run of back issues of Ian Hamilton's poetry magazine *The Review*—an activity that was part of a growing realization that I wanted to make my living in the world of literary journalism rather than as an academic; that the evaluative judgments, general racketiness, and closeness to the actual process of creative writing were much more appealing than being on an academic treadmill. Anyway, I was reading *The Review*, and I looked up to see the Merton Professor of English Literature, John Carey. He was a critic I greatly admired (and I admired him, too, because he was chairman of examiners when I got my congratulatory first, so I regarded him as a scary judge of talent), and this admiration gave all the greater force to a thought that suddenly hit me: If I stay in academia, and have a brilliant idea for a thesis, and write it up and get a junior research fellowship, and then turn it into a book and get a fellowship, and then a readership, and then, if I'm really lucky and work hard, a chair, perhaps even the Merton Chair itself—if all these amazing things happen, and I have the best possible career anyone can imagine, I get to spend the rest of my working life in this room.

I say we don't decide things, but that was one of the few times when I did. I realized that I wasn't going to be an academic and that I needed to find something else to do. I started to spend more time doing bits and pieces of journalism for student and local magazines, and touting for work from the London literary press, beginning with *Poetry Review* and *Literary Review*. These were the beginnings of a bid for freedom.

And there is another irony here—again, defining irony as Jonathan

Coe did, as a form of pain. Because I don't know whether I would have become a writer while my father was still alive. I think I would have found the level of risk difficult—financial risk, which is what would have bothered him, and me in telling him, and psychological risk, too. So, terrible though this is to say, my father's death gave me a degree of freedom. Anthony Powell says somewhere that there's nothing quite like having a father go bankrupt to force a man to think for himself. My father's early death was a version of that. His life was not inherently tragic; he wasn't inherently a sad man. If he had lived to be alive today, pushing eighty—even if he had lived to be seventy, not an unreasonable wish—he would have had decades of comfortable retirement to balance the years spent doing his boring job. He would, perhaps, have found things he wanted to do—the move to Norwich was a good start. He might have made a new life for himself, or even have just resigned himself to the fact that he was going to potter about, enjoying his hobbies. But none of that happened. He didn't have that long, balanced life, with years of drudgery evened out by years of suiting himself; he had a truncated life, with years of drudgery followed by an untimely death. That made me determined to not do what he did. Whatever else I did with my life, I wasn't going to spend it doing something I hated: because, as I learned from his death, life is short. If you have any degree of choice—which, as I've already said, most of the people who have ever lived haven't—you should, especially when you are young and unencumbered, set out to try to do whatever it is you most want to do. My father, who almost never gave direct advice—he was a wise man in that respect—was explicit about this. "When you are young," he told me, "you must try and do what you want to do. If it doesn't work out, you can always go and make some money when you get older—but you never get back that chance just to try things out." It was good advice, and I tried to take it. Indeed, broadly speaking, I think I did take it. First, though, there was a nervous breakdown to have.

The panic I had experienced that day at the Bodleian turned out to be the beginning of a series of attacks. Any situation I could not get out of at will was a problem. This, I now know, is classic agoraphobia—which, contrary to what the term is sometimes taken to suggest, has to do not with wide-open spaces but with the agora or public sphere. You are not frightened of the space per se, you are frightened of panicking when in the space; you are frightened of fear. It's the most complicated of phobias, and one of the hardest to treat, and it was my new constant companion. In a weird way, it was like having a new best friend. Fear of the fear became a structuring principle of my days. I wasn't frightened all the time, but at all times I was aware of the possibility of feeling fear. It was there in the corner of my eye if I chose to look. I always knew where I was in relation to it; it was like a private compass point, visible at all times, but only to me.

I started feeling anxiety, which had a way of spiraling into panic, every time I was in a situation that I couldn't get out of. It would happen to me even just sitting in the pub. In that instance, something about the experience of behaving normally, having a normal conversation, would somehow mean that my freedom was impaired (my freedom to get up and run away without looking like a complete idiot), so I would have to get up and run away like a complete idiot. That sensation was with me not quite all the time, but at least once a day. My world began to shrink, and to consist entirely of places and situations where I felt safe: that meant my room, and the journey home. The mere act of turning for home, of giving up whatever I was trying to do outside, brought relief.

It couldn't go on. That's easy to say, of course: lots of things that we feel can't go on do just that. But a fairly big panic attack while I was walking down Cornmarket Street—a longish Main Street shopping hell that for some reason was always a particular nexus for my phobic feelings—made me realize I had to do something, even though I had no idea quite what that something was. So I went to see a G.P. The first great relief was that he took me seriously. I was wired up to an ECG machine and he tested my heart—uselessly, I now know, since a resting ECG may not tell you much, but never mind. He then said that the best thing for me would be to go to a specialist, but that the referral would take some time. He wrote me a prescription for Valium for the interim and explained that it worked best when used to get over specific crises, rather than taken as a general panacea. And that was more or less that.

It would be untrue to say that I felt better immediately, but I found some relief in the thought that I had at least taken some action and that somewhere in the distance, if I listened very hard, I would be able to hear the hoofbeats of mental health professionals riding to the rescue. There was, though, a longish wait. I think it was a couple of weeks before I had a letter from the Warnford, the local bin, as it was usually referred to— the local mental health hospital. I was given an appointment for an assessment in three months. The time did not fly past, not at all. I spent it mainly reading back issues of literary magazines and mulling over an idea I had had for a novel, a cookbook that turned into a murder story— which was eventually my first book, *The Debt to Pleasure*. But mainly what I was doing was not working and not feeling, which, in its way, is a specialized, highly demanding, indeed exhausting, form of mental labor.

When the time for my appointment came, I took a bus to the Warnford and made my way to a Nissen hut, where I was given an assessment by a psychiatrist and the therapist with whom I was to work. She was a trainee, an Israeli in her early thirties with whom I had nothing in common but with whom I found I got along—I didn't know then how rare and how essential that was in a therapeutic context. We had one session a fortnight over a period of a few months, and though I can't really remember what we talked about, it helped. In fact it didn't just help; the phobia swiftly, and apparently definitively, just went away. Spontaneous remission, you might call it; "flight into health," if you were a Freudian; good therapy, if you were my Israeli; or some combination of the above. The turning point, or what felt like the turning point, was a session when I came in with something she had asked for, a timesheet giving a breakdown of a typical day. It was divided into fifteen-minute sections. I told the truth and gave an account of a day much like the one I described earlier. My therapist freaked. "You don't do any work at all!" she said. "Nothing!" Her outrage was useful: I realized that my general sense of something lurking in the bushes, waiting to jump out and get me, might be usefully addressed if I gave some attention to the thing actually lurking in the bushes of my daily life, namely, my unwritten—untouched, unbegun—thesis. I decided that I had to get out of the life I was leading—

well, I say "decided," but what happened was that I realized I couldn't go on, and needed to act on the consequences of that resolution.

I don't think my exhausting, strenuous efforts at not working were what was really wrong with me; but they were a vivid symptom. By turning to face the symptom, I began to feel that I was no longer running away—which is what I was really engaged in doing, all day and every day, and was one reason why running away played such a big role in the phobia. So I made a plan, and the first part of it was not to apply for money for the third year of my Ph.D. At the moment I was enrolled to do an M.Litt. (equivalent to a master's degree)—that 50,000-word thesis on a critical subject. If I took money for the extra year, I would have to do a D.Phil. (a Ph.D.), which would be 90,000 words, and would also have to be, by strict rubric of the degree, a "substantial, original contribution to knowledge." Those three words were like grenades. "Substantial" meant long, with lots of footnotes. "Original" meant it couldn't be a review or an overview of things that had already been discussed. But the real killer was "knowledge"; it wasn't to be a collection of thoughts or opinions or ideas or insights, however interesting: I had to find out something new. In those days, as a direct result of this grim rubric and the lack of support for graduate students trying to grapple with it, the average completion time for a D.Phil.—which was funded for three years—was between six and seven years, and the dropout rate (or "noncompletion" rate, as it was called in Oxfordese) was more than ninety percent. It might have been easier to take the money for the third year and to spend another twelve months in subsidized misery, but I realized that that way lay, perhaps literally, madness. So I decided to go home to Norwich when the grant ran out, in late summer 1986, finish my 50,000-word thesis in one big go, do as much journalism as I could, and try to find a job.

As I write, it occurs to me that what may have helped more than anything else to relieve the phobia was the fact that, by giving up on graduate work, I was giving up on an ambition I had inherited from my father. I was beginning to live my own life, and therefore beginning, implicitly, to acknowledge that he was dead. That's sad to admit. But it was true that his death gave me one fewer person to disappoint—and to become a writer, as Cyril Connolly once said, you have to do a certain amount of living down your promise. This usually takes a few years, and it would have been hard to do with my dad's unspoken worries and disappointments looming over me. Leaving Oxford was an implicit admission that I no longer had to worry about pleasing him. It wasn't that I simply woke up one morning to find that the phobia had gone away. It wasn't even a question of realizing that it had gone away. It was rather that the fear gradually faded, first in the number of times it came. For a while, the London Underground was a particular nexus, not when the train was stuck in tunnels (which is what gives me the willies now, to such an extent that I can't take the Tube anymore), but when it was rattling along between stations. The fear faded in frequency, then in severity, becoming less acute and unignorable and more like a few moments of anxious discomfort which, I learned, would soon fade. Then, as the specific occurrences went away, its steady presence in the corner of my mind went away, too—it was no longer the compass point, the monster in the cupboard. Sometimes you don't so much get over something as forget about it, and that was what happened here.

The scary part of the plan to go to Norwich and look for a job was that I was now living at home with my mother, for the first time since—well, in a sense, for the first time since I had left for boarding school at the age of ten. Every other time I had been home—to Hong Kong or Alderfen or Norwich—it had been in the context of living my real life somewhere else, at boarding school or university; I had always been in an institutional framework, with somewhere to go back to and work to get on with. Now I was at home until I could manage to get away. That was a source of strain from the beginning. Julie resented the idea of my being there in order to not be there; I was trying to keep my distance and avoid becoming so enraptured with home comforts that I would never manage to leave. No, that's not right. The sense in which I was scared of being at home was less practical than that: it was somehow a fear of losing the autonomy I had earned by all that time away. We were involved in a passionate struggle, and all without a word spoken. My mother loved having me at home so much that she hated it—hated it because it was going to end, and

On holiday in Derry, 1984.

would end because I would leave her. So she tried to show, by a certain cool-
ness and formality and adherence to boundaries, that that was fine with her;
as far as she was concerned, I might as well leave right away.

This was the longest period Julie and I had ever spent entirely in each
other's company. I wish I had clearer memories of it. The main thing I remember was a six-week holiday we took in Ireland together, spending
two weeks in Courtmacsherry in County Cork, in a borrowed bungalow
belonging to Miriam Bailey, an old Murphia friend from Hong Kong; two
in Clifden in Galway; and two with friends in Buncrana, County Donegal.
It was a good look at Julie's talent for being busy. I've said that she never
did anything, which is cruel and true in only one sense; in terms of being
on the go, of outings and shopping and cooking, of arranging drop-ins
and excursions and whatnot, she was a blur of motion. I am that rare variety of person who is content with an entirely unoccupied day—in fact,

On the Giant's Causeway.
My mother's caption reads: "John as Yogi."

it's something I crave, in the same way I crave regular episodes of solitude. I love doing nothing. (It's quite a rare love, I've noticed, even among people who describe themselves as lazy. Speaking as someone who is genuinely lazy, I'd say genuine laziness is quite rare.) I obviously did not inherit this taste from my mother, who, when she had time that seemed empty, set out to fill it.

As for her Norwich life, it was very much like that—busy with things she had devised to keep herself busy. She had good friendships, though she never attempted to have a close male friend after my father died. She once, rather embarrassingly, told me that she was "monoerotic" and that she had never felt attracted to any man apart from him. This may not have been biographically true, but she came to feel that it was true. She

was of that generation of widows who regarded their lives as being officially over when their husbands died.

My relations with Julie were now difficult. Nobody tells you that the
hardest part about being an only child isn't so much the early years, when
you are the sole focus of your parents as parents (I don't say of their attention, because you may well not be getting that). The trickier part
comes later, when the first of your parents dies. I daresay other only children, less emotionally illiterate and cut off from their feelings than I was,
and also with older parents who might reasonably be expected to die
soonish, are more prepared for this than I was. But I didn't know what to
do, or more precisely, what to think or feel, about the idea that I was supposed to look after my mother. It didn't help that she acted as if being
looked after was the very last thing she wanted. What this amounted to
was that I was backing away at the same time that she was pushing me
away, or pretending to.

In November 1986, festering at home in Norwich, I saw an ad for an
editorial assistant's job at the *London Review of Books.* In December 1986, I had
the biggest piece of luck I had had to date, when, after going for an interview, I had a phone call from Karl Miller offering me a part-time job in
the *LRB* office at a salary of £8,000 a year. It was the best thing that had
ever happened to me, intellectually and in other respects—but that is a
long and different story. As far as Julie was concerned, it meant that I was
indeed, finally and irrevocably, leaving home. The sense of disengage-
ment and stasis—one of whose meanings in Greek is "civil war"—between
us was by now immovable.

If there was ever to be a time when Julie might feel in a position to tell
me her secret, that time was now. My father, the person she most had to
protect, was dead—and, as I have discovered in the course of writing this
book, by the end of his life she had told him the truth. That happened, I
believe, in 1979. A letter of hers to me mentions a "breakthrough" in relation to "years of guilt and anxiety." It was a bizarre thing to tell me
about, since she had never before spoken to me of feeling guilty and anxious, or given me any reason to suspect what she might feel guilty about.
As for anxiety, well, she was usually worried about something—though

worry is a rather different thing from anxiety, since it tends to be pointed outward at others; it's another way of projecting a mood, with a big component of will to control in it. Worry is anxiety with an agenda. It is often a way of bullying people with love. Nonetheless, here she was, talking about her breakthrough. I think what happened was that she told my father her secret, and he forgave her. The documentary evidence that she told him comes not long afterward, in a letter from Bill to an accountant asking for tax advice. He gives a brief autobiography, and in it he says that "my wife is six years older than me," in other words nearly ten years older than she admitted to being. So she must have told him. I notice that my father, in stating her age to the accountant, would not lie about it, even though he had no contextual reason for stating the truth. This makes me think that it was much on his mind at the time; it may have been part of the reason for Bill's general sense of loss and disappointment at the time of his retirement.

Neither of them—but you know this—ever chose to mention the truth to me. The closest Julie ever came to telling me was not by dropping hints, or anything like that, but by letting me stay with Peggie—who lived in Norwich until autumn 1973—on weekends away from school, and then, subsequently, by letting me go to Ireland on my own. Peggie is tactful, and was aware that my mother's age was not something to be blurted out; it was she, indeed, who told the truth, years later, when there was a medical need for me to know. But she also knew that I was to be told only in an emergency. Once I went to Ireland and met the family, though, anything could happen.

In retrospect, I've wondered why my mother let me go, given her fears about her secrets. (It was I who wanted to go, by the way; I was desperately keen to find out about my Irish family, and in particular to meet my cousins.) I think, for one thing, that she couldn't have stopped me without making it seem highly fishy: if she was in contact with her family, why couldn't I be? And I also think that in the end—belying the warnings and dark hints she had given over the years—she trusted her family's tact. Dates of birth, in a family of seven sisters, aren't necessarily the kinds of things that are bandied about; there may well have been a sense that, given that my mother was forty when she married, she may not have been candid about her age at the time of the wedding, and so full disclosure would not be entirely tactful. If she trusted that, she was right to do so; it wasn't until fifteen years after my first visit to Ireland that someone mentioned the age of my uncle John, and even then, it was to my wife rather than to me, and by then I was so thoroughly indoctrinated to my mother's worldview that I didn't believe what I was told. In a sense, then, my mother was trusting the power of her own force field. She desperately wanted to keep this secret, and was good at suppressing things she did not want revealed; so she felt that her Inquiry Suppression Field would extend to Ireland while I was with her family, and help keep her secret for her. And she was right, it did.

The opposite may be true, too. She may have hoped that someone would let her secret out, and she would be free of it. She would do nothing to let even a hint of the truth out herself; but she may have wanted to be free of her secret nonetheless, and may have hoped, despite herself, that someone would bring the roof down on her. That would be only human.

But that didn't happen; no one told me the secret, and my mother never came close to doing so. This was not, I think, out of a feeling that I needed to be protected; rather, she felt she needed to be protected from me. To myself, I seemed an extraordinarily mild-mannered, calm, and irenic adolescent—to a fault, actually—but I know, because I was told, that to my parents I had become a tyrannical monster of sarcasm, silence, eye-rolling, parent-despising, moral superiority, boredom, and argumentative radical politics. All adolescents are like that. It is hard work separating from our parents. For Julie, this may have touched off too many memories from her own childhood. She was always prone to see things in terms of a struggle for the moral upper hand, and that was always going to be a contested area. This was one way in which our relationship was not like one between a parent and a child but more like one between competing equals. Children should seek their parents' approval, not vice versa. Children should seek to outdo their parents, not vice versa. Here, though, there was something much more like the competition to have the moral upper hand that is such a weirdly all-important factor in so much adult life, particularly in married life. (Why? I've never encountered an explanation for it. Why do we all so hate being in the wrong?)

This is why, in the final analysis, my mother did not tell me her secret. Julie didn't tell me her secret, because if she had, I would have had the moral upper hand. She could not bring herself to give me that weapon; she could not, or at any rate did not, trust me enough. I find that a hard fact to take, but there it is.

Was she right not to tell me? Thinking this over as calmly as possible, I can see why she didn't tell me when I was a child, or a teenager, or in my early twenties. By the time my father had been dead for five years or so, I can see less justification for keeping these things secret. I can understand why she didn't want to be judged by me. Julie was forgetting something, though, something that counts as a very, very important fact from my point of view, and something I try never to forget when I think about what she did. That something is this: If my mother had not lied, I would never have been born. My father had only two wishes for his own family life, when he came to have one: He would not use money as a means of control over his children; and he would have more than one child. Julie was forty when I was conceived, which in 1961 made it long odds against having one child, let alone any more. That makes the calculus pretty simple. If she hadn't lied to my dad, they would never have gotten together as a couple, and I would never have been born. So I can't find it in my heart to be too critical of what Julie did in 1960 or thereabouts, because without it, I wouldn't be here.

Keeping the secret, however, is a little different. By the 1980s, the habit had become entrenched. She was never going to tell me, and she never did. It would have been a decisive shift in our relationship. Perhaps it would have been the start of a more real relationship, in that my mother would have been removing a degree of control in return for an increased chance of trust and intimacy. But she didn't, and so we stayed stuck where we were.

I did make one attempt to shift it, or to clarify and express what I felt, at the start of 1987. I don't remember exactly what prompted me; it must at some level have been the feeling that I had now definitively left home. Whatever the reason, I wrote my mother a letter.

> I was intending to write less to tell news and more to thank you for having put up with me over the last few months so kindly and uncomplainingly when I must have seemed (and to tell the truth sometimes felt) to be at a very dead end. From Dad's death I learnt that it's always best to say things when you think of them and when you want to rather than to wait for a later occasion—so I thought I should tell you that I love you, and that if we have occasional disagreements and irritations, or if I seem thoughtless, it doesn't alter the fact that I love you and always will.

Perhaps, if we had been closer, I wouldn't have felt the need to write that; I would have been confident that she knew. Having to spell it out implied a degree of distance and strain; and as Jonathan Raban wrote in his introduction to *The Oxford Book of the Sea*, "people write about the things which give them trouble." True. But despite all that, I'm very glad I wrote the letter. It didn't have any particular effect on anything, but I'm still glad I wrote it.

As for how I know it had no particular effect, that's because of one of the nasty surprises I had waiting for me when I went through my mother's belongings after her death. I found that in 1988, by which time I had been living and working in London for almost two years—in other words, two years after I had left home for good—she put the house in Norwich up for sale and made plans to emigrate to Majorca. I've said very little in this book about my mother's fluent Spanish, love of Spanish culture, interest in the Balearic Islands, and long-standing wish to live on the Mediterranean. The reason I've said so little about these subjects is that my mother spoke no Spanish, never said a word about anything to do with Spain or the Mediterranean, and had been to Majorca only once, on a week's holiday. She liked the climate, which she found helpful for her arthritis, but still . . . This plan to sell the house and move to Majorca was a gesture of pure "Look what you made me do," a sulk or tantrum. The idea was that she would present me with one of her beloved faits accomplis. Then I would realize just what a terrible son I had been, and at the same moment realize that it was too late to make amends. It was her way of saying, with unambiguous clarity, "I see so little of you, I might as well be living in a different country."

This would have been her all-time definitive fait accompli—but it didn't happen, for a reason that hints at an ambivalence on her part about making such a stark move. (Although I was the main intended target, I wasn't the only one. It was intended also to show her Norwich friends and her Irish family how little she cared for them, in return for how little they cared for her.) The year in question, 1988, was the peak of the last UK property boom, and the price my mother demanded for our house, £189,000, was a little toppy. I say "demanded" advisedly. She had an offer for just below the asking price, and this is how she responded to it: "The price is £189,000. I am not interested in a lower offer."

That's Julie at her flintiest. It also gives a glimpse, perhaps, in its ab-solute unbending take-it-or-leave-it-ness, of the fact that some part of her did not want to sell the house. Later that year, the property market crashed and Julie lost the chance for a windfall on the Norwich home that would allow her to buy some nice place in Majorca and still have capital left over. She stayed on in the house in Friars Quay, with too many stairs and a view of the river.

· 3 ·

MAYBE I COULD HAVE HAD the same childhood that I had, and the same genetic inheritance, and the same degree of emotional illiteracy, and not have had psychological difficulties at some point. Maybe. But I didn't get away with it.

In January 1990, I took a day off work and went to the Lake District with my then girlfriend for a long weekend. The first day was very wet, not just damp, but so foggy and saturated with rain that we felt as if we were walking inside a cloud. The second morning, the cloud cover had lifted and the weather was good enough to walk in the impressive new boots we had bought during the downpour the day before. We set out along the valley and then up one of the fells, toward the stream and waterfall that allegedly inspired Coleridge to write "Kubla Khan." It was about three miles along the flat and then fifteen hundred feet or so uphill.

Before long we came to Coleridge's waterfall. It was narrow and small and not overwhelming, but I was glad to have seen it. By now the cloud had come down again and we were walking through it; we could see probably about a hundred feet ahead.

We started upward. Somewhere we lost our way and, without realizing it, wandered off the path onto a steep slope of scree. As anyone who has ever walked on it will know, scree is semi-scary fun to walk down, half surfing on the slates as they slide over one another—there's a sense that you're bringing half the mountain down with you in a man-made avalanche. Walking up it, however, is no fun at all. You slide down half or three-quarters of a step for every one you take upward, and trying to go faster makes the slates slide faster, so increased effort results in decreased progress.

On this particular slope, I was getting seriously out of breath and longing for the top of the fell for which we were headed. Instead of doing what I should have done—stop to compose myself—I pressed on, hurrying and simultaneously falling back. The effort was like those you make in nightmares, running only in order to stand still.

And then suddenly we were at the top of the slope, and equally suddenly—miraculously—we were through the top of the cloud in an absolutely clear, transcendentally blue sky. Because the cloud base was dead flat, at about a thousand feet, it was like climbing above the world, only now to be cut off from it by an obscuring blanket of white. All we could see were other hills above a thousand feet—it was stunningly beautiful and strange, and it felt as if we had been transported from a low fell in the Lake District to the highest point in the Himalayas.

It was too much for me. (This is a terrible thing to admit, but even describing that moment brings a wave of anxiety.) The crucial factor was that I was already desperately out of breath and on the point of hyperventilating from exertion. Whatever the reason, I found myself in the grip of a full-scale, 10/10 panic. My heart was going at a rate that I *knew*, just knew, was impossibly fast. I couldn't breathe, let alone see straight or think straight. It felt as if my mind had broken. I wasn't just going to die; I had disintegrated. There was nothing to hold on to. I didn't want to sit down, because I feared that the exertion of getting up again, on top of the effort my heart was already putting into its three thousand beats per minute, would kill me. But in order to go back down the hill—which I knew with absolute, chemical certainty was the only way I would survive—I would have to go along the path, now visible at the top of the scree slope we'd just climbed; and the initial stages of the path were not down but up.

Well, I did it—though not without being basically dragged by my girlfriend. It was a few minutes before my heart started to slow down; and then, as we began to descend, we bumped into a party of fell walkers going up the hill. They were delighted with the freak weather. "You can come here for twenty years and not get a day like this," one of them said, beaming. Well, I thought, thanks. But actually I felt better just by having met other people, even if they were (I thought at the time) insane. We weren't alone in the world, as it had felt for a moment at the top of that slope, cut off by cloud. No doubt it was this very thought, just below the surface, that triggered the panic.

I had panicked before, or so I thought. Yet those other experiences were nothing like this. They had been frightening and unpleasant; this felt like a glimpse of genuine psychic disintegration. It would not be true, quite, to say that I was never the same again. But it would be a little bit true. I did not immediately give myself over to panic on a daily basis, and I did not immediately, there and then, become agoraphobic. The next day, cold and clear, we walked from the B&B a good few miles over the hills and down into Grasmere to visit Wordsworth's cottage, and then back, and I was fine all the way—just the fact that we were most of the time in eyesight of places where people lived was enough to make me feel anchored, safe. So I did not succumb to the phobia immediately, by no means. When we returned to London and I went back to work, I was fine—there was no lurking sense of imminent ambush by fear. The specific circumstances of that huge first panic attack were a help. How often would I have walked several miles and then up a mountain? How often would I be cut off from the sight of other people by cloud cover? If being able to see people, or places where people lived, or buildings in general, was going to relieve the fear, then how much of a problem was it going to be in London? My attitude was, Maybe I'll put mountain-walking holidays on hold for a bit, but otherwise I'll be fine. The problem was, though, that I had relearned to panic. I had learned that getting out of breath plus feeling anxious could bring on—to use my girlfriend's term—a "wobbly," I could inflict on myself a truly horrible thing, a "near-death experience," in the words of one psychiatrist; and I could do it anytime, anywhere, without notice. I had learned how to panic.

The phobia really moved in to stay later that same year. In May, I took a three months' leave from work to try to write my first book. This was *The Debt to Pleasure*, the same one for which I'd had the idea about five years earlier. The idea was fairly complete, and so now all I had to do was the ton of work of actually writing it. My attitude was that I would one day wake up in the morning and find that I had written it. I discovered, to my disappointment, that it didn't work that way. To write the book, I would have to write the book. How unfair was that? Still, my girlfriend had a job in Barrow-in-Furness, one of the bleakest towns in England, on the Cumbrian coast. If I took unpaid leave from the *LRB*, I could go there for three months and start my novel. The World Cup was on at the time, so I would have something to keep myself entertained. My girlfriend went on a reconnoitering expedition and rented a cottage for us in a village called Bardsea, just outside the small town of Ulverston. (Birthplace of Stan Laurel, trivia fans.) There was a Tibetan Buddhist monastery just down the road. The cottage was within a short walk of the huge expanse of Morecambe Bay, whose big, calm sky and flat mud stretches were entirely deceptive: it's a lethal expanse of water, where the rapidly moving tides, shifting currents, quickly descending fogs, and sinking sand regularly kill people. You could look at it, but you couldn't walk on it. Levels of pollution were so high that there was hardly any bird life.

Trouble, though—the start of what I think of as my main encounter with the phobia—began on the way up. My girlfriend had to see someone outside Woodstock—a puppet expert or a makeup guru, I forget which. She dropped me in the town for a wander and a bookshop visit and gave me directions to the house, about a mile away across country. I pottered about happily enough and then set out to meet her. It was a sunny day, warm for an English May, and I was walking down a country lane with a sudden feeling of happiness and freedom. I thought, "I've left work, I can go anywhere and be anything I like. I'm free."

Kierkegaard said that anxiety is freedom. In other words, if you feel

anxious that's because you are out from under the shadow of certainty—
and the price, or corollary, of that is anxiety. This may not be true always and everywhere, but it was true for me that day. Almost at the exact
moment I had the thought "I'm free," I felt a wave of fear. It was unspe-
cific and all the more frightening for that; I couldn't have said what I was
frightened of, just that I was frightened—purely terrified. I had to hide
but didn't know how or where, since I was trudging down a country lane
with a field on each side. I was too far from Woodstock to turn back, or so
I felt, and even if I did turn back I had no way of getting in touch with my
girlfriend, so I would have to set out again on foot anyway. I tried to hide
behind a clump of trees on one side of the road—somehow I thought
that if I could get out of the light, out of all that sense of exposure, the
terror would ease. I saw a car coming and leapt out from behind a tree to
try to hitch a lift—a lift to anywhere, since anywhere would feel safer
than here. The driver, a woman on her own, did not stop; I'm not surprised. I must have looked a sight, a pale young man bursting out of a tiny
copse with staring frightened eyes and his thumb imploringly in the air.

The feeling passed, as it does—though at the time, of course, you
never remember that. I managed to walk to the house, meet my girlfriend, and head off for Cumbria. But this time the phobia was not paying a casual visit. In retrospect it seems all too clear that the anxiety was
linked to the fact I was making my first concerted attempt to write fiction. I felt free, or at some level I had decided that I was free; I was going
to write. The immediate cost of this was a crushing anxiety that focused
not on the question of writing—I had no nerves about that that I was
aware of: I felt that either I'd be able to do it or I wouldn't—but on the
question of panic.

This is when panic became institutionalized in my life. I was scared of
panicking, and knew all too well that I could panic. By extension, I was
scared of the kinds of places where I might panic—the kinds of places
where I would begin to feel anxious, and where the anxiety would then
spiral into panic because I was in a place or a situation that I couldn't escape. Wide-open spaces were, and to this day still are, the worst trigger for
the anxiety. The rational component of this is that if I'm in the middle of

a wide-open space and begin to feel trapped in it, it's by definition difficult to get out of, because—duh!—it's wide and open. As for what the irrational component is—the trigger behind the rational trigger—I don't know. But I would find it far, far easier to walk five miles down narrow urban streets than five hundred yards across any kind of open plain. In fact, I don't think I could do that except under duress, or in the company of someone I trusted. Some confined spaces are okay, others not so, and at different times. Large enclosed spaces were and are difficult—big museums, galleries, convention centers. The key factor here is the distance from an exit: if there's one within easy distance, I'm usually okay. It's worse if I'm tired, and very much worse if I have a hangover.

In Bardsea, the panic settled down and turned into a phobia. The house had no phone and was at the end of a lane about four hundred yards from the village proper. About halfway to the village there was a phone booth, which was the first place I felt safe when I went out, and in the village itself there was a pub, where I was safe also. Getting to the pub was quite a drama; some days I could do it—I'd go there for lunch—some days I couldn't. I couldn't drive—which, I see in retrospect, was a big part of the problem—but I could cycle, at least when I wasn't feeling too phobic. I could ride into Ulverston every now and then to do the shopping, but the ride back was much more difficult, because it was uphill, and would trigger my spiral from breathlessness to anxiety to panic. I began to dread it and then to avoid it. This was the second time I sought help. After a month or so, I went to a G.P. in Ulverston, who prescribed beta-blockers. At the library I checked a drug dictionary and found that beta-blockers are contraindicated for asthmatics, so I couldn't take the pills I'd been given. I went back to the doctor, who said, in effect, Oops, but not to worry because the danger was probably exaggerated. A couple of weeks later I had a visit at home from a very nice psychiatric social worker who gave me a questionnaire. He told me that when he and a colleague did workshops for people with agoraphobia, his colleague always said that "no one has ever died from a panic attack." He himself didn't feel you could say that, since you couldn't really know if it was absolutely true, but he hoped I would find it a reassuring thought.

I spent the days waiting for the start of the World Cup and trying to write my book. It wasn't going well: I was finding it almost physically impossible to sit still and concentrate. I did fragments of work here and there, made the occasional note or two, but neither the book nor I was going anywhere, and we both knew it. I ran out of money and split up with my girlfriend, though I continued to stay in the cottage out of a sense that going anywhere else would feel too much like a defeat—not about the relationship, which had already been defeated, but in relation to my unwritten, unwritable book and my hopes for it. The World Cup came and went. I watched it entirely on my own. At the end of the three months I went back to London with about five pages of notes for my book and a full-blown case of agoraphobia.

Once I was back in London, back in work, and back in a routine, the symptoms eased. I was always aware of the possibility of panic, and was always calculating where I was in relation to a possible attack. I was like a spy or a gangster, calculating lines of escape and places of safety. I was never alone; the anxiety was a constant companion. But the encounters with the fear were avoidable, and I could get around the city without encountering many of the blank or trapping spaces I most feared, so I reached a kind of accommodation with the phobia. As a result, over the next year or so it got steadily worse.

At this point, if I were reading this book, I would probably wonder about the question of courage. I've often wondered about it myself, before, during, and after encounters with my own fear. Would it be a lot simpler if I were just braver? If I simply advanced toward the anxiety whenever I felt it? Is the problem that I am just not brave enough? That I am, in fact, a cowardy custard?

The answer, I think, is: Maybe. I am in fact something of a physical coward—thanks, again, to that overactive imagination, and a too-great ability to imagine pain and injury. That can't help, in relation to something that is about fear. But on the other hand, I have fought hard against the fear, and have staged many, many head-on battles with it. These battles often, or usually, aren't externally visible, and can look to the external world like a man walking around the corner to buy a newspaper. In my head, though, it's a direct encounter with my deepest fear, a pure and harrowing drama, one in which I'm facing down the thing I most dread. I'm well aware that this is ridiculous and, in both the teenage and the non-teenage senses of the word, sad. But there it is, and I've done it many, many times. In the year in question, after I got back to London, I would have these battles several times a day. I would think: If I can go downstairs from the office and walk to the coffee shop the long way around, down the featureless city block where I get anxious, and manage it without stopping or slowing or turning back, I will have won, and that little victory will make me a little more confident, and next time I go up against the fear I will be a little more confident still, and I will win a bigger victory, and then a bigger still, and finally the phobia will have no choice but to leave me alone, and then I will have won, and I'll be free, and the whole process will have begun right here, right now, because this is where it stops. This is what I would think, and this is what I would do, over and over again, and it didn't work. The victories never mounted up to anything decisive. It never went anywhere. I have come to feel, in fact, that by staging these battles with the fear I was helping to institutionalize it as part of my personality, part of my typical day.

When you have a phobia like this, it profoundly feels that it is clinging to you—so that it is logical to think that you can fight it off, kill it off, beat it into submission. What is very difficult to accept is that in reality, you are clinging to it. *You* are clinging to *it*. Realizing that, then working out what to do about it, is hard.

One thing that made me realize I needed to go to plan B—which in practice meant get some help—was an experience I had one day while sitting and watching a video. It was James Cameron's craptastic underwater epic *The Abyss,* and I may be the only person in the world who has felt he had an important realization while watching it. Anyway, there's a scene where water is flooding into the heroes' submarine (actually there are about a dozen scenes like that, but bear with me) and everybody is rushing around frenetically trying to save the day. The heroes fight the on-rushing tide of water, and struggle to close a valve or a door or something, and they are desperately worried, right on the edge, they look terrified, and it's not clear whether they're going to make it, and they look even more terrified, and I was watching them be brave and look terrified and do heroic things and I thought: "But I feel like that every day. I'm just as frightened as that when the lift isn't working and I have to walk up the stairs, or I come to a city block with no doors or shelter or place to hide, or when the train stops in a tunnel. I go through fear like that every day." And thinking that, I felt, first, a wave of sadness for the misery I was inflicting on myself, and second, a realization that I had to do something about this, I needed to get help.

Another factor made me feel I needed to act. That was that I had met and fallen in love with my future wife. If I had been, in general, miserable, then maybe I wouldn't have felt the need to address the phobia and its consequences. In a landscape of general miserableness, the phobia wouldn't have stood out. But I was, in large parts of my life, happy, as happy as I had ever been, and that made me want to actually live my life, and not spend so much of it cowering. When you are frightened you are not really living; life is washing over you, and you are not really inhabiting it. That's how I felt. Because I now liked my life, I wanted to live it.

So for the third time I found myself going to a G.P., telling him my troubles, and getting a referral. My G.P. in those days was an amiable Italian doctor in Bloomsbury. He had the air of a man who disapproved of mental weakness, but despite that he wrote a letter, handed it to me, and told me to take it up the road to the Psychology Department of University College Hospital, about half a mile away. It felt odd trudging up the street with that letter, but I did, saw a senior therapist, got a referral, and began a course of psychotherapy that lasted for years.

I am not, and would never claim to be, a poster boy for psychotherapy. It is not a panacea. But it has helped me in pretty much every aspect of my life. I once heard Nicholas Mosley say something like that to Sue Lawley on *Desert Island Discs*; she replied that people often said that but then never gave specifics, so would he please enumerate the actual ways in which he had been helped? In that spirit, I would say that the things psychotherapy has helped me with have to do with feeling my feelings as and when I'm supposed to feel them, rather than mediated into mysterious mood swings or (worse) emerging in the form of panic. It helped me face painful feelings related to loss and abandonment; it helped me make sense of myself; it helped me deal with the illness and death of people I loved; and it helped me write. It did that by helping me spend more time in my own head without panicking. It helped me sit still, which is something you have to learn to do if you're going to write books.

It also helped me realize something that, for me, feels important. I have come to think that the two dominant models of the human personality are both false. One of them, the principal one in the West, sees the self as an edifice, a stable and enduring structure, like a building. In this version our personalities are not necessarily small or simple; they can have many different aspects; they have places from which one can take a different perspective, they have nooks and warrens, secret places, internal courtyards, harems, minarets, dungeons, unexpected phantoms, Bluebeard's chambers; they can be open-plan (knocked through) or closed and souklike—but essentially, for all their complexity, they are fixed and stable. We may find new things about ourselves over time, but that's like finding a room behind a door you'd never noticed in a ramshackle mansion. We are what we are; our self is us, and our self is here for keeps. In this version of things, my fears would just be part of who I am, fixed, an internal compartment of my permanent self.

The other view, a more Eastern one, regards this vision of the self as fundamentally mistaken. It sees the personality, the fixed self, as a kind of optical illusion. We are a wave, a fluid sequence of mental states and perceptions, passing through time. When we look back at the path the wave has traveled, we see a trick of memory, which makes it seem as if that self were still traveling with us—but just as in a wave the water stays where it is and only the energy moves forward, so it is with the personality, which is only in this moment, right here, right now. We remember past moments (or we think we do—we continually convince ourselves that we do) and we invent continuity with that earlier self, but it is a fiction. We are only who we are right now, and the stability and continuity of the self is a comforting illusion. We tell ourselves stories to arrange these successive selves into a single unity; we make stories to make a self. In this version, my anxieties would be no more than something I kept doing to myself, a story I was telling myself over and over again.

I find that neither of these accounts of identity is quite right. We are not fixed and permanent, and the Buddhist or Humean emphasis on fluidity is right insofar as it stresses that; but we also don't make ourselves up out of ourselves, moment by moment. The second of these views just doesn't feel right. I'm not exactly the same person I was yesterday, or a year ago, or a decade ago. Yet it is also true to say that I'm not an entirely different person. There is a continuity between our past selves and our current ones; this is something we feel in our deepest being. And that feeling is not entirely an illusion. Indeed, we often wish that there were less of a continuity, and all of us have aspects of ourselves that we wish we could simply slough off. But it doesn't work like that.

I would suggest that instead of regarding ourselves as either a building or a wave, we should see the personality as more like a literary work, a poem perhaps, with themes and subjects and imagery, and motifs that run through it but are not quite (or not necessarily) the same thing as stories. We have narratives, but we are not made out of narrative; we have stabilities, structures, but they are things we hold in place by internal tensions, braced by thematic energies. We hold ourselves in place with meanings—or if not meanings, with parallels, balances, rhythms, echoes, patterns. A life is a set of events but it is also a set of themes and meanings, and it is often the meaning that determines the event, and not the other way around. In other words, what you said and did with your first love, for instance, is given content by what you choose to make of it, much more than by the actual words that were spoken and the deeds that were done. Some people decide that their first love is the great event of their lives, and others can barely remember it a year or two later, and they might be remembering the exact same sequence of events. More than a building or a wave, what we most truly resemble is a work of art. That's something therapy has brought me to think.

What therapy didn't do for me directly is cure the phobia. It's much more manageable now—I've flown around the world, been all over the place, and I live my life as well as I can. But I'm not entirely free of irrational anxiety, not really. I don't know if I ever will be. Still, I can live with not being free of it, since it is part of who I am, and I have no choice about it. Anxiety is freedom. Freedom is anxiety. There are people for whom that is not true, and I envy them; I truly, deeply envy them. They don't know about their own luck. But I'm not one of them, and that's just the way it is.

That, too, is why I've never tried to cure the fear by taking medication. Many readers will have wanted to bang my head against a wall and order me to take Xanax (or another benzodiazepine tranquilizer) or Prozac (or another SSRI antidepressant) and just medicate my way through the fear. That, after all, is what most people now do. As Adam Gopnik wrote in *The New Yorker,* talking is out, and taking is in. To many people, the idea of deliberately not taking medication to help with a condition like mine is like refusing to use a prosthesis when you have a missing limb. It's a willful refusal to accept the available help.

I disagree. I don't disagree for everyone, and I don't see this as an issue where you can make general rules. In my own case, though, and with the single exception of when I fly, I won't take pills. That is because I don't want to be mentally blurred, or assisted, or comforted, or calmed, or eased, or tranquilized. I want all my faculties, even if some of those faculties sometimes turn against me and make me feel anxious. That anxiety is part of who I am, and in order to write books, I feel I need all of me, even the parts I don't want. If I thought that the pills were just curing a physical condition, the way my inhaler takes away the symptoms of asthma when I wheeze, I would take them. But I don't see my phobia as a purely physical condition. It lives in my mind, and it's part of my mind, for better or worse. And I need my mind to be the way it is in order to write.

To put it another way, I think that my phobia has some meaning. It's trying to tell me something, even though I don't usually know what. Writing and therapy are linked, because they are both about a search for meaning. To take the fear away with antidepressants would for me be to say that the fear is just a meaningless chemical accident.

· 4 ·

S O AS 1991 TURNED INTO 1992, I had a girlfriend who was on the way to being a wife; a therapist; a novel I had been incubating for some years and "working on" for almost two; a principled aversion to taking medication; and a room of my own. I had the freedom and the anxiety, which for me was its price. So naturally my book wrote itself, yes?

Ah, no . . . and this is a hard thing for me to accept; but I'm not sure I could finally have been able to get on with the book if it hadn't been for one more loss. It happened in the summer of 1992, and it was the loss of my mother as she had been, of Julie as I had known her.

In the summer of 1992, Miranda and I went on holiday to Scotland. I was working at Penguin Books at the time and had landed a parallel job writing restaurant reviews for *The Observer*. That gig, as we say in show business, was due to start in the autumn, and I planned to do some Scottish eating and sprinkle it through my columns in the next few months, thus making me look more adventurous and wide-traveling than was actually the case. But there was another component to the holiday plan: we would borrow my mother's car for the course of the two weeks. I would get lots of driving practice, and when I got back to London would book, take, and pass my driving test. I had gotten to thirty without learning to drive, no doubt mainly because I'd always lived in cities; however, it was now time to do what a man's gotta do. So Miranda and I went up to Norwich, stayed the night, and then drove off in Julie's car, with many a strong injunction about not crashing it, about returning it clean, making sure we put unleaded petrol in, and calling her every evening to let her know we were okay. (I should say here that my mother, who had never warmed to any of my girlfriends, strongly approved of Miranda. The first time they met, Julie opened the door to us, said hello, took our coats, told Miranda to go upstairs to the sitting room and help herself to tea, and said to me, *"You mustn't let this one get away."*)

So we set off and drove around Scotland for two weeks, heading as far as Ullapool in the distant northwest and then working our way back. Ullapool was delightful. We were staying at the also delightful Altnaharrie Inn, accessible only by boat, and without telephone or electricity, so that night I called from the pay phone by the boat dock and checked in with my mother. Julie sounded a little distracted. Miranda and I crossed, had dinner, spent the night, and the next day drove to Fort William, where we were staying at the utterly grotesque Inverlochy Castle, a "baronial pile" where Queen Victoria had spent quality time, now an over-the-top grand hotel, the kind of place where they make you feel like an escaped homicidal maniac if you aren't wearing a tie. It was raining—it's always raining in Fort William. I called my mother after we got there, at about six-thirty, but there was no reply. That's odd, I thought—she must have gone to her Greek friends Costa and Reula for supper. But that seemed strange: she hadn't mentioned it, and she'd been there only a couple of nights before, so between dinner courses, at about nine, I popped back to the room and called again. No reply. If Julia went out in the evening she was always back by then, so I began to be properly worried. At the end of the meal, say ten or ten-thirty, I called again, and there still wasn't a reply, so I called the neighbor, who had a key, and explained my worry. I let ten minutes pass and then called my mother's number again, and it was busy. That's when I realized something really was wrong.

Julie had had a stroke. She had fallen on the stairs and, according to the ambulance men, spent many hours there, unable to move. In their opinion she had been there all the previous night and all day. This was obviously a disaster, but there were several providential aspects, among them the fact that if I hadn't been calling every day—which I was doing only because I'd borrowed her car—I would not have known that something was wrong; no one would have had any reason to notice Julie's condition for a few days, and since she couldn't move, she would have died there on the landing.

Miranda and I drove down from Fort William to Norwich overnight, about as long a drive as you can make in mainland Britain, with a few hours' sleep in a fleabag hotel somewhere. The first time I ever drove at night was through Glencoe Valley at about one in the morning, with the mist descending, Miranda asleep beside me, and an extraordinary vision of a stag standing on a crest just at the end of the valley, lit by the headlights as they bounced off the mist. It was the only moment I've felt a shamanistic presence, as if that animal were somehow a watchful or presiding spirit, strange and creepy, on a very strange and frightening night.

When we got to Norwich, at about six p.m. the next day, Julie was in intensive care, which is where she stayed for the next forty-eight hours or so. Then she spent a couple of weeks in a ward in Norfolk and Norwich Hospital; she was transferred to what was supposed to be a convalescent hospital. There was next to no medical care at the hospital, and the patients were essentially left to rot. My mother was there for a couple of months, then went to a residential home in Sparham, in northwest Norfolk, for a few more months. Then she moved to the flat I had bought for her in Wimbledon, after selling her house in Norwich, about fifteen minutes by car from where Miranda and I were living in Battersea. When I say I bought it for her, I don't mean I paid, but rather that I arranged the sale of her house, and her move down to London with enough of her stuff to live with. She moved in May 1993, so all of this took nine months or so.

By the end of this period, Julie was nowhere near fully recovered; physically, she would never be the same. She would never drive again, never walk more than about two hundred yards. One of the great appealing factors about her flat was that it was within easy walking distance of a Catholic church, so she could go "under my own steam," as she always put it, to Saturday-evening Mass. (Evening was her preferred time, rather than morning; I don't know why. The exception was Mass on Christmas Eve, which Mum always avoided on the basis that "the smell of Guinness would knock you down.") The period of inactivity she had undergone in hospital, in addition to the stroke, had permanently slowed her down.

I don't want to make these months sound easier than they were. Julie's cognitive powers did not come back immediately. The doctors had said that most of the function she would get back would return within the first two weeks. This proved not to be true. The first two weeks, when the initial bruising from the stroke subsided, gave her about forty percent of what she was to get back. The rest of the recovery took a year or more. I suspect, from what I now know about strokes and doctors and the National Health Service, that the medics knew perfectly well it would be like that, but they gave me the bleak two-week prognosis in order to minimize the amount that was demanded of them. Obviously, if they had told me it would take a year for her to recover fully, I would have asked what they were going to do to help over the course of that year. This way they got to wash their hands of her recovery after a fortnight. The policy at the hospital where she was supposed to convalesce, which had no resident doctor, seemed to be to ignore the patients until their relatives could stand it no more and either took them home or began paying for private residential care. The only moment of animation I saw from the medical staff there came when I said that I had found my mother a place in a nearby residential home. "We mustn't miss out on this," the visiting doctor in charge said, not to me but to the ward sister who would be handling my mother's transfer; this was the lone note of urgency or real concern that I heard from any medical staff at any point during my mother's hospitalization.

She recovered enough, though, to be able to live on her own. That had been a big worry for me while she was ill. I had a terror that I would have no alternative between seeing her in paid care for the rest of her life, which she would hate, would make me feel guilty about, and which we could barely afford; and having to look after her myself, which, frankly, I dreaded, not least because of my sense that I had only just begun to live my own life. So the fact that she slowly, ever so slowly, got sufficiently better to live on her own was a great relief all around. The Wimbledon flat was in assisted living, with emergency alarms in the rooms if the residents needed help and a warden who dropped in every day to see if they were okay. My mother decided to resent this at the start, but very soon became firm friends with Maureen the warden. She made one other very close friendship in Cloister House, as the place was called, and enjoyed being on nodding and gossiping terms with the other residents. She was appointed to the residents' committee—another thing I learned only after her death. I had been particularly nervous about her cooking—whether she would be able to manage without malnourishing herself or burning down the building, or doing both simultaneously. But she managed fine, or fine-ish, or fine enough, with only the occasional mishap. It has to be said that the microwave oven, which she had always spurned, came into its own. One day she put a tin of condensed milk to boil and turn into toffee, then forgot that it was on the stove. It exploded and left an impressive toffee-bomb stain on the stovetop and on the ceiling. She made an impression on the workman who came to repair the damage. "She's a nice old lady, but she didn't apologize or anything, the way most people do," he said. "She seemed sort of . . . defiant." That was Julie. Never apologize, never explain.

I noticed, though—and it helped once I had noticed—that there was a direct correlation in Julie between her anxiety and her level of cognitive functioning (especially her short-term memory), her mood, and her temper. When she was anxious, she would also be forgetful and irritable and depressed, and vice versa; when she was calmer and felt more in control, she would be able to think and remember better, would be much chattier, and was consequently happy. Once I had spotted that and was able to allow for it, coping with her moments of anger or snappishness became much easier. In general, once she got into her flat on her own, surrounded again by her own belongings—her stuff—she calmed and eased and grew happier. This was the final phase of her life, and unlike the others it was not marked by a change of name. She was still Julie, Julia,

Mrs. B. T. J. Lanchester, Mum. But there was a change of character, or rather, an easing of character. My mother let many of her worries go. She did not project anxiety in the way that she had; she did not use worry as a controlling mechanism; there was not a constant sense that she was radiating grievance. Instead, a sweetness that had always been present, but that she hadn't often allowed out to breathe, was increasingly manifest. Julie had her gentle, yielding, trusting side; it was just that she hadn't often trusted it. Now, more and more, she did.

Some of this had, no doubt, to do with the stroke, but a large part of it was due to the shift in our relationship. We had, as I said, been locked in stasis, an undeclared civil war, the basic gesture of which was her pushing me away for fear that I wanted to run away, and me always edging halfway out the door, physically and emotionally, for fear of being caught and forced to stay put. I felt that I had left home many, many years before, and I had no intention of being maneuvered into moving back. Now, though, there had been a crisis, and I had surprised both my mother and myself by wanting to be there to help her. That was, from my point of view, the great plot twist: I didn't run away because I didn't want to run away. I wanted to go and see her in hospital, I wanted her to get better, I wanted her to move to London so that we could be near each other. I won't pretend that it wasn't stressful and difficult and painful. I'm not sure I could have done it without being in a stable relationship (in fact, I'm sure I couldn't have), and also without being in therapy, where for all this time I was going mainly in order to let off steam about my mother and all my various griefs and fears and anger for her and about her. (That's one of the things that happens in therapy that is easy to describe: you go there to complain, in order not to suffocate the other people in your life with your complaints.) But I did want to do it, and I knew that and she knew that, and it brought an easing between us.

I've used the word "ease" more than once, and that is for me the thing that chiefly changed in the last phase of Julie's life. She was easier, easier on herself and easier to be with. We could sit together and do things together without a sense of being locked in struggle. A big contributing factor to this was that we saw so much more of each other and spoke to each other much more often. I would call at least every other day—not that there was usually much to report on either side—to check in. (I remember she once said, with a newsreader's intonation, "It's been a quiet day here at Cloister House"—somehow her inflection implied the existence of noisier alternatives, old-age pensioner rioting or raves.) Miranda and I would either take her out or have her over to supper once a week, usually the latter, and usually on Saturday night, when I would go over and pick her up after evening Mass. One of Julie's proudest possessions was a mink coat my father had bought for her in Hong Kong. It had originally been floor-length, but she had had it altered into a jacket that came to below her hips. With this on and her walking stick, and wearing tinted glasses, she would cut quite a figure waiting outside the church. Once when I was going to pick something up from her flat, I saw her on the way to her doctor's—it was only about two hundred yards away—and had that moment of fresh vision you sometimes have when you unexpectedly see someone you know too well to see at all. She had her mink and stick and shades and looked indomitable, and brave and stylish and dotty and practical-minded and in a world of her own, and I was taken off balance by the type of pure love that you feel most readily toward your own children.

The change in her was symbolized by the flat. This had a small bedroom, a tiny second bedroom or study, and a sitting-dining room, and they were all utterly chaotic. You could hardly move for the overflowing stuff—books, papers, clothes, and CDs in particular, the bounty of the mail-order catalogues to which my mother, after her stroke, had become addicted. The contrast with the ultraneat way she had always chosen to live was inescapable. She had always been someone who would not consider the day done unless everything had been tidied up and squared away—it wasn't a question of not leaving the washing-up for the next day, it was a question of not leaving the washing-up for fifteen minutes. Now her home was like a bomb site. It was possible to see this as a loss— obviously, it was a loss—but I don't think it was only that. Her obsession with tidiness and order didn't seem to have brought her much happiness, and although there was something oppressive about the chaos of her flat, there was also a sense that she had stopped minding about everything quite so much.

The years at Cloister House were a kind of coda to Julie's life. She felt acutely what she had lost, and spoke with great wistfulness of her years in Norwich in particular—the contrast, I suppose, had to do not so much with loneliness, since she had been alone there, too, but more with her health and her relative freedom of movement. (Not that she had actually used that freedom much, just as my father hadn't much used the theoretical freedom he had won by earning a good living. People are always reluctant to ask themselves what price they're paying for things they think they value, and whether they're actually using freedoms they think they have.) She spoke of her own good times being past: *"Et in Arcadia ego,"* she was fond of saying, never failing to add her translation: I, too, have lived in Arcadia. So there was loss and sadness at having ended up in this small Wimbledon flat at the age of seventy-two (though, of course, admitting to only sixty-two).

Once this was accepted, however, Julie's life wasn't so bad—and it was to have some consolations, in terms of things she had always wanted. She had her friends and her routines, and saw much more of me. She liked the regular treats that were not hard to line up in London, such as trips to Bentley's Oyster Bar, where she had gone on her second dinner out with Bill, and where she had drunk her second martini. She enjoyed meeting my friends and felt no need to qualify the sharpness of her opinions. "How's X?" she asked me once about a friend who had been depressed. "Has he lost that awful hangdog look?" "I was very disappointed by Y," she said on meeting an old girlfriend of mine. "She looked like a cottage loaf." In the taxi on the way home after a party where she had met, for the first time, my agent, she announced, firmly, "He's very nice. I quite fancy him." Sometimes her remarks were pure Alan Bennett. "He didn't seem at all well," she once remarked of my entirely healthy father-in-law. "Touch of Parkinson's, I think." More than once, friends who met Julie for the first time would tell me that they thought she was "sweet."

For all these years I had been someone who wanted to write. That is, for a certain type of young person, an identity in itself, almost a job in itself: "wanting to write." It has to do with a sense that although you aren't actually doing any writing—meaning writing a book; I had done quite a bit of other kinds of writing—you have a secret identity, being a writer. This, your real self, protects you from the possibility that your other, external self becomes too real. It's like being back at school and having a note saying you're excused from homework, only here you have a note saying you're excused from life. You don't have to try too hard, work too hard, or care too much about anything, because it's all a preliminary for the real task of being a writer—or rather the larval or preliminary stage of "being" a writer, which is wanting to write.

I should say in defense of my younger self that, even at the time, I knew this was a crock: I knew that writing was something you did, not something you were, and that there was no such thing as "being" a writer or "wanting" to write; the only thing that had any reality at all was actually writing. I knew this, but I found it impossible to act on the consequences of that knowledge. I had made a start on my first book and then conked out; I had now been sitting on the idea, incubating it, for more than seven years. My book was in the perfect state of suspended animation: I wanted to write it, and yet there I was, doing a highly successful job of not writing it.

A book must be an axe for the frozen sea within us. Kafka said that. In my case, writing the book needed an axe, or not one but several—the death of my father, a grown-up relationship, some therapy so I could be with myself for long enough to do the work, and finally, I believe, my mother's stroke. It was not as if my mother had died: she was very much present, in many respects more present than she had been since my childhood. But she was not the same. The Julia I had grown up with wasn't there anymore, and that was the final thing I needed to break up my particular frozen sea.

That is because by writing I was, on some level, reaching out to her, trying to get in touch with her, trying to get her attention. And I could not do that while there was a chance of actually getting her attention in life. While the mother I grew up with was present (or semi-present, or absent in her unique way), it was she with whom I was struggling. I wanted her gaze on me, and I wanted not to be anywhere near her, at the same time. I wanted to be absent-present in something resembling the same way she was. Once she had had her stroke, she was, to use a phrase many people used about her, "never the same again." That meant that it was now impossible to contact that person she had been, and that was what made me begin to reach out to her in the form of writing. I couldn't get her attention in the way I had wanted it, so now I tried to get her attention on the page. And at the same time I knew that she couldn't properly read what I was writing. That was the last trick pulled by fate and my unconscious: because Julie's cognitive faculties weren't what they had been, she couldn't really read anything the way she had been used to—so she couldn't read my book. That was what I needed in order to begin writing it.

I've said before that motives are difficult to unpick. Perhaps I'm proving the point here. What all this boils down to is: Once my mother wasn't able to read my books, I finally began writing them.

· 5 ·

B Y THE END OF 1994, I had finished *The Debt to Pleasure*. I handed it over to Miranda, the first person to read it, on December 31 (and immediately came down with the flu). I told my mother about it shortly afterward, and she was pleased for me, as pleased as she could possibly be. She hadn't been able to be a writer herself, for complicated reasons, but was delighted that I had managed to write a book. (The other things she would most have wanted me to be were a don and a priest—the latter an ambition she once let slip to one of my teachers at school, who lost no time in passing the news on to me.) She came to a dinner celebrating the news that a publisher had bought my book, and came to the launch party, too.

There were, however, moments of difficulty, as there always had been surrounding my writing. She would "open the window and fling her chest out"—she lent copies of it to, for instance, her G.P. I found that out after her death, when I saw a polite note from him in the returned book. But sometimes it was as if my gaining some attention as a writer rubbed a sore nerve. A piece I wrote about how I became interested in cooking only in my twenties was brought to her notice by friends of hers, because

I had talked about her influence on me. "It was only by starting to cook myself that I learned how much care and attention—how much love— had gone into all the meals cooked by my mother over the years. I am glad I found out about that," I wrote. My mother's response: "Lots of people showed it to me, told me about it, but I didn't think it was anything special." That, admittedly, was when she was in the residential home, and relations between us were spiky. When my book came out, there were glimpses of the same attitude. It surfaced in particular over prizes. When I won a Betty Trask Prize, I invited her to the ceremony, run by the Society of Authors, a couple of weeks in advance. David Lodge, a writer Julie admired, was to be giving the prizes. It was something she said she looked forward to. But when the day came, I was called by the warden of the assisted-living facility, who said that Julie had gotten into her bathtub the night before and not been able to get out. Rather than pull the alarm cord, which was right beside the tub and was specifically for that purpose, she had sat there all night until the warden's rounds that morning. So obviously, she wouldn't be coming to the ceremony. Okay, I thought—too much buildup, too much excitement. The next time I won a prize, the Whitbread First Novel Award, I told her two days before. Seamus Heaney, another writer she admired, would be there. She was delighted. Then at two p.m., with dinner and the ceremony to start at seven, she rang to say she couldn't face coming. Simple as that, she couldn't face it. I wasn't able to talk her out of that frame of mind. Okay, I thought. Lesson learned. The next time I won a prize, the Hawthornden, with the ceremony at the National Portrait Gallery, I kept the news to myself for a month and then, on the day, called her at four p.m. to say that a taxi was picking her up at six. That ceremony she made. She seemed pleased to be there.

There was clearly some tension here, involving if not envy, then a kind of generational rivalry. This is a tension that, I've noticed, exists more often in relations between different generations of women. Fathers and sons can be competitive: sons want to outdo their fathers, and there is a patricidal component to that; not all fathers are willing to be outdone. But there is a sense that fathers and sons are competing at some existential level, to see who does better on a basically level playing field. It has often to do with who is more of a man, or what kind of a man it is best to be. With mothers and daughters, it's different. Younger generations of women often have completely different opportunities, both in terms of the practical things they're allowed to do and in terms of the psychological support they're given in doing them, and perhaps especially in respect to the reigning assumptions about women and their lives. Daughters often have objectively better life chances than their mothers—and this inevitably causes some generational tension, a kind of envy. The daughter thinks: "It's my turn." The mother thinks: "If I'd had the chances you have. You don't know how lucky you are. You'll never know how easy you have it. You'll never know what it was like for me." I think my success—in this context, I have to call it that—as a writer touched on some of those feelings for Julie. She was pleased for me and proud of me, and at the same time part of her wondered whether she might not and should not have been the person garnering the applause and attention. I had had opportunities that Julie hadn't had. I would say those opportunities had to do less with time or ambition or education or anything practical as with psychological factors. But she might not have seen it that way. Between parents and children it should be the case that, as a friend once told me, "Their pluses are never your minuses." That should always be true. But alas, it isn't, not always.

In the summer of 1997, I was at the Hay-on-Wye festival doing the last book event attached to the publication of *The Debt to Pleasure*—something that I'd been devoted to for about the past eighteen months, and that made me feel like an employee of my own book, perhaps the vice-president in charge of public relations. I had a call on my mobile from I no longer remember whom—I suppose it must have been Maureen, the warden. My mother had had another stroke. I got through the "event" and hurried back to London and to St. George's Hospital. My mother was conscious and not in danger; it had been a smaller stroke than the first.

If the years after the first stroke in 1992 were the coda to Julie's life, the next year and a bit were the coda to the coda. Although the later stroke was smaller, it had more of an effect on her speech and short-term memory, and she minded that, especially the sensation of fumbling for words and picking the wrong one: her language had been such a central and powerful part of her that this was a very intimate betrayal. The memory problem meant that she was not quite as reliable managing on her own. I would occasionally go to take her out, only to find that she had forgotten I was coming, and had already eaten—which in practice tended to mean she had gotten someone else to cook dinner for her. This used to make me angry at the time and then, usually when I was on the way home from dropping her off, intensely sad. Her quality of life was markedly less good from this point on: she watched a lot more TV, went out less, and was less present when she was present. It was a worry. This is the cruelest of the reversals that happen when you look after an ailing parent: that instead of their worrying about you, you worry about them. You begin to be your parents' parent. The terrible difference, though, is that when you're being a parent to a child, they're growing up, growing away with every day that passes, becoming stronger and more independent; with a parent, all these processes are going the other way. That's the hardest thing about this passage of life, when, in the words of a *Doonesbury* cartoon, "you find yourself talking to your parents and your children in the same tone of voice."

I suppose I knew on some deep level that my mother's death was coming. I didn't necessarily know it would be soon. Bear in mind that as far as I knew, she was not yet sixty-seven, and it wasn't so unreasonable to think that she had a good few more years to live.

"I won't be around for much longer," she told me once when I'd gone to pick her up from her flat in 1998. She had been saying this for as long as I could remember—at least since I was ten years old. But even people who always talk about the fact that they are going to die one day do eventually die.

"Rubbish. You'll see Finn"—my son, who was three months old— "walking down the road outside Trinity College Dublin, sticking his waistcoat out."

"Do you think so?" my mother said, her face lit up.

I picked Finn up and handed him to her.

"He's a handsome haggis," I said, and then, feeling the extra weight he'd gained, as I lifted him, "and he's also a heavy haggis."

"He doesn't like being called a haggis," my mother said very firmly.

Your relationship with your parents changes when you have children. You see how much your children mean to you, and in many cases—in my case—you realize for the first time what love means, full, unconditional love. There are a couple of lines by W. H. Auden:

> If equal affection cannot be,
> Let the more loving one be me.

In a relationship with a spouse or partner, I don't think anyone ever really believes that—we'd all secretly prefer to be the one who is at least a little bit more loved. (The French say, In love one always kisses, and the other always turns the cheek to be kissed.) That's not the case with your children. You want to love them more than they love you, just as you want them to live longer, be happier, and have more opportunities. It's this sudden sense of the expansion of love that transforms the world, to make it seem that you were always looking at it in black-and-white, and now it's in color. This is not to say that life is easier or fairer; just that now it's in color.

And then you think, This is how I made my parents feel when I was born. Because the flow of love between parents and children is so unstraightforward—being prone to blockages and kinks and diversions, periods of stagnation, reroutings underground, reversals of current—it is easy to forget how it once was, as pure and clear and simple as flowing water. (But then, the flow of water is also very complicated. Ask anyone who studies it.) The birth of your child reminds you of how things once were, except you are in a different role: this time you are the giver of unconditional love rather than its recipient. The switch in perspective is sudden, dramatic, jolting, and deeply moving. Very, very few things in life are a revelation—it's one of those words typically used to mean "better than expected, slightly surprising"—but this is, or can be.

I saw Julie in relative health for the last time in July 1998. It was the usual routine: she came over by cab, I cooked her supper. At about seven the phone rang, with the warden of the assisted-living facility in a state: Tesco had come to deliver some groceries and couldn't get into my mother's flat. She'd ordered some stuff and then forgotten about it. This was the kind of confusion or slip she would make, sometimes scarily (leaving things on the stove, forgetting to turn taps off), other times, like this, not scarily at all. The groceries were sitting in the hallway and the frozen things were thawing. I drove over, sorted out the shopping, and started leaving. As I was going out, my mother said:

"I do miss you, you know."

There was a real weight of feeling and love in her words. It came out of the blue, and was so unlike her that I stopped dead.

"I know, Mum. I miss you, too."

I went home. We spoke on a Friday, two days later, for the last time. The next morning, I was standing in the kitchen when the phone rang. It's only now, when all the people I love most are together in our house, and the phone rings, that I realize something: For years, every time the telephone rang, I was worried that it would be bad news about my mother. I wasn't even aware until after she died that part of me was going through a tiny cycle of fear and relief every time somebody phoned. I knew the call would come one day, and that was the day it did. A friend of my mother's had gone to see her after breakfast, but there was no reply when she knocked on the door, so she'd gone to get the warden. When they went in, my mother was lying on her side in bed, unable to speak or move. They called an ambulance. Miranda and I called a friend who agreed to take Finn for a few hours, and we drove to St. George's Hospital, where my mother was in the ER. Her head was turned to one side and her eyeballs were fixed in the corners of her eyes. She had had a massive stroke, and she would not move or speak again.

I spent the next three weeks visiting St. George's Hospital every day, and essentially waiting for my mother to die. It's not a time or set of feelings I would hope ever to live through again. I vividly remember driving around the small, half-untarmacked car park, hoping I wouldn't be able to find a space, because that way I could put off the walk down to the main building, the elevator ride to the fifth floor, and the experience of sitting with my silent, immobile mother for an hour or so. I remember looking at things on the drive over and wishing I were doing them instead—sitting in that park, going to that greyhound track, dropping in on those friends who had lived over there. I would take the slow route, around Clapham Common, rather than the quick route down by Wandsworth. When the traffic was bad, I felt the way a schoolboy feels when a test is postponed. When the automatic gate of the entrance to the car park was jammed, I sat happily in the queue. Don't honk for the man to come and fix it—he'll be along in his own good time. What's the rush?

Visiting people in hospital is hard work. Visiting someone you're madly in love with who's in only overnight, for something laughably minor, and is in a good mood, is hard work. Everything else is harder by degrees. I don't quite know why—perhaps it's because the sick have their attention by necessity directed elsewhere, so you always feel as if you're making small talk. Either that or you're talking about things that are all too important.

With my mother there was no real talking at all. Occasionally she would seem to utter fragments of words—but only fragments, the beginnings of a word or sentence. One day we took Finn to see her, hoping he might get a reaction from her. I asked my mother if she was pleased to see him, and she said something that could have been "course," as in "of course." It didn't get any better than that.

Most of the time I just sat with her. Sometimes I read to her, usually poetry, because she loved it, and usually from the old Oxford anthology edited by Sir Arthur Quiller-Couch. Sometimes I told her about what had been going on elsewhere in our lives, which meant that I talked mostly about Finn. And a lot of the time I sat and held her hand.

The doctors asked me whether I wanted them to attempt to resuscitate her in the event of another seizure. I said no, since I had a clearish memory of her asking me to say that. So "DNR" was written on her chart. But this caused me anxiety, not so much about my mother's wishes, because I was pretty sure what those were, but about the teaching of the Catholic Church. This mattered to me not for my sake but for hers. I knew it was something she would want me to get right. And so, for the first and thus far only time in my life, I found myself taking her advice that "when you're in trouble, you can always turn to the J's." I called the Jesuit residence in Farm Street and asked to speak to the duty father. I explained my mother's circumstances, said that I wasn't Catholic but she was, and asked what the Church's teachings were in this case. He said that the Church would not want "artificially to prolong life." I asked him if this meant the DNR instruction was, in the circumstances, appropriate, and he said he thought that it was.

It's easier now, in hindsight, to see that what made things so difficult was the fact that I wanted my mother to die. That was the only possible release, for her and for me. No one could imagine that she was going to recover, and in the weeks after her stroke there was no improvement, so death was the only way out. But I could not bear to see that quite so starkly at the time. And I also wanted her to live, to have another twenty or thirty years with her, not for any good reason, or any reason that a consultant could tick off on a quality-of-life chart, but simply because she was my mother and I loved her and I wanted her to live as long as possible, and because I knew I would miss her horribly when she was gone. We want the people we love to live; wanting someone we love to die is an insult to our whole psychology, our deepest instincts.

So it was a relief, in a way, even though it did not feel like one, when the ward sister called on a Thursday morning and I set off to hospital with Miranda. I had only just gotten up and was desperate for caffeine. There was a branch of Seattle Coffee Company en route, and it would have been simple to stop for a fix; but I'm deeply grateful that I didn't, because if I had, and had taken five or ten minutes to do it, I would never have known whether that was why I wasn't there when my mother died. She had had either another stroke or an embolism in her lung. The people at the hospital asked for my permission to do a postmortem and said they would call me with the results, but they never got around to it. So I never knew what it was that killed her. I suppose that's fair enough, since there were so many other things about her I didn't know.

There's a lot to do when somebody dies. "The probate years," a friend of mine once called the period of life when you find yourself dealing with all of this. My experience of my parents' deaths was like that both times—in addition to the grief, there was so much administration to get through that it was like finding myself in charge of a small business. After I found the identity papers and the will—which she'd lodged at her bank—I began the business of registering for probate, paying off bills, clearing the balance owed to the tax man, settling my mother's utilities accounts, closing her bank accounts, canceling standing orders, stopping her various subscriptions and her mail, returning unopened all the various mail-order bits and pieces that arrived in the days after her death, arranging for real estate agents to view and value the flat, first for probate purposes and then to put it on sale. Then there was the task of arranging her funeral, and going to see the priest to discuss the service, which was to be part of the regular Wednesday-morning Mass, six days after her death; he was a polite South African, a new priest who barely knew my mother, not the previous father whom she had known and liked, which was a pity. There was also the cremation to arrange, which would take place immediately after the service, and the question of who would and who wouldn't go on from church to that; then the funeral lunch afterward, and the question of who would and who wouldn't go on to *that*.

And then, the day before the funeral, talking to Miranda after dinner, I had the biggest surprise of my life. (I should say that Miranda remembers this conversation differently. She says she tiptoed around the subject carefully, and had reasons for thinking I would react badly.) We were chatting about nothing in particular when she said,

"There's something you don't know about your mother."

This in itself was an unexpected sentence. The next one was:

"I think your mother might have been a bit older than she said she was."

And then she told me that Peggie—who was worried that my mother's doctors might be acting on inaccurate information—had told her my mother's real age. In that moment, I knew; although it was the single biggest out-of-the-blue surprise I'd had, I knew it was true. I also had a sudden sense not only of what my mother had done, but also of how she had done it. I realized it was true in the way that people realize that their spouse has been having an affair: I was gobsmacked with surprise, and yet I was aware that somewhere in my unconscious, I had already known. Some kinds of knowledge have a chemical certainty to them, and they are usually things that touch on our deepest feelings—that is to say, they touch on love.

I felt the life story my mother had given out, in dribs and drabs, through stories and by implication and anecdote, take a giant lurch. I also felt the truth of a profound thing once said by Edmund White: "Family life binds strangers together." My mother, I realized, was much more of a stranger than I knew.

This, I suppose, is where we came in. The things I found out immediately after my mother died sent me on a journey to find out more about her, and about my father, and by extension about myself. I think I had always known there were things I wasn't told, but I had no idea of their extent. I had no idea of the consequences they had had for my mother. I wanted to know the story, and the meaning of the story—or what it means for me now, anyway. There's no guarantee that I won't see things differently in five or ten years' time. In fact, I expect to. That didn't deter me from telling the story today, in the present. I came to feel I had no choice.

What, more than anything else, I wanted to know was my mother's sense of what her own life had been. This became the most crucial matter, the central question: What was Julie's sense of her own story—did she see her life as a connected narrative, or as a series of things that had simply happened one after another? If she did see it as a story, what was the story about? Was this a story about a person who had told a lie, and who kept paying for it? Was it about a woman who had escaped, twice, from home and from the convent, but who despite that had never quite managed to be happy? Was it a story about a woman who more than anything else wanted to write, but whose circumstances had arranged that she couldn't write, because she couldn't tell the story she wanted to tell more than any other—her own? Was it a story about a woman who was saved by love, and who in turn gave everything up for love—a story about sacrifice? Or was it perhaps not a story at all—did she deliberately not connect the dots, for whatever reason—to protect herself from what that might make her feel, or because she chose not to second-guess those former selves? Did she think there was one self she had been who was the real self, truer to her inner being than the others, and was that Julia Gunnigan, or Sister Eucharia, or Julie Lanchester? Was it one of her fictional selves, even Shivaun Cunningham or B. T. J. Lanchester? Or was the answer to every one of these questions, at different times in her life, yes?

Those were the things I most wanted to know, and those were the things I did not find out. Julie quite simply gave nothing away about her innermost feelings. She never spoke to anyone about these things; she never wrote a word about them; she left no evidence, not the tiniest bit. I've had to imagine myself into her skin and work out what she thought and felt. The likeliest thing is that her life story did not, to her, quite add up; there were fundamental ruptures and discontinuities in it. There was some sense in which she was not fully present to herself.

There are times when storytelling is indispensable; there are times when we have to tell a story about something to make sense of it. Julie couldn't tell the story of her own life. For reasons I have explained, I don't think she could tell it even to herself. That left me with a deep, unappeasable wish to connect the dots and tell the story for myself—and also, perhaps, I presume to think, for her. I don't think she could bear to tell the story of her life, but I believe that she did want it told. I hope so. We can want things that we can't bear.

I've come to think that the most revealing thing I know about Julie are the last words she said to me in person. "I do miss you, you know." But she said it while I was right there, said it while I was standing in front of her. You don't have to miss me, I'm right here, is what I might have said. But that would have been obtuse. I don't think I was ever fully there for my mother, and I don't think anyone else ever was, either; and I think the reason for that is that she was never fully present herself. Some part of Julie was never in whatever space she herself was in; she was always under what the Catholic Church calls a "mental reservation." She was telling the truth when she said she missed me: she did. She always had—always.

Now that I know so much more about her life, I think, and feel, that this was the core of it for her, this sense that her attention was always slightly turned away, turned inward; she knew it, too, I think, knew it and regretted it and could not stop it. I know now both why she so much wanted to write her own story and why she felt she could not. She passed that ambition on to me, and did it without ever explicitly telling me about it; she let it sink in, by osmosis, or like ink-dyeing. But it isn't that that made me a writer. More than anything else, what made me a writer was the way she left me reaching for the one thing I could never quite have, even when she was alive, and that I now can never have: her attention. I had to wait for it to be gone before I began to write, and now I know I will always be reaching for it, and will never get it. That's just the way it is. I reach for it every time I sit down to write, this thing I will never have, this thing that was always already lost to me, and that I am reaching for as I sit here even now, writing this sentence.

In the end, though, one thing I do know is what I should put on her grave. Last week I wrote to the parish priest in Manfield, where the Lanchesters are buried, apologizing for the delay in finding an inscription for my mother. I'm expecting a call from the stonemason in a few days' time, telling me that the inscription is ready, and then I'll drive up to North Yorkshire, where my parents' ashes are buried, and look for the first time at the carved words:

AND HIS WIFE JULIE LANCHESTER,
WHO DIED ON 6 AUGUST 1998,
AGED 77 YEARS

There is something abrupt about summarizing my mother, who was several people, with the one-word name "Julie" and the one word "wife." But she herself said that was the role in which she was happiest, so I don't think she would object. As for the age, that decision seems simple. It is at last time for her to be free of her secret, which did not make things easy for her in life, and should now leave her in peace.

ACKNOWLEDGMENTS

I would like to thank my aunt Peggie Geraghty. Without her generous help I would not know my mother's full story, and I could not have written this book. That is not to say she agrees at every point with this version of events and people. The same thanks are owed to Siobhán and Vincent Geraghty. I would also like to thank, and with the same caveat, my uncle John Gunnigan. In addition, I thank his wife, Mary Theresa, and their children, Pat, Louie, Thaíg, Marianne, John, and Jane. Thanks to the Stauntons—especially Margaret, Marion, Jane, and Rosín—the Kerrs, and the Brownes, for the unfailing kindness, hospitality, and friendliness they have shown me. I thank Bernadette Duca, and her children, Bernard and Moya; Joan, Alf, Adrian, and Richard Linden; Miriam Bailey, John Kelly, Clair Wills, Andrew O'Hagan, Nicholas Jenkins, Jon Riley, and Anna Jardine. Any errors or omissions are mine, all mine.

It's hard to know where to begin with the writers from whom I've learned about Ireland, because, to borrow a compliment that William Empson paid T. S. Eliot, I'm not sure how much of my mind they invented. I would like to make particular mention of Brian Friel, Seamus Heaney, Greta Jones, Roy Foster, J. J. Lee, Seamus Deane, John Banville, and Colm Toibín. For the period of my mother's life during which she was in the convent, and just after she left it, I owe a debt of understanding to Monica Baldwin, Elizabeth Kuhns, and especially Karen Armstrong.

I once found myself listed in the acknowledgments of a book—an anthology—and couldn't work out why I was there. After thinking about it for a long time I finally remembered that I had once photocopied something for the editor. That, I suspect, is the smallest thing for which anyone has ever been thanked in an acknowledgments section. I don't know the biggest thing for which anyone has ever been thanked, but for her support while I was writing this book, I nominate my wife, Miranda.

The photographs on pages 182 and 186 are reproduced by permission of the Imperial War Museum.